SEPARATED TOGETHER

THE INCREDIBLE TRUE WWII STORY OF SOULMATES STRANDED AN OCEAN APART

KENNETH P. PRICE, PH.D.

Separated Together. The Incredible True WWII Story of Soulmates Stranded an Ocean Apart. A Personal-Historical Memoir

Kenneth P. Price, Ph.D.

ISBN 9789493231092 (ebook)

ISBN 9789493231085 (paperback)

ISBN 9789493231269 (hardcover)

Publisher: Amsterdam Publishers, The Netherlands

info@amsterdampublishers.com

Separated Together is part of the series Holocaust Survivor True Stories WWII

CONTENTS

ADVANCE PRAISE

Dr. Kenneth Price's book *Separated Together* is not only the story of a miraculous reunion, but this testimony itself has something of the miraculous about it. September 1939: Sonia's husband Abe was stranded in New York, while she and her two children were left in Poland, to be swept up in the horrific whirlwind that was the Holocaust. Somehow Sonia was resurrected from the ashen earth of Auschwitz. Somehow she was able to embrace her husband Abe once more. Somehow the two of them made a new life in America – but without their murdered children. Dr. Price relates this powerful tale with insight and eloquence, in all of its pathos and drama. It is sure to transform you.

Dr. David Patterson, Hillel A. Feinberg Distinguished Chair in Holocaust Studies, Ackerman Center for Holocaust Studies, University of Texas at Dallas

Kenneth Price's book, *Separated Together*, is a great accomplishment in the realm of Holocaust chronicles. It gives a deep insight into the enmity against the Jews as well as their brutal mass murder, their suffering, their humiliation, and their deepest despair. Yet it also reflects their attempts at survival and the survivors' search for a new existence after the war. This is an important book in the world of the Literature of the Holocaust.

Dr. Zsuzsanna Ozsvath, Ackerman Center for Holocaust Studies, Leah and Paul Lewis Chair in Holocaust Studies Professor Emeritus, The University of Texas at Dallas, Author of *When the Danube Ran Red* (2010) and *My Journey Home: Life after the Holocaust* (2019)

Separated Together is a powerful work about survival and renewal whose narrative spans generations and is sure to inspire new generations in the 21st century who need to learn the bitter and inspiring lessons of the Shoah.

Rabbi Abraham Cooper, Simon Wiesenthal Center, Los Angeles

Ken Price, a creative and scholarly clinical psychologist, has produced an uncommonly thoughtful chronicle of two people's debasement by but ultimate victory over murderous Nazi oppression. It's a true story that reads like a novel. It's inspiring as well as sobering – inspiring because it shows what the human spirit can overcome; sobering because it is a cautionary tale of what the Jews have been subjected to for thousands of years and of what, like other oppressed groups, they are at risk for today and into the future. This beautifully written book is uplifting even as it is frightening. Price has written something notable.

Dr. Gerald C. Davison, Professor of Psychology, University of Southern California, Los Angeles

I'm sure this is a labor of love, it shows. This is a compelling personal story whose intimate look at the human costs and triumphs of the transitions of history tells the story of people losing a world and finding a new one. Beyond a story of the Holocaust, it explores the way that people lived and the way that they rebuilt their lives.

Daniel Greenfield, Shillman Fellow at David Horowitz Freedom Center

Just finally finished your book and WOW!!! Terrific work, it knocked me out, told me much I didn't know historically which was the greatest pleasure for me, lots of fascinating historical stuff and *such* a truly wonderful tribute to Gloria and family.

Very, very impressed and really knocked out by it all. Kind of wiped me out in the best way possible. Congratulations on a wonderful accomplishment, really well done!

Henry Jaglom, writer, film and stage director & producer, author of *The Third Stone on the Second Row: A Family Memoir and a Brief History of the Jewish People*; son of Simon Jaglom, Director of trade in Danzig pre-1939

This moving memoir describes the lives of a Jewish couple married before the war but divided during the Nazi occupation of Poland as the husband had found himself in the US at the outbreak of the war. Miraculously, his wife survived and they were reunited in 1946 and made new lives for themselves in the United States. It is a remarkable study of human resilience and should be read by all those interested in the fate of the Jews in the tragic twentieth century.

Dr. Antony Polonsky, Albert Abramson Professor (Emeritus) of Holocaust Studies at Brandeis University, Chief Historian, Museum of Polish Jews in Warsaw

What a great achievement you have accomplished with your magnum opus. It's an admirable and complex work merging history, emotion, social science, and love. You accomplish the tremendous achievement of synthesizing the histories, personalities and characters of Abe and Sonia while presenting the dramatic story of their lives. The prose is clear and the narrative flows. The format is excellent – following the parallel lives of Abe and Sonia from childhood, through courtship and marriage, through their wartime separation, their moving reunion, and afterwards as survivors.

There is an erudite interweaving of historical chapters on history of 20th century, Poland in 20th century, rise of Nazism, political events of 1930s, the Final Solution, and politics in the West – a great introduction for history students.

You have a nice way of injecting your own voice into the narrative, including touches of humor, bringing the reader closer to the story. Thank you for giving me the opportunity to read your work, at once popular and scholarly, and to revisit the extraordinary lives of Sonia and Abe.

Helen Schary Motro attorney and author of *Maneuvering Between the Headlines*, 2005; daughter of Zalman Schary, the cousin who persuaded Abe to come to America in August 1939 for a "short visit." She divides her time between Tel Aviv and New York.

Thank you very much for sending me a copy of your manuscript. It gives me great pleasure to offer a brief review of your book *Separated Together*.

I am also a child of immigrants. My father was born near Krakow, Poland. He moved to Vienna in his teens and escaped with my mother from Austria in 1939, managing to reach the U.S.

Your narrative is a story of resilience, first and foremost, of a family that found each other after unspeakable loss and separations who managed to put losses behind them and live a most productive and meaningful life. For other survivors, including my father, the adaptation did not turn out so well, although the next generation – my generation – has fared much better.

You are a masterful storyteller and historian, weaving within the story of Abe and Sonia, the history of the Nazi's and their systematic annihilation of the Jews. As a psychologist, you show remarkable sensitivity and insight into your protagonists and other trauma survivors, the situations they faced and how they survived without major psychological damage.

The stories are compelling. The characters brought to life; the reunion and "second life" inspirational.

This book is a wonderful addition to the library of Holocaust memoirs. I can see this book turned into a moving and successful screenplay and movie.

Ron Fischler, M.D. FAAP Pediatrician, Associate Clinical Professor of Pediatrics, University of Arizona College of Medicine, Phoenix, AZ

As a Holocaust scholar, author, researcher, filmmaker, I have read many Holocaust memoirs and conducted hundreds of survivor interviews. And although each one is unique and each one has resonance, this story told by Ken Price of his parents-in-law is unique beyond unique! It is not only a Holocaust story, it is also – to borrow Dickens' title – a 'Tale of Two Cities!'

Where else have you heard of one spouse in Poland, while the other is at New York's 1939 World's Fair? Where else have you read about a Jew volunteering to go to Auschwitz? Or a woman, whose children were murdered, actually saying, "I have ONLY met good people in my life"?

The story of Sonia and Abe is, to be sure, a tragic story – How can it be anything but tragic when your children are murdered? – but it is also a story of triumph, of remarkable resilience, and at its heart, a story of love.

Besides being a gripping, personal account of Sonia's endurance and survival during the war coupled with her husband's struggling immigrant life in the United States, this story continues long after the war is over. We see the re-creation of a family, as Sonia and Abe reunite in 1946. They not only begin a new life in their new country, they find joy again as well. They have a second little girl and boy; they become proud and loving parents, and grandparents, and throughout the thread of the 'new' family that they create, their love for the 'old' family is never far from anyone's memory.

This is a story of love and resilience, and ultimately, of hope. It is a story that must be [told] – so that others may learn and hope as well.

Ann Weiss, author of _The Last Album: Eyes from the Ashes of Auschwitz-Birkenau_, Norton: 2001

Separated Together is so much more than the everyday garden variety Holocaust story. I know so many personal journeys of Holocaust survivors have hit the bookstores, but I think this book is special. I love the style, the attention to detail and tying in historical, Biblical and literary references. I am caught up, breathlessly agonizing as Sonia makes an escape from the Warsaw Ghetto and by returning to it saves her life. I love Abe's aphorism about Yesterday, Today and Tomorrow and how he chooses to live in Today.

Memory, faith and longing over time and space sustained both Abe and Sonia through adversity and hardship, becoming in the end, a uniquely American epic. For those who wonder, how did WWII and the Holocaust come about, the author offers a clear historical background to explain what led to the World War, targeting of the Jews, and Germany's quest for land and power. After reading this book, one can no longer say, "I had no idea, I didn't know." Prepare to be woke.

Jackie Wald, Book Reader, Editor and Reviewer

Dr. Ken Price has produced a unique and interesting book here to honor his in-laws from WWII. Rarely do you hear about a son-in-law praising his in-laws, especially his mother-in-law. However, Dr. Price not only praises his in-laws, he also reveres and honors them by writing their story of survival. Few sons-in-laws would dedicate six years to writing and researching the story of their in-laws, but Dr. Price does so and shows brilliantly how these two people illustrate how to live a healthy life. His father-in-law, Abe Huberman, was a refugee to American in 1939 when war broke out in his home country in Poland. He stayed in the U.S. and built up a life from nothing and waited patiently for the war to end so he could be reunited with his beloved wife. Dr. Price's mother-in-law, Sonia Huberman, was stuck in Warsaw when war broke out with Abe's and her two small children. Sonia suffered in the ghetto in Warsaw and then was deported to Majdanek and Auschwitz. Her children were killed in the camps, but she survived the war, in part, by knowing her husband was waiting for her. After 1945, she made her way back to her husband and she and Abe built a life together in the United States and had two additional children. Dr. Price is most insightful when he takes the therapeutic training and psychological insights he has gained over a lifetime of work, especially having worked with U.S. veterans and their trauma for years, when reviewing the lives of his in-laws in order to teach us the lessons of how one lives a good life despite hardships. This story is about hope, love and survival and is told well by Dr. Price. It shows us in dramatic form what superhuman feats we are capable of if we have a will and desire to do them.

Bryan Mark Rigg, author of *Hitler's Jewish Soldiers* **and** *The Rabbi Saved by Hitler's Soldiers*

This book is dedicated

To my Heroes

Abraham Huberman

and

Sonia Jaglom Huberman

And to

David and Lusia Huberman

The Children

Who didn't live long enough

To become Heroes

INTRODUCTION

Many years after the Second World War, Sonia and Abe Huberman's 19-year-old daughter, Gloria, spent a summer in Israel visiting family. She recalls one of her adventures:

"My cousins, Dani and Raquel, led me on what was supposed to be a two-hour hike in the Galilee on the famous Wadi Amud trail. We were admiring nature and listening to Dani talk about the history of the Galilee. As time passed, we finally noticed we hadn't seen any other hikers in ages. We realized we had been walking for five hours and woke up to the fact that we were lost. We were exhausted and hungry. Our throats were parched, and we had no water left to drink. I, for one, was frightened. Suddenly, Dani spotted a flight of steps cut into the side of a tall, steep mountain. It looked like Jacob's ladder reaching to the sky. At the base of the steps was a small iron gate and a sign reading "Stop Military Base No Entrance." We were all alone and desperate, so we ignored the sign and began climbing the narrow steps. As I climbed, I could barely catch my breath. My legs felt like they were made of concrete. Halfway up I felt that I couldn't continue. I couldn't take another step. I would just give up and tumble down the mountain, ending my suffering. Then I thought of my mother and my father. I knew their story of love and defiant courage and their refusal to ever give up. So, I took a deep breath and with renewed energy I pushed myself to raise one foot above the other. I climbed to the top of that mountain and to our rescue."

PROLOGUE

"You have to be lucky in the way you're born and lucky in the way you die." Abe's words echoed in Gloria's thoughts as we stood underneath the small tent in the Shearith-Israel cemetery in Dallas, while I delivered Abe's eulogy.

The past few years hadn't been easy for Abe. He had suffered from lymphoma and heart disease. Our family physician had saved Abe's life a number of times, most recently by discovering a blockage in the arteries of his neck. Abe had felt too weak to walk a hundred feet. After surgery, he felt – as he put it – "like a new man." Now, he could easily manage the 15-minute walk to his synagogue in Lido Beach, New York. But it was the small stroke that he suffered following one of his stays in the hospital that really changed him and set him on his downhill course. He lost his peripheral vision; his memory and concentration deteriorated. His thinking was no longer sharp as it had always been, and he began to take long naps throughout the day.

In September 1989, Abe took a sudden, serious turn for the worse following complications of pneumonia. Fearing the end was near, Gloria flew up to New York and brought Abe and Sonia back to Dallas. During the flight, Gloria tried to make Abe comfortable.

Although obviously uncomfortable, he didn't complain. They made it home on a Saturday afternoon. Abe went into our guest room to sleep. That night, he was restless and confused. None of us got any sleep. I peeked into Abe and Sonia's room to check on him. I witnessed Abe sitting on the edge of his bed clapping his hands together and speaking strangely as if talking to someone. He was up and down the whole night. He was struggling, but I didn't know with what.

On Sunday morning, Gloria was making herself busy in the kitchen when Abe walked in, straight and tall. Speaking to her in a strong, clear voice, he announced, "Gloria, I'm hungry." Gloria was so excited that Abe was feeling better. She imagined that he had undergone some kind of miraculous recovery. She set about preparing breakfast for him. After eating with gusto, under Gloria's approving eye, he said he was going to wash and get dressed.

"Daddy," Gloria told him gently, "you're not going anywhere; you don't have to get dressed."

He nodded and headed back to his room. He washed himself, put on clean pajamas and lay down on the guestroom bed. Gloria, thrilled that he had recovered, began preparing his favorite foods for his post-nap lunch.

It happened that that Sunday was the second day of *Succoth*, a Jewish holiday, also known as the Feast of Tabernacles, which recalls the 40-year wandering of the Israelites on their way to Canaan, and celebrates the renewal of life. I had gone to religious services at Congregation Shearith Israel in the morning, acting as the family's representative. When I returned home around 1 PM, I rushed to the guest room to check on Abe. My face fell. I joined Gloria in the kitchen and whispered weakly that Abe wasn't breathing and had no pulse. With difficulty and with tears in my eyes, I got the words out of my mouth, "I think he's gone." In Jewish tradition, when a person dies on Shabbat or on a special holiday, it is a sign he or she is a *Tzadik* – a righteous person.

I now understood what had been going on the previous night: Abe had been wrestling with the Angel of Death.

Three days later, on a beautiful fall day, we laid Abe to his eternal rest. Our friends stood all around us. They had come not just to comfort us, but to honor the memory of a man they had come to know, respect and love from his many years of visits to us in Dallas.

During that first week of mourning, someone asked Sonia how she could bear to lose her husband. How would she take care of herself, when her husband had always taken care of her? "We had a wonderful 54 years together," my mother-in-law replied, "and, now, while I miss Abe, I have to get on with the next stage of my life, with whatever God has in store for me." That was Sonia – practical, honest, and direct. My only gloss on her words is that while she and Abe had been married 54 years, they had been together for only 47 of those years.

Accidentally, Abe had found himself living in the *Goldeneh Medina* – the Golden Land. But contrary to the image of many in the old country, the streets of New York were not paved with gold. The reality was that America was the land of golden opportunities, where even a penniless immigrant who spoke no English could become a success if he had talent and worked hard enough. Left behind in war-torn Poland, Sonia would personally discover the depths of sadism and depravity to which men and woman from across the European continent could sink. She was also to discover the wellspring of strength, courage and bravery within her, which guided her in successfully navigating the River Styx that led her through the European Hades.

Across the "pond," Abe was navigating through the unknown American territory with even less knowledge of the dangers he would face and the customs of the Land's inhabitants that he would encounter than earlier explorers of the unknown land, Meriwether Lewis and William Clark. Lewis and Clark at least had a local, native guide, Sacagawea, who could interpret for them and teach them the customs of the strange territory they would traverse. Abe

3

had relatives who were immigrants themselves and busy with their own lives. Except for cousins Fanny and Goldie, many of the others appeared to have lost interest in if not compassion for their immigrant relative, who was no longer the rich cousin from Poland, but was now a burdensome, unemployed, impecunious stranger.

Abe would come to remind them of *The Man Who Came to Dinner*, a hit comedic play that debuted at the Music Box Theatre in New York on October 16, 1939, two months after Abe had landed in the port of New York and just six weeks after the German invasion of Poland. Abe's personality was far from that of the play's main character, Sheridan Whiteside, an arrogant, overbearing guest who came for dinner but never left. Whiteside overstayed his welcome, while Abe came to be loved by all who knew him.

Long before the challenges of the Second World War, Abe and Sonia faced other challenges. And those bring us to earlier times in places far away.

1

SONIA: THE EARLY YEARS

Sonia Jaglom was born into an upper middle-class, educated family of great *yichus*, or pedigree. Her father's family, the Jaglom clan, comprised wealthy and influential businessmen. Their roots go back to a man named Moshe, who lived in Antipol, Lithuania or Byelorussia in the 1700s. His son, Baruch Avraham (b. 1792), was the first to have taken for himself the name *Yahalom*, after Czar Alexander I decreed that all his subjects must take surnames. "Yahalom," meaning "precious stone," was the third stone on the second row on the breastplate of the Biblical High Priest. In modern Hebrew, "Yahalom" means "diamond." "Yahalom" became "Yaglom" in Russian and later "Jaglom" when the family used the German cognate when they moved to Central Europe. Baruch was Sonia's great-great-grandfather. To this day, the family is distinguished in the fields of business and the arts in the United States, Europe and Israel.[1]

Sonia's mother's maiden name was Hurwitz. On her mother's maternal side, Sonia was the great-granddaughter of Rabbi Dov Berish Meisels (born in Szezekoeiny in about 1800 and died in Warsaw on March 17, 1870). In 1856, he became the Chief Rabbi of Warsaw. In 1861, in the run-up to the 1863 Polish Rebellion against

Russian rule, Meisels took an influential position supporting the Polish Nationalists, together with the Archbishop of Warsaw and Father Wyszynski of Warsaw. As an intimate of the Polish patriotic leaders, Meisels was able to forestall planned pogroms against the Jews by a group of Nationalist antisemites (with tacit approval from ruling Russian antisemites). As a Polish patriot, Meisels was arrested late in 1861 by Russian authorities. After serving several months in prison, he was expelled from the country. He then moved to London where he was promptly invited by the Jewish community to become their Chief Rabbi. He declined the honor and was permitted by Russian authorities to return to Warsaw in 1862. His activities during the 1863-1864 failed rebellion are unknown to us, as are the following six years until his death.[2]

The year 1911[3] was an especially important year for births. Sonia was born seven months after future U.S. President Ronald Reagan made his first appearance in Tampico Illinois and barely one month before the famed Gospel singer Mahalia Jackson was born in New Orleans. Sonia came into this world in a small town, Brest-Litovsk.[4] She moved with her family to the predominantly Jewish town of Pruzana (also known as Pruz'any) when she was about three years old, about the same time that Archduke Ferdinand of Austria was assassinated, which sparked the Great War, known today as the First World War. Evidence shows that Jews lived in Pruzana as early as 1450, as history records the existence of a synagogue there in 1450. The synagogue apparently remained standing for some 400 years. In the first decades of the 1900s, Jews in Pruzana made their living primarily as craftsmen, artisans and traders. The town was variously occupied by the Russian army and German and Austro-Hungarian troops in the First World War and in 1920 briefly by the Bolsheviks, until they were driven out by troops of newly independent Poland. German troops occupying Pruzana from 1915 to 1918 behaved decently to the Jewish residents, even supplying food to the Jewish kindergarten that German functionaries opened in 1917 to serve the needs of more than 100 Jewish children ranging in age from four to eight. This is likely the

"Abramowitz" school that Sonia recalled attending. The earliest photograph we have of Sonia is one taken with her classmates in the 1918-1919 school year. Perhaps the most famous child of Pruzana was Rabbi Joseph Dov Soloveitchik (1903-1993), a Talmud scholar and religious philosopher. He immigrated to the United States in 1932 and became the head of Yeshiva University's Theological Seminary and the unparalleled *doyen* of Orthodox Judaism in the United States.

Sonia was the third of four children – her brother, Miron ("Meir" in Hebrew) the oldest, Manya her older sister and Rachelle her younger sister. She grew up in the countryside surrounded by ducks, chickens and a cow. Her first language was Russian, which she spoke at home and in school. She knew Polish from her environment but became fluent later when Pruzana came under Polish rule in 1919, as Poland became an independent state for the first time in modern history following the end of the First World War. She also learned Yiddish, the *lingua franca* of Polish Jews at home, and studied Hebrew with a tutor who came regularly to her house.

She knew her paternal grandparents, the Jagloms, who were prominent in her community. Although her maternal grandparents had passed away before she was born, she knew most of her mother's seven sisters, two brothers, and their children from the family get-togethers and celebrations that she attended.

Her father, Isaac Mordecai Jaglom, had been married previously and his wife had borne him two sons. She died from an illness which at that time had no successful treatment. It was not long until Isaac remarried a woman who would become Sonia's mother, Golda. She was quite beautiful and when Isaac married her, the boys from his first marriage were in their late teens or early twenties. The family story holds that the boys, Sam and Daniel Jaglom, were so enamored of their attractive stepmother, who was not much older than them, that they did not believe they could remain in the same house with her. The boys were able to procure visas and they immigrated from Poland to the United States in 1912, settling in New York.

Sonia's father was employed by his brothers as an accountant. While the family was traditional, observing for example Jewish dietary laws, they were not deeply religious. Her father told her that to be a good Jew you don't have to be religious; you only have to be a good person and be good to others. Sonia was closer to her mother than the other children. Golda suffered from anemia and as a result of fatigue, spent much of her time in bed. It fell to Sonia to be nurse to her mother.

Sonia's parents were modern in their world outlook and so sent Sonia to a Russian and later, Polish school, as her father had studied in a Russian school in his youth. Isaac was educated, spoke Hebrew, and was familiar with the *Tanach*, the Hebrew Scriptures. While fluent in Yiddish, the parents spoke Russian at home except for the occasional adult conversations in Yiddish. In those days *yichus*, or family heritage, was considered very important and marrying off a child to a spouse with *yichus* was every parent's dream. Marrying someone with a lot of money wasn't necessarily the goal; a brilliant *yeshiva bocher*, a Talmud scholar, was preferable in that social circle to a man of means who was an unmannered oaf. Sonia had *yichus* on both sides: the Meisels and the Jagloms. While the Jagloms were prominent and wealthy, Sonia's father was not. He was middle-class, but considered himself a "gentleman." When he went out with his friends in Pruzana – often to play cards – he dressed in his usual suit and tie. To a formal event he donned white gloves. He may not have been a man of independent means like his Jaglom brothers and cousins, but at least he looked the part.

European history is a story of fluid and constantly moving borders. The basic Western concept of sovereign nation-states originated with the Treaty of Westphalia in 1648, which ended the 30 years' and 80 years' wars. But the borders of modern European and Middle Eastern nation-states were established close to their present form following the First World War, when the Austro-

Hungarian and Ottoman Empires were defeated in war and dismembered in the peace treaties that followed. After the war, Pruzana found itself within the borders of the newly independent Poland. The town had two high schools, a Polish and a Jewish high school. The Russian school no longer existed, and Sonia found herself at that point studying in a Polish government school.

She had many friends, both Catholic and Jewish, though her closest friends were Jewish. Sonia recalled few instances of antisemitism. The only incident she told us about was an experience in high school. One of her teachers started his class by saying, "I want the Jews on one side and the Christians on the other." There were about seven Jews in the class. One Jewish boy stood up and announced, "Let's go to the principal and complain."

To their relief and satisfaction, the principal, an older man with friends in the Jewish *intelligentsia*, told the youngsters to go back to the class and sit in their usual seats, and he would talk to the teacher. The Jewish teenagers kept their seats. Unlike later years when Germany was to come under Nazi rule, freeing antisemites in neighboring countries to unveil their suppressed anti-Jewish attitudes and behaviors, Poland was still a civilized society, where many of those in authority protected their Jewish charges from home-grown future Nazis. In another few years when Sonia moved to Warsaw to attend a teachers' college, antisemitism in higher education was apparently tolerated, including a *numerus clausus,* or quota for Jewish students. In college, Sonia experienced professors requiring Jewish students to stand or sit in the back of the classroom (on so-called "ghetto benches") while the non-Jewish students sat in their seats.

Fear of antisemitism led her brother Miron to leave Poland. It was common in those times in those places (Russia, Poland, Hungary, Baltic states, etc.) for Jewish men to be drafted in the Army where they faced persecution informally by their fellow servicemen or formally and brutally by many of the officers (especially in Hungary). Despite this reality, a not insignificant number of the soldiers in the Polish army were Jews. At the start of the Second World War in 1939, about 100,000 Jews were serving in the Polish army. Jews were generally prevented from rising to officer ranks above lieutenant. They were typically posted to logistical rather than combat units, except for physicians, who were allowed into the medical corps.

Facing the draft, Miron managed to get a visa and find passage, not to his preferred U.S. destination, but to Argentina. He left Poland in 1924, never to return. When Sonia was about 17, another member of the family left. Her father, according to family lore, thought it would be a good idea to immigrate to the United States. He had hoped to immigrate with the whole family, but the American Consul in Poland wouldn't grant him a visa for his wife and children. After his eldest sons had immigrated to the United States and Miron to Argentina, Isaac thought it might be a good idea to immigrate, too. Though he couldn't bring his family with him, he left Poland alone and sailed to America.

One family story has it that Isaac had been afraid that he would not be able to pay the dowry for his three daughters and claimed that it would be easier to marry off his daughters in America without having to pay a dowry. The other family story – probably the more accurate – is that Isaac was working in a government-licensed liquor store and was caught selling liquor under the table without paying government taxes. A police source warned him that he was on the verge of arrest and might want to find a way to leave the country. This second version is supported by the fact that Isaac fled Poland precipitously for Denmark, likely with the help of his well-connected brothers. He easily obtained an immigrant visa from the U.S. Consul ("Quota #3017") on November 9, 1928. He set sail from Copenhagen on S.S. Frederik VIII on January 31, 1929 and landed in New York on February 11, with five dollars in his pocket. Isaac apparently did fall in love with America. After two months he wrote his wife a letter from America: "People are free. You can do what you want. You can get a good job." He wrote that he wanted to stay in America and would work to bring the family here as soon as possible. He did find employment in New York and dutifully sent 30 dollars (approximately 150 Polish Złotych at the time) per month back to the family in Poland. According to Sonia, the money was appreciated.

When Isaac first arrived in America, at age 58, without knowing any English, he found a job in a factory. He went to night school to learn English and then succeeded in getting a job in a school. After two years, he sent affidavits to Sonia's mother guaranteeing that he would support her and their children and they would not be an economic burden to the United States, which was in the midst of the Great Depression. Sonia brought the affidavits along with a visa application to the American Consul in Warsaw; but the Consul would not give them the visas to go to America. He offered a visa to Golda to join her husband, but not to the rest of the family. Golda wouldn't leave her children behind, so she refused to accept the visa and they all remained behind in Warsaw. She and the girls kept hoping that the Great Depression would end, after which they would be able to get visas for all of them to join the family in America.

Sonia's mother had inherited a pair of diamond earrings. One earring she had sold so that Miron could afford passage to Argentina. Now that Sonia was moving to Warsaw to attend a teachers' college, Golda sold the second diamond earring to pay for Sonia's expenses at the college.

One of Sonia's friends, Hania, a classmate of hers in college, who had grown up in Krakow, had a friend, Tovah Leah, who had recently married a man named Avrum (diminutive of Abraham). Tovah and Avrum owned a radio receiver, a model of German engineering: a *Telefunken*. Hania visited the couple frequently on Friday nights, along with other invited guests. They visited, noshed on snacks or ate a formal dinner and listened to music broadcast through the Telefunken. For sure, they must have listened to Big Band music broadcast from America over the shortwave. Hania invited Sonia to join her at Avrum and Tovah Leah's apartment for

Friday night *Shabbat*, and Sonia accepted the invitation. Sonia's younger cousin, Anna ("Hanka"), described Sonia as "a strikingly beautiful, tall willowy blonde with blue eyes." Little did Sonia guess that her Friday night visit would alter her life story dramatically.

---

1. Jaglom
2. *Jewish Encyclopedia,* 1906.
3. A number of official documents generated after the war list Sonia's birth year as 1909, though Sonia always told the family that her birth year was 1911. It was not uncommon for birth dates to be advanced or retarded by immigration or other officials. In the ship's manifest of Sonia's sailing to the United States in 1946, her age is given as 17. My guess is that some official asked Sonia her birthdate and she gave the correct answer of September "seventeenth" which was misunderstood as age 17, even though that was ludicrously impossible. We have chosen to use the birth year that Sonia used.
4. In Polish: Brzesc-Litewski, or Brzesc nad Bugiem, commonly known by its Jewish inhabitants as "Brisk".

2

ABE: THE EARLY YEARS

It's a true saying: 'Money can't buy happiness.' But without money you have plenty of unhappiness. When you will know my life story, you will understand why I was so money-conscious and why I gave so much to my children. - Abe Huberman

Abe Huberman was a thinker. He was a man of great depth and a wonderful observer of life. He was a practitioner of self-examination, who made a point of passing on to his children and grandchildren life lessons that he had learned. One of his greatest gifts to us were the memoirs or essays of his reminiscences that he wrote every few years. They were thoughtful, detailed and moving.

Abe was born in November 1904, some nine months after the outbreak of the short Russo-Japanese war and barely three weeks after New York City's subway system opened for business, and the same year Henry Ford's horseless carriage models B and C made their debut. The next year, 1905, the Russo-Japanese war ended with a Japanese victory and concluded with the Treaty of Portsmouth brokered by then U.S. President, Theodore Roosevelt. It was also the year that the Imperial Russian, Czarist government was engulfed in revolution and violent riots. At the time, eastern Poland remained under Czarist rule.

In his own colorful language, Abe told the story of his birth at 2:30 AM to Rivka and David Huberman:

In a little town in Poland, called Kozienice [or Kozinetz, in Yiddish], near Radom, a number was changed in the City Hall register: the living population of the city was increased from 1,200 to 1,201. (Official census records suggest the population was closer to 4,000. But no matter.)[1] *I arrived in this world crying very loud. This was my announcement that I am here. My mother, Rivka, told me that my crying was not a cry of complaint – not 'Why have I been brought into this world of happiness but also much misery?' No, it was a prayerful cry – for good luck in life. [I was born to a] wonderful, wonderfully intelligent and very good-natured mother of good character, and to a father, David, a pious, honest, religiously observant, smart man, who, alas, was not too successful in business. My coming into this world brought a lot of happiness to my parents because I was the second child and the first boy who survived childhood. Their greatest wish was to have a son, who could help support the family and say Kaddish for them after they passed away.*

Kaddish is the traditional prayer recited after the passing of a close relative. Often called a "prayer for the dead," it is, in reality, a prayer to help comfort the living by reminding them that God's ways are unknowable. Traditionally, only sons are required to recite the Kaddish, which is why religious Jews in Europe used to rejoice when their first son was born – they had someone who could say Kaddish for them. Parents commonly called their first son *mein* [my] *kaddish.*

Like today, the birth of a child was cause for celebration. Unlike today, if parents wanted to have a family of four children, they would have six or more children, knowing well that some of them would die young and never reach adulthood. Between 1911 and 1915, more than ten percent of European newborns, died at or shortly after birth. In comparison, neonatal deaths in Europe by the 1970s were, on average, one-and-a-half percent. David and

Rivka's first child, a daughter, had died of disease in infancy. Following Abe into this world were sister Tovah Leah and three brothers, Aaron, Moshe and Yitzhak, all of whom survived childhood. Aaron, three years Abe's junior, was tall, blond, very smart and admired by the whole family. He fell ill with pneumonia at age 17. Rivka, David and Abe, rushed him to Warsaw to see Dr. Belenco, who took one look at him and exclaimed, "What did you bring me – a dead body? It's too late, I can't do anything." In a last futile attempt to treat Aaron, they took him to a sanitarium in Otwock, a town some 15 miles southeast of Warsaw, on the right bank of the Vistula river below the mouth of the Swider river. Aaron turned his head to the family with his last breaths, saying haltingly, "Such a beautiful world, with so many people. I was hoping and planning so many beautiful things and now they are going to bury me deep in the ground." With that declaration, he closed his eyes and died. At a young age, Abe became acquainted with illness and loss.

The town named Kozienice has existed at least since 1390. The name comes from the root word "koza," meaning "wild goats" or "stags." Many wild animals, especially goats lived in the surrounding forests and became the favored prey of Polish kings who frequented the area in the 15th and 16th centuries. Jews are documented as residents of Kozienice by the year 1616, when they (all 75 of them) were granted a Royal charter to reside in the town.

Kozienice came to prominence as a center of Hasidism, as it had been the home of Rabbi Yisroel of Kozienice (1740-1815), who came to be known as the *Kozinetzer Maggid* ("the storyteller of Kozinetz") and was the progenitor of the Maggid five-generation dynasty. Hasidism originated in the 18th century as a subtype of Judaism that emphasized joy and dancing in prayer. Although its leaders were typically learned in Jewish texts, the average Hasid tended to be less educated in the Talmud and more likely to immerse himself in stories of mysticism and to attach himself to a particular *Rebbe* who was venerated as a religious leader with special knowledge and alleged, special magical abilities. The *Kozinetzer Maggid* was considered in his own time and almost two centuries later as a holy man, great scholar, mystic and maker of miracles.

From pictures we have seen of 18th-century towns in America's West, we imagine that Kozienice must have looked similar. Its streets were unpaved, muddy and filled with ruts during the rainy season. There were few sidewalks, no electricity, no running water and no indoor plumbing. It was not until 1931 that Kozienice finally joined the modern world of electrically powered lamps.

The Hubermans lived in a two-story house made of wooden planks and beams. Small as it was, the house consisted of four apartments. The other three families were headed by a tailor, a shoemaker, and a tobacconist who rolled his cigarettes by hand. The residents' businesses were in the front of the house, and they lived in the back, on the first or second floors.

The Hubermans' apartment comprised a single room. In the middle of the room stood a little wood-burning stove made of bricks and cement that served for cooking and provided heat in the winter. Their furniture, as it was, consisted of two metal beds with "mattresses" – bags of straw placed on top of the frames. Once a year, before Passover, the old straw was replaced with new – it was the only time they could afford it.

Next to the stove were two benches and a wooden table used for eating and for supporting the sewing machine that Rivka used in her dressmaking business. Rivka slept in one bed with Tovah Leah and Moshe. Abe slept with his father and his brother Aaron in the other bed. The other children slept on straw mattresses on the floor. There were also two barrels in the house, one filled with clean water and covered with a linen cloth to keep bugs out, and the other a receptacle for the family's dirty water. The dirty water was spilled into the street every morning. As all the neighbors did this, it made the streets in the winter like a sheet of ice, leading to many slips and falls. One kerosene lamp hanging from a nail on a wall provided light for the one-room home. On many occasions, David mistook a fly on the wall for the nail, resulting in a dropped and smashed lamp. The family lived in the dark until David could walk to the store the next morning to buy a new lamp and a container of kerosene. Early in the morning, townsfolk could be seen trekking through the dusty or muddy streets on the way to Herschel the Baker to buy bread. In August or September, everyone was storing up potatoes for winter meals. David usually bought five large sacks of potatoes, which were stored in their small, dusty and musty "basement." Cool in the summer and cold in the winter, the basement was their "refrigerator."

Kozienice was known as a center of shoemakers, who not only repaired shoes but manufactured them by hand. David, who only had a grade school education, made a living manufacturing and selling shoes and shoemaker supplies such as leather, wooden dowels, nails, cloth and bristle brushes to other shoemakers. He toiled six days a week but barely made a living. Abe estimated that at one point his father's entire stock of merchandise would have been worth about 30 dollars. Rivka, who had graduated from high school (known as a *Gymnasium*) in the big city, Krakow, had her own business; she was a self-employed dressmaker. Although talented, she didn't earn much money. In a town of poor people, even a capable and popular seamstress didn't earn much, especially since it was not uncommon for housewives to endeavor to make clothes for their own families.

From the age of six, Abe accompanied his father on his daily rounds, calling himself his father's "right-arm." Before the onset of winter, his father typically hired two farmers with wagons to ride 15 to 20 miles outside of town to buy wood for their wood-burning stove in order to be prepared for the freezing Polish winter. His father carefully inspected the wood in the lumber yard, looking for especially good quality dry wood. At home, the wood was stowed in a storage room, known simply as the *Kammer* ("the room") in the backyard. Frequently, recalled Abe, they would find that bundles of wood had been stolen from the *Kammer*. For this reason, they installed a large strong lock on the door.

"How times change," Abe used to say. *"In America they steal diamonds, mink coats, silver and other valuables, even automobiles. In the old country they stole wood for the stove and clean laundry from the attics, where the laundry hung for four to five days to dry."*

Abe's childhood recollection of the family's clothes laundering apparently made a big impression on him. He was awed by the laborious routine of the washerwoman:

Once a month, the washerwoman came to our house to do the laundry, a task that took two days. She was middle-aged, short and stocky, but what muscles she must have had. She started her toil by first soaking then soaping and washing the laundry in a big round wooden tub called a ballia. The next step was to boil the laundry in a large kettle on the stove. And then, carrying the wet laundry wrapped up in a blanket, she schlepped it six to eight blocks to the river, where she rinsed her load and beat every piece of laundry with a heavy wooden klapke [a "beater"] against a wooden board. Returning home, she used krochmal [starch] on the colored clothing and whitened the whites with some kind of mixture of water and diluted blue paint. The final step after squeezing water out of the laundry by hand, was to carry the clothes up a stepladder to the attic, where she hung them on clotheslines to dry. Since the attic was shared with other families, it was not uncommon for clothes to be pinched and disappear. There were times, other than winter, when members of the family slept in the attic to watch over the drying laundry to protect it from pilferage.

The washerwoman wasn't the only one doing heavy housework. Besides not having electricity, there was no indoor plumbing. As in Biblical times, townsfolk walked to a centrally located well to fill pails with water for home usage. Typically, long lines of people waited to fill their water containers. It was a social time, and youngsters sent to get water for the family used the opportunity to visit with their friends. Abe had memories of fetching water during the cold Polish winters when the outside air plummeted to ten degrees below zero. The area around the pump caught the water spilled from the spigot and the pails, and turned to ice with the onset of winter, frequently leading to the designated water carriers slipping and falling, spilling the water they had waited so long in line to pump. Abe fondly recalled how nice the folks were, allowing the kids to re-fill their pails at the head of the line, instead of forcing them to go to the back. It was common to carry a full pail of water in each hand to balance the load. The well-to-do townsfolk didn't fetch their own water; they hired a water carrier (*vasser tregger*) to bring pails of water to them: three cents in Polish money for two pails worth of water. The town's storekeepers, not as financially well-off as the townsfolk might have thought, often fetched their own water from the pump at night, so that they wouldn't be embarrassed being seen by their fellow townspeople as unable to afford to hire *vasser treggers*. David suffered from the same pride or embarrassment. Often, he and the kids went out at night to get their water to avoid being noticed, taking the 20-minute walk daily, whether it was a sweltering hot summer day or a freezing cold winter.

Thursdays were market days. Local farmers came to town to sell their chickens and eggs, potatoes, wheat, corn, beets and carrots. In turn, the farmers shopped in the town's stores for kerosene, soap, candles, shoes and material from which the wives would make the families' clothing. According to Abe, the Polish Catholic farmers and their Jewish customers and shopkeepers got along well. A Credit Union existed in town and was run by Jews and Polish Christians. It was known for giving out low-interest loans to the town's artisans and shopkeepers

The Huberman family was so poor that they couldn't afford to buy enough food to feed the whole family daily. Abe recalled going to bed hungry on a regular basis. He told us how his little brother Aaron looked up at his father and asked wistfully for a piece of bread. From time to time, recalled Abe, David managed to procure a piece of bread and cut it up into small pieces to parcel it out to the children. As a small child, Aaron's dream was a to get a whole slice of bread for himself.

Occasionally, the family visited their cousin Paula and her parents in Warsaw. They were very well-to-do and even owned a dog, a black and white little dog named Brilush. When little Aaron saw the family give the dog bones from dinner, with plenty of meat still on them, he whispered to Abe, "I wish I could be a dog in Auntie's house."

The family generally arose at 7 AM. Toilet facilities were an outhouse shared with other families. This meant that there was often a queue and a wait to use the facilities. Abe remembered that during wintertime his father often returned from the outhouse with icicles hanging from his beard. Abe accompanied his father to the synagogue for morning services every day at 8 AM. In addition to a place for men to gather for prayer, the synagogue was also a place for visiting with other townsfolk and for getting news of the outside world.

After religious services, the men gathered around Zalman the watchmaker. Zalman – apparently better off than most of the other men – got a newspaper every day from Warsaw and related to all the men news about Poland and the outside world. The men would return home and tell the family over breakfast, such as it was, the news of the world. Famished, David and Abe along with the rest of the family, dove into the meal that Mother had prepared that morning: potatoes cut into pieces, swimming in a soup of a little milk and a lot of water. The milk was fresh. Rachelle, the milk woman, traveled to a nearby farm at 5 AM to buy milk, which she brought back and sold to the townsfolk. Rivka typically bought a half-pint or pint of milk (straight from the cow and unpasteurized, of course) from Rachelle. The second meal of the day was supper. For supper, Mother mashed potatoes, drizzled some oil on them and fried them in her cast iron pan. For practical reasons, the water used for boiling potatoes was recycled and used to wash the dishes.

Sometimes, when Rivka could afford it, she bought a few ounces of butter and added them to the potatoes. At other times, she was able to buy some rice or kasha, and on occasion – for the Sabbath –

some fish or a real treat: chicken. There was a common saying at the time, that if you saw a poor woman buying an orange or a chicken in the middle of the week you would ask who was sick. If a poor person was splurging on "luxuries," some family member must be sick and in need of chicken soup or some fresh fruit.

Typical of Abe's positive outlook, he thought his mother's meals were wonderful – the food she made was absolutely delicious! Whatever food she prepared was delicious because he was so hungry. Despite the privations he endured as a child, as an adult, Abe always talked about how warm his family was, how close the community was, and how happy he was. In contrast to the recollections of many Polish Jews, Abe recalled that he never experienced antisemitism as a child.

As a young boy he went to a one-room Jewish school, known as *heder* (literally "room" in Hebrew/Yiddish), where he learned about Jewish traditions and the Bible as well as how to read Hebrew. He remembered "as if it were today" going with his father to Heder for the first time to discuss with the teacher, Rabbi Mayer Chill Shtroyae, about school tuition. His father told the Rabbi that he wanted Abe to learn all the Jewish traditions, but most importantly, to learn to pray well.

Growing up in Poland, Abe became fluent in Polish, but apparently never learned much Russian. At home, the family spoke Yiddish, that traditional European Jewish language, a descendant of Middle High German. As his family was religiously observant, Saturday, or the Sabbath (*Shabbos* in Yiddish), was a day of rest from work; but it was a day of study for him. Typically, he accompanied his father to the synagogue for Shabbos services and then to the home of the town's Rabbi for lunch, which was followed by lectures on the Bible and the Talmud. Abe preferred to join his less observant friends in play, but out of respect for his father, he put aside his disappointment and observed the Sabbath by study alongside his father.

For ordinary folk in Kozienice, the Sabbath was a respite from hard work, the time to which they looked forward all week. On Friday afternoons, about half an hour before Sabbath began at sunset, a beadle[2] walked down the streets (we can only imagine what that must have been like in the winter, with a couple of feet of snow on the ground) going door to door knocking on people's doors with a stick to remind them that Sabbath was coming and it was time to close the stores and get the family ready. This meant setting the table with a tablecloth, putting out candlesticks, preparing the food – a *challah* (braided egg bread, home-made or from Herschel the baker), maybe a chicken if the budget allowed, and sides like kasha and potatoes (the Hubermans' staple). Sometimes, a delicacy like pickled herring would miraculously appear on the table. Chicken was the most substantial entrée that ordinary people could sometimes expect to see on their Sabbath table. It was expensive for working people but could not compare with the extravagant price of red meat or fish other than herring. Impoverished as Abe's family was, he did not see either of those on his plate until he reached adulthood and financial success.

In spite of material poverty, the family was rich in love. In spite of the hunger in his childhood, Abe was emotionally well nourished. The respect and love within the home helped form Abe's character – self-confident, secure and optimistic – as much as the hunger shaped his ambition.

---

1. Kaplinski, *et al.*
2. A house of worship usher or caretaker

CATASTROPHE IN KOZIENICE AND THE PIGEON STORY

The Catastrophe

Kozienice was home to more than 220 Jewish businesses, primarily trades and crafts. At its peak, more than 70 percent of the population of the town was employed in the manufacture and sale of footwear. Kozienice also hosted a foundry, a flour mill, a sawmill and a slaughterhouse.

Jacob ("Yankel") Birnbaum opened the first mechanized shoe factory and employed 20 workers. In addition to Yankel, prominent shoemakers, recalled by Birnbaum's son-in-law Issokhor Lederman, a former Kozienice resident, were: Yankel Breitman, David Huberman, Messrs Meltzer, Fleischer, Korman and Lederman. They sold their wares to the large Russian market and also to trade fairs in Lentsche, Lublin and a variety of other Polish towns.

Hoping to increase his income, David undertook a new business venture. He bought shoes from four shoemakers in Kozienice and traveled across the border to sell them in Russia. The new business seemed a success. Life would be good.

On his final trip to Russia, he hired a driver and horse-drawn wagon filled with six crates of shoes to take to the nearest station to catch a train to Russia. When he got to Russia and began his rounds to local stores to sell his merchandise, he discovered, to his horror, that every last shoe was gone. Instead of shoes, every crate was filled with stones packed neatly in straw. He had had confrontations with a rival businessman back in Kozienice and was convinced that his rival had stolen all the shoes and replaced them with the worthless stones. Depressed, but incensed, David found the local police station and reported the theft. The Russian police promptly arrested him on the charge of filing a false claim, leading one to conclude that it wasn't the rival who had stolen the shoes, but local Russian businessmen in cahoots with the Russian cops. But David was forever convinced that it was his competitor in Kozienice who did the deed.

It's not clear whether David had used his savings or had borrowed money to buy the shipment of shoes. In either case, the outcome was that David Huberman was forced to declare bankruptcy. There would be no more money for buying shoes to sell.

Abe's world was turned upside down. He was 11 years old and understood that the family was in trouble – bad, serious trouble. Whether on his own initiative or encouraged by his humiliated father, Abe dropped out of school. That was the end of his formal education. From that point, he became his father's partner as family breadwinner.

His main job was to buy locally sourced foodstuffs such as butter and eggs, then sell the "farm-fresh" staples in the the big city, Lublin, a three-hour train ride distant. In Lublin, he bought or traded his groceries for such things as kerosene, tobacco, soap and brought them back to sell in Kozienice. His margins were razor thin. Usually, he bought a one-way ticket from Kozienice to Lublin. For the return trip, he boarded the train without a ticket. Instead of riding in a coach car with seats, he stuffed himself in a "steerage" car, under one of the bench seats, scrunching as close to the wall as he could, holding on to his merchandise. All the while, he prayed he wouldn't be found out by the conductor who, as he made his way down each car punching tickets, would kick his heavy leather boot under each bench seat trying to catch children he knew were often hiding under the seats, hitching free rides on "his" train. Sometimes, the price of the return ticket that he didn't buy was the only profit from his business trip to Lublin.

Even little brother Moshe contributed to the family upkeep. Abe remembered Moshe as a brilliant student and a natural-born businessman. At the age of eight, Moshe started his first business. He bought school textbooks from high school students at the end of the school year and sold them at the beginning of the next school year to new students going into the grade. Though a creative and clever little boy, Moshe wasn't a risk taker. He was slow and deliberate in making decisions, unlike his older brother, Abe, a major risk taker, as his life would show.

The Pigeons don't come Home to Roost

Abe had learned one important business lesson early in life. Sometime, around the age of six or seven, Abe and a boy a few years older than him were outside playing. A flock of pigeons flew by and the older boy remarked that those were his pigeons. Enthralled, Abe said he would like to own some pigeons, too. If he would pay a few *złote*, the boy offered to sell him some.

In his mind Abe now had a mission. He had to find some money, so he could buy a few pigeons from his friend. Rivka, his dressmaker mother, always had some change lying around in the house. Although a good, honest boy, Abe was not perfect and had the ability to be silly and mischievous. He noticed where his mother had put a few coins and covered them up with some papers. Not long after, Rivka was looking for change for a customer and wondered aloud, "Where is that change?" Abe found the "misplaced" coins and brought them proudly to his mother. Within a week, Abe again found a few *złote* on the floor. He picked them up and moved them to a hiding place. They did live in a one-room house without much furniture; nonetheless, Abe's stash was not discovered, and Rivka apparently never missed the few coins. The next time Abe went out to play with his friend, he proudly handed over the *złote* and asked for his pigeons. His friend pointed little Abe to three or four pigeons and said, "OK, those are now yours." Abe ran over to them but they promptly flew away. Abe looked at his friend, puzzled and teary eyed. "Don't worry," comforted his friend, "Come out tonight at 9 o'clock, and you'll find your pigeons outside the house." Of course, Abe's bedtime was before 9 PM, so he was never able to commune with his late-night pigeon visitors.

Abe was young, but he wasn't stupid. That was the first time – and maybe the last time – that he was fooled in a business transaction. He enjoyed telling the pigeon story as a warning not to trust anyone, even a friend or an acquaintance who offered an investment that sounded like a fly-by-night scheme.

While David needed and appreciated Abe's help, he felt guilty that he was not teaching his son a trade. He contemplated turning him over to a watchmaker so Abe could learn the watchmaking trade. By then, nearly 12 years old, Abe insisted that he wanted to be a businessman like his father, not a skilled tradesman. To convince Abe that father knew best, David appealed to the town's Rabbi, whose opinion was respected by all, to talk sense into the boy. After listening to David's argument about what was best for his son, and Abe's rejoinder, the kindly Rabbi winked at Abe, turned to David and announced, "We have enough watchmakers. If the boy wants to be a businessman, let him do what he wants." Though disappointed, David respected the Rabbi's decision, and he never raised the issue again.

Abe took advantage of the Jewish holidays to become a little businessman. On *Pesah* (Passover) he delivered dresses on behalf of his aunt, Etka, earning from each of her customers a *grosz* or two as tips. On *Shavuoth* (Feast of Weeks), he sold green, leafy branches to neighboring housewives for holiday window decorations. On

Purim, it was customary to send plates of food, like an apple and a piece of cake to friends. The Hubermans took the gifts they received and exchanged them with other friends, so they actually only had to prepare one plate of their own to send. Abe spent the day delivering food parcels and earning tips from all the recipients. He remembered David Dufche, a tall man with a long red beard, a wealthy tannery owner, who tipped him ten *groszy,* a big copper coin worth a few cents, a nice tip thought Abe at the time. On *Succoth* (Feast of Tabernacles), Abe sold willow branches (*hoshanos*), which were used for religious services on the sixth day of *Succoth* (known as *Hoshanah Rabbah)*. Abe wrote in one of his memoirs:

This was a very risky business. If you couldn't sell the hoshanos by 10 AM you had to throw them away. I was trying to outsmart my competitors, who were all standing in front of the synagogue. So, I stood a block away from the synagogue, and sold my merchandise to customers before they reached the synagogue.

4

ABE DEMONSTRATES HIS BUSINESS ACUMEN AND BECOMES A CEO

After dropping out of elementary school, Abe worked full-time helping his father rebuild his shoemaking and supply business and when he had time, running his little Kozienice-Lublin "supermarket" business. He was a small child, a cute boy with a delightful sense of humor and a knack for joke- and story-telling. Undoubtedly, he charmed the local shoemakers and perhaps the storekeepers in Lublin as well, enabling him to actually earn some income for the family from the adults who enjoyed visiting and trading with him.

During his teenage years, Abe learned about the shoe business in particular and business in general from his father, his customers and vendors, and everyone he ever ran into. Whether a natural talent or a learned behavior, Abe could talk to anyone. As the saying goes, "he never met a stranger." By the age of 15 or 16, he reached his adult height of five feet six inches. By today's standards, that's short for a man. But in those days, the average height of a man in Central Europe was five foot five. For Abe, physical height was not important and never an issue. In fact, he was much larger than his physical size. He was a big boy and later a big man – in his character, his faith, his love of family and country, his love of people and most of all, his love of life. He never saw himself as short. And neither did anyone who met him.

Between 1918 and 1926, David, with Abe's help, established a shoe factory with four shoemakers, and began to earn a better living. As it turned out and as the years passed, Abe became the businessman and David turned into the helper. Abe wasn't just selling shoemaker supplies, but also manufacturing shoes. One specialty product he sold was slipper-socks. It was perfect for indoor wear during winter months.

He learned how to source leather and found and hired shoemakers to make footwear. He also opened a store to sell finished products. His brothers all worked for him. As we learned earlier, Kozienice was known as a place to go to buy good-quality, reasonably priced, hand-made shoes. Moshe, the brother Abe described as brilliant, became a shoe "broker." Moshe's job was to position himself at the train station nearest to Kozienice. As people alighted from the train, Moshe scoped out the well-dressed, those who he thought had come to buy shoes, along with those he thought ought to buy shoes, and solicited them. His sales pitch was that there were plenty of shoemakers in Kozienice, but their merchandise was quite expensive. If they wished, he would take them by carriage to the store in Kozienice that featured the best-quality footwear at the lowest prices, and he wouldn't charge them anything – he would get a small commission from the owner of the store. Naturally, he took them to the family store. While Abe did stock some shoes available for immediate purchase, generally it was usual for customers to have their feet measured, to choose the style of footwear they wanted, the color, the type of leather and so on, to pay for the number of shoes they wanted to order and then depart for home. When the shoes – sturdy men's boots or stylish women's shoes – were finished, they would be delivered to the customers.

Though the business, nominally run by his father in Kozienice, was now going well, Abe decided that it was time to move his headquarters to Warsaw. He opened a store and a warehouse in

Warsaw, at 28 Nalewki Street. From the one store that sold shoes manufactured in Kozienice, Abe developed the business into one that manufactured shoes to be sold in his store and in other retailers throughout Poland. He sourced leather from a leather broker in Warsaw, and distributed the raw leather to shoemakers in Warsaw, who then delivered the finished products to Abe's store. He named his company in honor of his father, *Hadebut*, standing for "Huberman David Boot Co."

Moshe proved himself such a talented and capable businessman that Abe decided to make Moshe the store manager. While Moshe stayed in Warsaw, Abe hit the road as head of "outside sales," traveling around the country taking orders. Abe had an instinct and a knack for selling. He never indicated that he was the owner of the company; he suggested he was merely a salesman. In that way, he could learn what the customers really thought about the products. And if a customer wanted a discount or something special, Abe told him that he would get back to him after he returned to Warsaw and had spoken to the company's owner. They were a good team, Abe and Moshe. The business was doing so well that Abe procured a visa to travel to Colombia, South America sometime in 1926. His first cousin, Samuel Awerzstern, had immigrated to Colombia from Poland some years earlier. Abe could easily afford the cross-Atlantic voyage by then, and he felt totally comfortable leaving the business in Moshe's hands while he was gone.

Before he could buy a ticket for the trans-Atlantic passage, Abe got a letter from his father, who had remained in Kozienice to run his small business. Their Kozienice branch was in trouble; customers weren't paying for their merchandise and David had no money to pay for raw materials nor to pay the workmen. Not one to ignore problems or to leave problem-solving to someone else, Abe cancelled his international travel plans. Taking the train to Kozienice, Abe met with his father. Gently and diplomatically, as was his custom, Abe explained what he needed to do. Without any objection from his father, Abe closed down the Kozienice branch of the business, paid outstanding bills and commissions due workmen and moved all the remaining merchandise and supplies to Warsaw. He rented and furnished an apartment in Warsaw and moved his parents into the apartment, close enough so that he could watch over them and take care of his father, who would pass away in 1930.

In the early years in Warsaw, Abe worked day and night building his business. Reminiscent of his childhood when he or his father slept in the family attic to protect their well-worn laundry from pilfering, now Abe slept in the warehouse where he stored his large inventory of valuable merchandise, lest it falls victim to thieves. He wasn't about to repeat his father's disastrous experience of losing his merchandise to robbers or competitors and his business to creditors. It was cold in the unheated warehouse. But Abe feared neither the weather, nor potential burglars. He was brave. He was fearless. And he was building a successful business to support himself and his entire family.

By 1930, Abe employed 30 shoe-contractors, each of whom employed approximately ten shoemakers, who worked from home fabricating shoes. In Abe's store, office and warehouse, he employed three shipping clerks, a cashier and two leather cutters. He also employed three traveling salesmen, as well as his brother Moshe, the store manager. Abe parceled out leather and other materials to the contractors on Sundays and the contractors brought finished shoes to the store on Fridays and got paid. By Polish standards, and even by American standards, *Hadebut* was a very successful business and Abe was a rich, self-made man. He was the quintessential capitalist businessman. He discovered a need and built a company to fill customers' needs. It is true that he had some experience working with his father from the age of six. But what he learned from his father primarily was how to *not* run a business. Now, Abe provided work and sustenance for his own family as well as a good income for his employees, who, in turn, spent money on their personal needs, thus helping to support the entire downstream businesses and community.

Warsaw was a long way from Kozienice. And Abe was a long way, at the age of 25, from the little boy who went to bed hungry and slept with his father and brother on an uncomfortable, straw mattress. The only thing missing from Abe's life, was a wife with whom he could share his life and good fortune.

5

THE TELEFUNKEN MATCHMAKER

"My matchmaker was a Telefunken radio," Abe wrote in his essay that he titled "My Happy Marriage." High-quality German radios were expensive and relatively rare in those days. Abe's sister, Tovah Leah, lived at 30 Franciszkanska Street in Warsaw, with her husband, Avrumche, and their little son, Dadjo (David). They were fortunate enough to own a high-end Telefunken radio. It was common for friends and relatives to visit Tovah and her new husband in their apartment to listen to the radio. Abe, along with his brothers Moshe and Yitzhak and their mother, were among the frequent visitors to Tovah Leah's home.

One of Tovah's friends, a frequent visitor to the Telefunken "salon," was Hania Roth, from Krakow. As a gentleman, Abe would always hire a vehicle (horse and buggy) and accompany Hania home – except when the visit was on a Friday night. As she was religiously observant, Hania wouldn't ride in a buggy on the Sabbath, so after visits on Friday evenings, Abe walked Hania home. He had no romantic interest in Hania but thought it his duty not to allow a young single woman to walk or ride home alone. Though not dangerous, traveling home by herself was not something Abe thought was proper. Hania was apparently totally and blithely ignorant of Abe's lack of romantic interest in her. She interpreted his gentlemanly behavior as a sign of his love for her. In her heart, she pined for Abe.

Hania and Sonia Jaglom were both students at the same teachers' college in Warsaw and they also lived in the same apartment building. One Friday night, Hania suggested to Sonia that they spend the evening with Hania's friend, Tovah Leah, and listen to entertaining shows on her radio. Always proper, and a bit shy, Sonia protested that she hadn't been invited and therefore didn't think it appropriate for her to just show up at a stranger's home. Ultimately, she allowed Hania to persuade her that Tovah Leah and her family were such fine people that they would welcome Sonia without having issued her a formal invitation in advance. As it happened, who else was scheduled to visit Tovah Leah that night? None other than Tovah's devoted brother, Abe.

Hania and Sonia had just arrived at Tovah's, when Abe walked into the apartment. His eyes met Sonia's, and as he recalled years later, he "felt like an electric shock went through my whole body." As an inexperienced suitor, Abe was probably anxious, and tongue-tied – the opposite of how he behaved in a business situation. To break the ice, as he helped Sonia remove her overcoat, he pretended to tear a button from her coat. While he thought that was funny, Sonia didn't, exclaiming, "You have some nerve! You don't know me!" Totally mortified, Abe apologized profusely and stammered that he was just trying to make a joke. Considering how enamored he was with Sonia at first sight, this was not an auspicious beginning. Abe's heart sank as he thought that this beautiful young woman might end their relationship before it even began.

In the end, they spent some two and a half hours together at Tovah's apartment drinking tea, eating pastries, and having a wonderful time. The color came back to Abe's face as he relaxed and imagined that he had rescued himself from the abyss that he had created. He convinced himself that he had made a good impression on Sonia and would likely succeed in taking first steps to court her.

That night, Abe walked Hania and Sonia to their apartment building at 22 Sliska Street. He took a cab home – though he didn't remember the ride; as far as he knew, he could have flown home on wings of love. Abe was totally smitten with Sonia. She was beautiful, refined and educated, having had all the advantages and opportunities in her youth that his poverty had denied him. That same night, he told his mother, "This is the woman I am going to marry."

Sonia was also taken by Abe because of his character. Later, when describing to her mother why she was attracted to Abe, she explained, "I have watched the way he treats his mother. Any man who treats his mother with such kindness and respect is certain to be a wonderful husband."

The following week, Abe and his supervising family spent Sunday afternoon with Sonia and Hania at Tovah's apartment. Abe hired a horse and buggy to take the girls home. Privately, he made a date with Sonia to go out to a nightclub, where they danced, drank tea and ate pastries. From then until around April 1933, they went out together almost twice a week. In June 1933, Sonia and Hania graduated from their teachers' college. Thoughtful as always, Abe sent both of the ladies sumptuous bouquets of flowers to celebrate their graduation. Upon receiving the beautiful bouquet, Hania gushed to Sonia that Abe was such a nice man. Although he was *her* boyfriend, explained Hania, Abe sent Sonia flowers so that she wouldn't feel bad that he had sent a beautiful gift to Hania. Sonia always had tremendous self-control and she exercised it at that point, keeping a straight face in front of Hania, while smiling inside, secure in the knowledge that his romantic interest was exactly the opposite of what Hania imagined.

On their next date, Sonia told Abe, with a laugh, what Hania had said, and the shocked Abe protested that he never gave Hania any indication that he was interested in her. He treated her like a lady because he was a gentleman. Abe wrote in one of his autobiographical essays "Besides shaking her tiny cold hands at hello and goodbye, I never gave her any reason to think that I dreamt about her!"

Another Sunday, after a visit to the Telefunken salon, Abe hired a buggy to take Hania home. Abe turned white when Hania opened her mouth and announced, "Abe, I want you to know that when you marry me, I shall not allow you to travel on Saturday." He "felt like a bomb had fallen on" him. Upon his arrival home, he related the story to his sister and mother, and they all had a good laugh – though they did feel sorry for poor Hania. From that point on, Hania had to make her way home from the salon by herself. Abe avoided her whenever possible. To her great disappointment, if not shock and dismay, Hania ultimately discovered Abe's lack of romantic interest in her when his dating Sonia became openly known to all their friends and family.

6

DATING

Telekinesis of Cash

As Abe got to know Sonia, he understood her situation. For one thing, her father had moved to America and routinely sent money to her and her mother. But it wasn't a lot. Sonia remembered that her father's monthly wiring of small amounts of money from New York to Warsaw enabled her and her mother to live adequately, when added to the money they earned. But Abe remembered that Sonia was certainly not financially well-off and lived frugally.

As Abe fell increasingly in love with Sonia, he progressively wanted to take care of her and support her. Since he also didn't want to embarrass her, he came up with a plan.

When they went out together, say to a theatre or a restaurant, Abe, ever a thoughtful gentleman, held Sonia's purse. Abe frequently put cash into Sonia's purse, anywhere from 50 to 100 Złotych or more, when he thought she wasn't looking. Abe wondered why Sonia never said anything to him about the money. He wanted to know, was the money enough for her needs? Did she need more money for her expenses? Was there anything else that he could do for her? But Sonia never said a word. Not a single "thank you." Not an acknowledgement that when she returned home and opened her purse, she discovered that cash had miraculously appeared in it.

Abe continued to gift Sonia a weekly supply of cash. And he never said a word. Sonia continued to receive the cash, with gratitude in her heart. And she never said a word. Years later, after they married, Abe finally asked Sonia why she never said anything to him about the financial support. She answered that she was embarrassed to accept the money that he gave her, but she really needed it and was grateful that he offered it.

It was a secret that they both kept. He did not want to embarrass her by openly giving her money, or by so doing, making it appear that he expected something in return. And she didn't want to embarrass and humiliate herself by acknowledging the need for the money and was grateful to him for doing the deed without embarrassing her. By each of them not verbalizing the little dance, Sonia kept her pride. And making Sonia happy, made Abe happy.

The Umbrella

During one of their dates, Abe noticed that Sonia carried a rather rickety umbrella. On the occasion of their next date, Abe took Sonia for a sleigh ride. The snow was deep and the temperature was well below freezing. Abe was wearing a heavy, fashionable fur coat and under it he had hidden an elegant yet practical umbrella; he surreptitiously slipped it out and allowed it to fall to the floor of the sleigh. When they stepped out of the sleigh, he pointed to the umbrella and remarked, "Sonia, look at this beautiful umbrella; someone must have forgotten it." Sonia immediately suggested that they should turn the umbrella over to the driver. It took all of Abe's persuasive abilities to convince Sonia that he would leave his name with the driver, and if someone approached the driver with a lost-umbrella claim, Abe would notify Sonia and he would return the umbrella to the rightful owner. Sonia was an honest woman, so it was not surprising that her first instinct was to turn the umbrella over to the driver. But, when Abe became so insistent that she keep the lovely umbrella, Sonia quickly realized that this was another instance of Abe's gifting her indirectly so as not to embarrass her. According to Abe, she never knew the truth. What Abe never learned was that Sonia once revealed to us with a laugh that she had figured out his subterfuge but played along with him because he seemed so pleased with himself.

Abe was sensitive to treating everyone with respect and understanding their feelings and needs. It was his nature to enjoy helping other people, often without taking credit for his assistance. His pleasure was in the feelings he derived from doing good deeds. As it turns out, the physician and philosopher, Maimonides (Moses ben Maiman, or the "Rambam"), considered the greatest Jewish sage since the Biblical Moses, wrote about different levels of charity and, in his opinion, the level of morality attached to each. Among the higher levels was giving charity anonymously.

We don't know if Abe ever studied or learned about Maimonides' levels of charitable giving. His instinct was to treat people fairly and honestly and to help them even when they were not even aware that they were being helped. Similarly, when kindly assisting Sonia, or later in life when providing goods to customers or acquaintances, Abe knew that he was performing a kindness when charging them well below normal retail prices. And when Abe donated money, often it was an anonymous donation – except when it was a donation to his synagogue or charity during a fundraising dinner when he wanted to set an example publicly to put pressure on other successful businessmen to increase their contributions.

7

ENGAGEMENT AND MARRIAGE

Engagement

After graduating from teachers' college, Sonia moved back to Pruzana. She missed Abe and couldn't stop thinking about him. Her family couldn't stop talking about him. In a small town, gossip circulates faster than water down a drain, and word on the street was that Sonia was going to marry the richest man in Warsaw and her family would owe Abe a big dowry.

Against this background, Abe's aunt, at the time living in Warsaw, made a point of meeting with Sonia's mother during one of her trips to Warsaw with Sonia. As a curious *yente*, the aunt boldly asked how much dowry they would be giving to Abe? "What?" Golda exclaimed in surprise, "My Sonia, the most beautiful and intelligent girl should give you a dowry?! Forget about it." At that, Golda got up in a huff, walked out of the meeting and took herself and Sonia on the next train back to Pruzana.

When Abe heard the story, he was mortified and upset. Eager to smooth over the situation and make a formal marriage proposal to Sonia, he took a fountain pen in hand and wrote to Sonia, explaining that he was a wealthy man and had no interest in receiving a dowry from Sonia's family. His only wish was to marry Sonia and take care of her, forever. He redoubled his efforts when he learned that Golda thought that his *yente* aunt was his mother. In another letter he explained that the aunt had no business asking for a dowry – she was neither his mother nor his *shadchan* ("matchmaker"). Receiving no replies to his letters, Abe took matters into his own hands. He found himself in Wilno (formerly Lithuanian Vilnius, which was annexed by Poland on February 20, 1922) on business and decided to go to Pruzana. He boarded a train at the Wilno station and reached Pruzana 16 hours later. According to Abe, it was a long trip, "*but when you are in love it was short.*" The story should be in Abe's own words:

When I stepped down from the train, I saw a policeman on the platform who apparently noticed me. He snapped to attention and clicked his heels, looking straight ahead. I think that maybe he was expecting a government official. I was dressed in my beautiful fur coat with a brown fur collar, and a sharp, black bowler hat. I ignored him as I walked out, and he departed. The weather was very cold, maybe 20 degrees Fahrenheit below zero. There was a lot of snow and ice and the only way to travel was by horse-drawn sleigh. I walked over to one of the taxis outside the station and asked the driver to take me to the nicest hotel in town. He drove me to the biggest hotel. The owners, Mr. Zukerman and his wife lived upstairs in four rooms and rented out three small furnished rooms downstairs. It was 9 AM and I was still cold from the ride. I climbed the stairs to the owner's apartment and asked Mr. Zukerman for breakfast. They served me a glass of tea, a roll with butter and two scrambled eggs. As I was eating, Mr. Zuckerman made conversation. He asked me my business in town and I told him I represent a big shoe factory in Warsaw and came to Pruzana to get orders for my firm. I never introduced myself as the owner of the factory. It was good for business, as the company would look bigger when I was just a salesman. And when a customer complained about quality or delivery or price, I always said, "I will talk it over with my boss." It worked perfectly. I asked and received from Mr. Zukerman a list of names and addresses of all the shoe stores in town.

I also told Mr. Zukerman that I have friends in town, the Jagloms. "Oh," he said, "they are nice people. You know they say that one daughter, Sonia, is marrying a very rich man from Warsaw." I became very anxious and questioned him further about what he knows about Sonia and her two sisters. Mrs. Zukerman noticed that he was talking too much. I observed that she tapped his leg with her foot under the table to signal him to quit talking.

Now, Sonia didn't know that I was coming. It was to be a surprise for her. It was around 10 AM. I wrote a note to Sonia that I was in Pruzana and would like to see her and sent the note with a boy to her home. The boy returned with a note from Sonia asking me to come over at 6 PM. I got very nervous and insulted that Sonia didn't invite me over immediately. As in all other little towns in Poland, you had trains running twice a day, at 10 AM and 10 PM. If a train had been available, maybe I would have been foolish enough to make a big mistake and take a train and leave. But I had no train, so I went out to make business calls to all the shoe stores in town. As usual, I did good business.

I calmed down during the day and took a ride to Sonia's house at about five minutes to six. I saw that they had done a little preparation. They had baked a cake and the house looked spotless.

Sonia explained that her mother had wanted Abe to come to the house unseen, after dark, because she was concerned about her daughter's reputation. If the many women and *yentes* who came to visit or passed by saw a man at the house, and if later the *shidduch* ("match") didn't work out, then people would talk, saying that Sonia had been involved with a man who didn't want her, her reputation would be ruined and no decent man would marry her. Then it was Abe's turn to explain that Golda had spoken in Warsaw to his aunt, not his mother, and that the aunt thought that Sonia's family must be rich because the father of the family was living in America (and everyone knew that in the *Goldeneh Medina* streets were literally paved with gold and everyone was rich) and therefore, this Jaglom family must be rich and could afford a substantial dowry. In the first place, Abe explained softly that his *yente* aunt had no business discussing a dowry. And secondly, Abe had – thank God – enough money. He loved Sonia and she would want for nothing if she married him. And he neither needed nor wanted a dowry.

Sonia and her sister, Mania, accompanied Abe to the station. Abe boarded the 10 PM Pruzana to Warsaw train, with Sonia's heart in his jacket's breast pocket and a substantial number of written orders for shoes and boots from Pruzana's storekeepers for the *Hadebut* company, in his jacket's other inside pocket.

When I came home, I was very happy. I said to myself, "mission accomplished." I told my mother about my trip to Pruzana and she was very happy to see me happy. I started writing letters, and after a few weeks, Sonia came to Warsaw and we met a few times in the week. I remember very well how hot it was in Warsaw in the summer. My mother had rented an apartment in Swider in the woods, full of pine trees. One Friday, I invited Sonia to visit us for the weekend. I'll never forget how beautiful she looked. She was wearing a white silk or satin dress with white sneakers. Her cheeks were the color of roses – without makeup. I don't remember, and nobody told me the way I looked, but I was very happy. Sometime in October Sonia's mother and two sisters moved to Warsaw on Ogrodowa Street. We decided to get married on March 10, 1935. Sonia's mother was a sick woman suffering from anemia, so my mother began the preparations for the wedding.

In Europe, to prepare for a wedding was a big job. Not like in America, where you shop for everything that's ready-made. In Europe, you had to select the material for the wedding dress and suit, go to the tailor for measurements and at least three times for fittings. You had to buy feathers for pillows and material for linens. You had to order shoes from a shoe maker (not a difficult task for me), furniture from a cabinet maker and you had to shop for food and cake. It was a big job. But my wonderful mother did everything with love. She shopped for Sonia for the finest materials and she went with her to the dressmaker.

In I. B. Singer's novel *Shosha*, the mother of the lovesick narrator, Aaron Greidinger, says to her son, "There is a saying that love is blind, but even love isn't completely without reason. A shoemaker's apprentice would not fall in love with a princess, and he certainly would not marry her." Responds lovesick Aaron, "Even this can happen." "What? In novels, not in real life," shouts back Mother. Abe was not a shoemaker's apprentice. He was the owner of the shoe company. He did find his princess. And she did marry him. Romantic love may have been a theme in novels and Hollywood movies; but for Abe and Sonia romantic love was, indeed, real life.

In the same year that witnessed the birth of Elvis Presley and the CBS Radio Network's hiring of Edward R. Murrow, who was to become the radio voice reporting on the Second World War to American listeners, Abe and Sonia got married. The ceremony on March 10, 1935 was performed by Reb Aharon Yechiel, himself the son of the *Kozinetzer Rebbe*, the famous Chassidic Rabbi, Reb Yerachmiel Moishele Hopstein. According to Sonia, Abe made a "beautiful wedding." They had big families and lots of friends and the number of guests surpassed 300.

Among the guests were 30 Hadebut employees and their wives. Inviting these tradesmen was the only thing about which Sonia questioned Abe. "How is it that for our wedding, such a personal and religious event, you invite 30 shoemakers?" Abe replied, "I make a living through them and they make a living through me. They are nice to me and I am nice to them. They are decent, hardworking men and I consider them friends. They make it possible for us to have what we have, and I want them to know that I appreciate their relationship with me and that I respect them." Sonia nodded her assent without argument. Though it was a beautiful, elegant wedding, it was understated and not elaborate. Even then, Abe understood that given the depressed economic circumstances in Poland along with the rest of the world, it wouldn't be appropriate for him to put on an expensive, showy wedding when so many were struggling. He knew that jealousy and envy of those who have by those who don't constitute inflammable substances that can combust when a match is lit by a party seeking power and looking for a scapegoat against whom to inflame the have-nots.

Nine months after their wedding, on December 26, 1935, Sonia gave birth to a boy, whom they named David, or "Dadjo" in Polish. He was named after Abe's father, as well as the second King of Biblical Israel. According to Abe, it was a relatively common name in Poland and his name wouldn't necessarily reveal his Jewish identity. Three and a half years later, Sonia gave birth to a daughter, Lusia.

The years between 1935 and 1939 were very good years for Abe and Sonia. Everybody was healthy. They had two beautiful children, whom they adored. And business was very good, as everybody needed shoes. Unlike dresses or pants that could be made at home by a talented homemaker, quality shoes needed to be manufactured by experienced craftsmen who had quality raw materials. Moreover, shoes needed to be replaced as they wore out or children outgrew them.

Abe was a hard worker, a good organizer and manager and an honest salesman. He had a great head for business and a wonderful eye for fashion and utility. He was not materialistic when it came to himself, but he delighted in buying whatever his wife desired.

Sonia, too, was not materialistic, but enjoyed dressing well and having nice things in her home. She did not need or want lots of things, but whatever she bought, she wanted it to be of fine quality and beauty. Abe's business acumen led him to diversify his financial assets. After deducting business expenses and salaries, whatever profit was left over that didn't need to be reinvested in the business, Abe invested in real estate. Years later he would give us business advice with a quip we thought he had coined, "They're not manufacturing land."

Abe bought a piece of land of about a quarter of an acre at 74 Zelazna Street in Warsaw, on which he built a six-story building. The ground floor was built out for retail stores, and above them five stories of residential apartments. Abe combined two apartments into one consisting of four bedrooms in which he, Sonia and the children lived. He also bought land at 65 Nowolipki Street on which he constructed a small building, though we don't know whether it was residential or retail. His other real estate investment was a lot he purchased at 36 Nizka Street. The lot boasted a stable and Abe planned to develop the lot. In the meantime, he collected rent on the stable. As for his store at 28 Nalewki Street, Abe apparently rented the space. We deduce this from the fact that after the war, Abe never made a restitution claim on this property.

For the first year of their marriage, Sonia continued to teach elementary school. Abe persuaded her to stop working, both for her comfort and his pride. Unlike today in the United States and perhaps elsewhere in the world, where it's more common for married women to work than for them not to work, this was not the case in pre-war Poland. Abe was very proud of his accomplishments and felt that if Sonia worked as a teacher (with a meager salary) it would look to outsiders like Abe couldn't afford to support his family. Sonia agreed to resign her position at the elementary school and to devote her time to her husband, children, and the community.

They had a very comfortable life. Sonia employed a cook, a housekeeper and a governess to help with the children. They lived a rich social life with their friends and family and a cultural life of theatre, concerts and charitable dinners. But they didn't use their wealth just to live well. In her memoir, *Never Far Away*, cousin Hanka wrote: "Generous to a fault, according to my mother, [Sonia] used to support many needy families."

In the summer, to escape the oppressive heat in their un-air-conditioned city apartment, Sonia would take the children and the governess to spend time in a resort in the mountains of Otwock, where it was cool and pleasant.

In the late 1930s, in Poland, life was good for Abe and Sonia. And Warsaw was a long way from the Kozienice of Abe's childhood.

8

CLIMATE CHANGE. THE SKIES DARKEN

There was another kind of business going on in Germany, Poland's neighbor on its Western border.

Before the First World War had come to its conclusion, revolution had come to Russia in November 1917, when the Bolsheviks, under the leadership of Lenin, ended the Romanov dynasty and 1,000 years of the Russian monarchy. From 1917 to 1923, revolutions, civil wars and wars among European states exploded as European stability imploded. So much for the "War to End All Wars."

Germany's economy was crushed by the war and burdened by onerous reparations that Britain and France had forced on it in the treaty that ended the war. Germans suffered food shortages and massive unemployment. The hyperinflation that pushed the price of a loaf of bread to billions of *Marks* may have been engineered, some say, by the government itself, in order to repay their debts with increasingly worthless *Marks*. In 1924, the United States implemented the Dawes Plan to make the payments more manageable. The Dawes Plan was a success because American banks loaned Germany money to rebuild its industrial base. The German hyperinflation was ended with the establishment of the *Reichsmark* as Germany's new currency (at an exchange rate of one trillion old *Marks* to one new *Reichsmark*). In June 1929, the Young Plan further eased Germany's burden of reparations by stretching out repayment to 59 years. The 1920s roared, not just in the United States, but in Germany as well.

Everything changed in October 1929, with the Wall Street Crash, the echoes of which were heard around the world, particularly in Germany. American banks called in their German loans and the boom was over. Germany plunged into an economic depression along with the rest of the world. Millions of workers lost their jobs and the majority received little to no unemployment insurance.

But let us back up to earlier events prior to 1929...

The Private becomes Führer

A future leader of Germany, a hitherto anonymous ne'er-do-well named Adolf Hitler, would become a famous veteran of the German army (*Deutsches Heer* or Imperial German Army) in the First World War. An Austrian from a small town near Linz, Hitler had moved to Vienna hoping to become an artist, but he was rejected from the prominent art academy at which he had hoped to study. The First World War would save him from destitution. When the war broke out, he initially dodged the draft in the Austro-Hungarian army. An admirer of Germany, he traveled to Bavaria and succeeded in joining the *Deutsches Heer* in October 1914. Eleven days after arriving at the Western Front, he was assigned to the regimental headquarters as a dispatch runner, carrying orders from the regimental HQ to the battalion HQ, rarely if ever crossing into lines of fire. While there was the danger of occasional artillery barrages, life in the regimental HQ was good – warm and well-fed – and relatively safe. Combat soldiers in the front line, suffering the horrors of trench warfare typically referred to the regimental runners as *Etappenschweiner* or "rear area pigs." Hitler was, in fact, awarded two Iron Crosses, Germany's highest military award. While Hitler would later exaggerate and fabricate stories of his alleged bravery and valor, the historian Thomas Weber convincingly argues that Hitler, like many other soldiers in the German army, likely earned his awards as a result of his obsequious service to the officers in his regimental HQ, not of military heroics. Hitler was promoted to Private First Class. Reportedly, he was never eager for additional promotions that might put him in the line of battle, nor were any offered to him. Several of his officers testified after the war that Hitler was seen as asocial, rigid and argumentative and showed no leadership qualities.[1]

Hitler ended his war in a psychiatric hospital in Pasewalk, Germany. Although he would later claim to have been a victim of an Allied gas attack, his attending psychiatrist diagnosed him as suffering from hysterical blindness. Later testimony reported that Hitler's second diagnosis was "psychopath."

Hitler remained in the newly renamed *Reichswehr* after the war and obtained a job in its propaganda department. On his own initiative, Hitler attended a meeting of the German Workers' Party (*Deutsche Arbeiterspartei*) DAP for short, on September 12, 1919. The group, comprising not more than a few dozen men met in the *Sterneckerbrau* tavern. Hitler loved the extreme nationalistic, anti-capitalistic, anti-democratic, and antisemitic principles of the DAP. He was seduced by the party's ideology and the party was seduced by his manic and magnetic, nationalist, supremacist, rhetorical skills.

The head of the propaganda department, Captain Karl Mayr asked Hitler to respond to a letter written to Mayr by one of the students in his indoctrination course. The letter asked for the government's position on the *Judenfrage*, or the Jewish Question. Hitler's answer, dated September 16 is the first written evidence of Hitler's obsessive antisemitism. It foreshadowed the themes about which he would write in *Mein Kampf*. In his letter, he railed against the Jews as an "alien race" and recommended "a properly planned legislative attack on and elimination of the privileges which the Jews, as distinct from other aliens living amongst us, possess." He likened the Jewish race to a "racial tuberculosis of the nation" and went on to say that the ultimate goal of the German nation must be the *Entfernung* or removal of the Jews altogether. "Only a government of national strength is capable of doing both, and never a government of national weakness."

Hitler's letter revealed the depth of his jealousy and envy of the largely successful, assimilated Jewish population in Germany. He merged this with the delusional, antisemitic hatred and psychotic conspiracy theories that he had absorbed during his years in virulently antisemitic Vienna and in Munich from marginal, drunken, beer hall "professors," and political cranks looking for scapegoats for Germany's lost war. It wasn't many years later before Hitler was able to merge raw emotional Jew-hatred with a carefully, albeit irrationally, planned *Entfernung* of Jews from social and physical existence.

On March 31, 1920, he was finally discharged from the army, allowing him to work fulltime for the DAP. He was instrumental in changing the party's name in 1920 to the *National Sozialistische Deutsche Arbeiterspartei* or National Socialist German Workers' Party, the NSDAP or Nazi, for short. The name was changed to emphasize its ideology of "genuine German socialism," setting itself apart from the alleged "class-warfare socialism" of the Weimar Republic and its Jewish leaders, which it wanted to destroy. By July 1921, the party had over 3,000 members, owned a radical, antisemitic, propaganda paper, the *Volkischer Beobachter* ("People's Observer"), and had a new partly leader to whom it had given dictatorial powers: Adolf Hitler. The party now had a noisy presence in the Bavarian province of Germany. By the end of 1922, the party boasted some 20,000 members, among them a high proportion of university students, graduates and professors in Munich.

In November 1923, with the leadership of the Weimar Republic in disarray, Hitler attempted a *Putsch* in Munich, marching at the head of a two- to three-thousand-man army of NSDAP thugs from the *Bürgerbräukeller* tavern towards the city hall. Munich police blocked the marchers, shots were exchanged, and some two dozen Nazis and three police officers were killed. Hitler succeeded in running away but was arrested two days later.

Instead of ending up in the seat of power in Berlin, Hitler found himself sitting in a court dock in February-March 1924, indicted for treason against the Weimar Republic. Hitler used the trial as a showplace for his considerable oratorical talents, on display for the packed galleries and given wide publicity in the press. He condemned the Treaty of Versailles and justified his attempted Putsch as an understandable attempt to revivify Germany's honor. The trial judges were sympathetic to him and his arguments. They sentenced Hitler to five years in jail. After eight months in Landsberg prison, he was released in December 1924. During his time in prison, he had been treated like a favored celebrity by prison authorities. He dictated to his early comrade and fellow prisoner, Rudolf Hess, his racist and antisemitic manuscript *Mein Kampf*, which Hess dutifully typed and likely edited.

After his release from prison, Hitler set about enlarging and strengthening the NSDAP. He decided that the best way to take over Germany and its government was not by violence but by participating in the political process. In 1925, Hitler began campaigning for his party's election to the German parliament. Funded by party members' dues, the U.S. industrialist Henry Ford, and the German industrialist Fritz Thyssen,[2] Hitler barnstormed across Germany pioneering the use of an airplane to transport himself and his team all across the country.

In the 1928 parliamentary elections, the Nazi Party received only 2.6 percent of the vote granting it 12 seats out of the 491 total seats in the parliament. But, more importantly, now the Nazis and their swastikas had a legitimate presence in Germany's legislature.

By July, 1932 the NSDAP had became the largest party in the German parliament, achieving 37 percent of the vote and 230 seats.

On January 30, 1933, Hitler was named by President von Hindenburg as Chancellor of Germany. Hitler repudiated the Treaty of Versailles, the Young Plan and the Lausanne Conference and ended further German financial reparations.

In preparation for the parliament elections in March 1933, agents of the Nazi SA (*Sturmabteilung*) paramilitary organization, the Brownshirts, acting on orders from the Minister of Propaganda, Joseph Goebbels, and Hermann Göring, were commonly believed to have set fire to the *Reichstag* (parliament building), gutting it on February 27.

The fire, clearly a Nazi operation and provocation was the pretext for the *Reichstag* Fire Decree, announced by President Hindenburg on February 28, which suspended all civil rights in Germany. No freedom of speech nor of press, no right to assembly, no right to privacy, no unlimited right to property no unrestricted personal liberty. Rudolf Diels, head of the *Gestapo*, noted drily that the Nazis "now had legal power to do anything, and victims had no appeal."[3] Nazi police, *Sturmabteilung* or *SA* and *Schutzstaffel* or *SS* arrested and abused thousands of Communists, trade unionists, Social Democrats and anyone else deemed by the Nazis a political threat.

Hitler needed a two-thirds majority in order to pass the Enabling Act, which would give him dictatorial powers. He joined in a coalition with the DNVP Nationalist party which had received over three million votes, yielding it 52 seats, and with the *Zentrum* or Center Party, the Vatican-controlled party, which received 12 percent of the vote and 74 seats.

With only the 120-seat Social Democrat Party voting against, the parliament delegates passed the Enabling Act (officially known as the "Law to Remove the Danger to the People and the Reich") on March 23, 1933, which allowed the Nazi cabinet to enact laws by itself, without the need for a vote in the parliament. This essentially made Hitler the dictator of Germany. The Center Party famously dissolved itself in line with the German-Vatican Concordat.

The head of the DNVP, Alfred Hugenberg, a wealthy newspaper magnate, owner of the Scherl press empire and (to all intents and purposes) head of the Krupp arms works, also dissolved his party and joined the Nazi cabinet. All parties other than the NSDAP were ultimately outlawed. The Reich cabinet, essentially irrelevant, would stop meeting after 1937.[4] After the death of President von Hindenburg in 1934, Hitler combined the office of President with his post as *Reichskanzler*, or Chancellor, declaring himself the ultimate leader or *Führer* of Germany. The one-party German parliament became a rubber stamp, if even needed, for Hitler's *Führer* decrees and what would become Nazi-controlled German aggression and genocide.

Poland

In the last decade of the 18th century, Poland had had its independence eradicated as it was dismembered, and its territory divided among Imperial Russia, Prussia (the German Empire) and Austria. Despite its attempts at revolution in the mid-19th century to throw off the yoke of its foreign rulers, Poland was to remain occupied by the three major powers of Central and Eastern Europe until after the First World War.

With the defeat of the German, Austro-Hungarian and Turkish empires by the French, British and American armies, the British and French governments had set about redrawing Europe's borders by carving out of the pre-existing imperial territories new or invented countries. Czechoslovakia, for instance was created from the territories of Bohemia, Moravia-Silesia, Slovakia and Carpathian Ruthenia as a democratic republic. It became a multi-ethnic state with substantial minorities of Germans, Hungarians, Ruthenians, Jews and assorted other ethnic groups.

One of the largest minorities were the three million ethnic Germans. They were included in the new state of Czechoslovakia as a result of the German territory, the Sudetenland, being ceded to the new state that was to serve as a buffer between Germany,

Austria, Poland and Hungary. The *leitmotif* of the border rearrangements after the First World War was self-determination for ethnic or national groups. In the event, the new borders were to plant the seeds of future conflict by creating states in which ethnic groups who couldn't tolerate each other were supposed to live in peace and harmony as equal citizens of their newly independent nations.

Poland, on the other hand, was a country with a long history of national independence on its own or as part of the Polish-Lithuanian Commonwealth. After 123 years of partition, Poland was reconstituted as an independent nation by the Western Allies as part of the Treaty of Versailles in June 1919. Poland, like Czechoslovakia, was recreated, in part, by the incorporation of territories containing non-Polish ethnic populations such as Germans and Ukrainians. A side-treaty, signed by Poland and the victorious Allies, known as the Little Treaty of Versailles or the Polish Minority Treaty, obligated Poland "to protect the interests" of the minorities who differed from the majority "in race, language or religion." Polish independence did not result in peace and quiet for Poland or its neighbors.

Between 1919 and 1922, Poland fought borderland wars with the Ukrainians, Soviets and Lithuanians. From late 1918, Poles living in the eastern German territory of Poznan and Upper Silesia revolted against German rule. The Trier Armistice signed in February 1919 formally ended the uprising, although fighting continued until June 1921. In the 1919 peace treaty, Germany accepted the relinquishment to Poland of Danzig, Poznan and West Prussia.

Poland's economy was largely agrarian and relatively poor. The modernization of Poland might have progressed, along with political stability, absent the Great Depression and the aggressive climate change in its neighbor, Germany, only four years after that.

Poland suffered greatly from the worldwide Great Depression. Poland experienced increased unemployment, saw bankruptcies rise, and people suffered economic deprivation. Sonia reported seeing many poor Jews with nothing to eat, begging in the street. There were a lot of poor people, the chronically poor and the *nouveaux* poor.

Wealthy Poles, including members of the Jewish community, with successful businesses, generally continued to do well financially. Sonia recalled not experiencing a lot of antisemitism in Warsaw. She believed that antisemitism was generally prevalent mostly in smaller towns, where she thought there wasn't as much contact between agricultural peasants and Jews, as there was in cities.

On the other hand, Abe recalled experiencing some antisemitism in the mid-1930s. He saw signs put up, or scrawled on the windows of Jewish shops, reading "don't do business with Jews." Some gentile customers asked Abe to come in the back of their stores rather than through the front door, so that people wouldn't see a Jewish man coming into their stores.

Antisemitism was so ingrained in European culture and history, that in times of peace and economic prosperity, when Jews were not actively persecuted by European governments, antisemitism for Jews who were assimilated or economically privileged, was an annoyance that needed to be accepted and managed. Abe was not a revolutionary nor was he interested in politics. He always saw himself as a businessman. So long as he and his family could live in peace and he could work unmolested, he was satisfied with his life.

Poland was a land of variegated complexities. Jews numbered about three- to three and a half million, or around ten percent of the population of Poland in 1939. In Warsaw, they constituted no less than 30 percent of the population. Jews were active in the fields of medicine, law, art, finance, and business. There were substantially wealthy Jews in Poland, such as Sonia's cousins, as well as predominantly middle-class professionals, businessmen and shopkeepers, but also blue-collar workers, and even the poor, the sick and the disabled. The Jewish population made tremendous contributions to Polish society. They often mingled with and earned respect from the Gentiles. At the same time, Poland had an undercurrent of antisemitism engendered by extreme Nationalists and the very conservative Polish Catholic Church.[5]

After the beginning of the Great Depression in 1929, the installation of Germany's *Führer* in 1933, and especially after the 1934 German-Polish Non-Aggression Pact and the death on May 12, 1935 of the well-liked Polish military hero, Marshal Józef Piłsudski, who had had a positive relationship with the Jews in Poland, conditions for Jews in Poland deteriorated. A government-approved boycott of Jewish businesses was instigated. The government spokesman Boguslaw Miedzinski explained the government's negative attitude towards the Jews, "Personally, I love Danes very much, but if we had three million of them in Poland, I would implore God to take them away as soon as possible."[6]

The Polish political party OZON or the Camp of National Unity, was formed in 1937 by Adam Koc, a retired army colonel. The party published and disseminated antisemitic posters in prominent locations around the country. One read "Buy only in Polish shops!" Another read "A Poland Free from Jews Is a Free Poland."[7] OZON competed with the more antisemitic party, the *Endek* or National Democratic Party that had been founded by Roman Dmowski in 1897. The Polish Catholic Church chose to support the NDP as an alternative to the "atheistic" Polish Socialist Party (PPS).

In February-March 1936, August Cardinal Hlond, Poland's Catholic Primate wrote in a pastoral letter that was to be read in all parishes: "A Jewish question exists and there will be one so long as the Jews remain Jews. It is an actual fact that the Jews fight against the Catholic Church, they are free-thinkers, and constitute the vanguard of atheism, bolshevism and revolution. The Jewish influence upon morals is fatal, and the publishers spread pornographic literature. It is also true that the Jews are committing frauds, practicing usury, and dealing in white slavery. It is true that in the schools, the Jewish youth is having an evil influence... upon the Catholic youth."

He was kind enough to add, "Not all the Jews are, however like

57

that." Hlond did, apparently, oppose wanton killing of the Jews in Poland, but he supported an economic boycott of the Jews.[8]

The *Sejm* or parliament passed a law forbidding work on Sunday, which negatively impacted Jewish businessmen who didn't work on Saturdays for religious reasons. Another law outlawed kosher slaughtering. In 1937, the government lifted all licenses on retail sellers of tobacco, the vast majority of whom were Jews. When the government reissued the licenses, they were given almost entirely to Polish Gentiles, thus depriving as many as 30,000 Jewish merchants of their livelihood. A numerus clausus (quota) restricted the enrollment of Jews in *Gymnasia* and universities. Many professors required Jewish students in lecture halls to sit apart, on "ghetto benches."

In 1938 and 1939, economic boycotts of Jewish businesses were undertaken, while violent pogroms against Jews resulted in hundreds of Jewish casualties. The pogroms were not directed or supported by the government, but the government was either unable or unwilling to stop them. Members of Piłsudski's cabinet, such as the former Prime Minister, Janusz Jedrzejewicz, spoke out against this government's antisemitic policies. In 1937 and 1938, though Koc had resigned from OZON, the government considered the idea of encouraging the emigration of the Jewish population. Given that 35 to 40 percent of all the taxes collected by the Polish government came from its Jewish citizens, the departure of the Jewish population from Poland would have been economically catastrophic (not even taking into consideration the loss to the nation of Jewish doctors, lawyers, writers, academics, etc.).

Germans' influence in Poland increased in those years as well. According to the 1931 census, out of 30 million residents, Poland had, in addition to the Jewish minority of 3 to 3.5 million, 4.2 million Ukrainians, at least 690,000 *Volksdeutsche* or ethnic Germans and 930,000 Byelorussians, with smaller numbers of Czechs, Armenians, Lithuanians, Russians and Gypsies. By 1939, the ethnic German population was around three-quarters of a million.[9] The ethnic Polish population was estimated to be around 22 million. There's evidence that many of the wartime, anti-Jewish attacks or pogroms were carried out by Ukrainians and *Volksdeutsche*.[10]

Wherever possible, people who fear for their livelihoods or their lives, vote with their feet. Between the First and Second World Wars, approximately 400,000 Jews emigrated from Poland. Had the world's borders not been sealed against large Jewish immigration to, for instance, the United States and the British Empire, in particular, Mandatory Palestine, it is likely that far more Jews would have emigrated from Poland. Despite the troubles for the Jews in Poland, Jewish life flourished. One prominent Jewish historian in Poland, Ezra Mendelsohn has argued: "... we owe a debt of gratitude to Polish freedom, which allowed the Jews in the 1920s and 1930s to participate in politics, open schools, and write as they pleased... The experience of Polish Jews between the wars was a combination of suffering, some of which was caused by antisemitism, and of achievement, made possible by Polish freedom, pluralism and tolerance... Interwar Poland was therefore bad for the Jews, in the sense that it excluded them from first-class membership in the state... I think we can say of Jewish history in interwar Poland that it was 'the best of times and the worst of times:' The best of times in the sense of the extraordinary creativity of Polish Jewry, the worst of times in the sense of the fulfillment of the bleakest prophesies, made mostly by Zionists, concerning the imminent fate of the East European Jewish Diaspora.[11]

Abe and Sonia did not speak about pervasive antisemitism in Poland. Prejudice didn't influence their sunny and optimistic personalities, and they chose to remember the good Polish people they knew rather than the bad.

In her description of Polish Jews, Lucy Dawidowicz, in her classic and relatively early one-volume history of the Holocaust, wrote: "Except for a thin stratum of wealthy and upper middle-class Jews, the preponderant majority were lower middle-class workers, small businessmen, and a proletariat, employed or unemployed."[12]

Apparently, though he came from serious poverty, by 1939 Abe found himself among a minority of Jews – as well as ethnic Poles – among the top of Poland's economic elites.

Germany prepares for War

In no way could Poland and its treatment of its Jewish citizens in the 1930s be compared to Germany and its Nazi government's crescendo of persecution of both the German Jews who had been living in Germany for centuries and those who had moved to Germany from other European countries for opportunities not available in their home countries.

Although in reality ruling with dictatorial power, Hitler kept Germany's judicial system intact in order to provide a veneer of law and respectability to the social order. On September 15, 1935, the parliament passed the notorious Nuremburg Laws, which made it illegal for German Jews to make a living, to own businesses or property, or to marry non-Jews, i.e., the "pure-blooded" German Aryans[13] German citizenship was stripped from the Jews. For many Jews who had financial means, escaping from Germany was their only alternative to living in a Germany which was making them non-citizens and ultimately, non-persons. The problem was that most countries in the world had shut their doors to Jewish refugees.

As Hitler consolidated his political power and terror organizations he created, the SS and the *Gestapo*, and incarcerated or murdered those who opposed him. The power of his one-man rule grew. He surrounded himself with like-minded Nazis. Heinrich Himmler was appointed *SS-Reichsführer* (head of the SS and the *Gestapo*); Reinhard Heydrich Himmler's deputy and chief operational planner of the murder of Polish and other European Jews; and *Reichsmarshall* Hermann Göring, Hitler's right-hand man, Plenipotentiary, Commander of the Prussian police, Commander-in-Chief of the *Luftwaffe* (air force) and co-architect of Hitler's aggressive war. Himmler was the architect of the "Final Solution," which was designed to be the genocide of the world's Jews. Germany's military, the renamed *Wehrmacht*, grew in numbers and strength as Hitler violated all provisions of the Treaty of Versailles which had ended the First World War and had placed strict limitations on German rearmament.

The generals of the *Wehrmacht* and the officer corps also grew in power and stature as they began to develop significant military forces under their command. Able at last to reverse their humiliation at Germany's defeat in the First World War and supposed disarmament, Germany's generals were satisfied. As they witnessed the tremendous growth in the power and ability of Germany's war machine, built up under the noses of the world by Krupp industries and other armament manufacturers, the generals were actually surprised when the Allied victors of the First World War refrained from enforcing the provisions of the Treaty of Versailles, which would have stopped Hitler as early as 1933 and as late as 1938. Of course, by 1938, the foreign policy of appeasement that had been adopted by the British and French governments, along with their lack of serious military preparations for the looming war, meant that stopping the *Führer* was considered unrealistic. Horace Wilson, advisor to British Prime Minister Neville Chamberlain, would later explain his government's obsessive adherence to the policy of appeasement thus: "Our policy was never designed just to postpone war or enable us to enter war more united. The aim of appeasement was to avoid war altogether, for all time."[14]

As early as August 1920, a Turkish intermediary had been recruited to begin negotiations to reconcile Germany and the Russian Soviet Federative Socialist Republic (USSR). On April 16, 1922, Germany and the USSR concluded the Treaty of Rapallo, which normalized diplomatic relations between the two and formalized the renouncing of all territorial and financial claims against each other. On August 11, 1922 the ink barely dry on Germany's signature on the

Treaty of Versailles, the German General staff officers had reached a clandestine agreement with Stalin for Germany to develop and train German airmen and armored forces in new tactics on the vast plains of the Soviet Union, given that armored forces, not to mention an air force, were forbidden to Germany by the Treaty of Versailles. Chemical weapons research was also carried out by the Germans in their Russian training grounds. While the Germans were supposed to reciprocate by providing the U.S.S.R. with technical and engineering help, the Germans gave very little while receiving very much in priceless experience. One of the German officers who trained in the Soviet Union was Hans Guderian, who went on to become one of the most famous *Wehrmacht* armored force commanders of the Second World War.

The agreement on German-Russian military cooperation and training in the USSR was terminated after Hitler became Chancellor in January 1933, but sources differ on which side was the prime mover in the termination. By 1933, over 1,200 German pilots had been trained at the Russian Lipetsk base.[15] At home, the German military had evaded the restrictions they had accepted in the Treaty of Versailles and pursued military advances. They trained pilots to fly airplanes in alleged civilian glider clubs. Likewise, they trained future infantry troops in sports clubs that presumably developed healthy athleticism in German youth.

Once Hitler had achieved power in Germany, he withdrew Germany from the League of Nations and began an intensive rearmament program in gross violation of the Treaty of Versailles. But it was as early as 1924, that the *Reichswehr* staffed an Economics Bureau to partner with German industry to establish a *Wehrwirtschaft* or war economy. In 1926 another bureau was set up, the *Truppenamt* or troops office, whose mission was to produce goals for the German military. It issued a memorandum that held that Germany would need to reoccupy the Rhineland and effect the return of Upper Silesia, the Saar region and the Polish Corridor. The memorandum made it clear that this goal could only be accomplished by Germany launching a European war.[16] The

British and French governments had been informed by their intelligence services of the German violations of the ban on German rearmament in the 1920s while Hitler's rearmament program was so blatant that it was impossible to ignore. An article on the German-Russian military cooperation appeared in *The Manchester Guardian* in December 1926 but led to no apparent alarm in the British or French High Commands. Neither Britain nor France took any aggressive action to enforce the ban on rearmament by Germany, so great was the reluctance, if not dread, by their peoples and their elected leaders to consider another war so soon after the slaughter of the First World War.

In January 1934, Germany concluded a ten-year Non-Aggression Pact with Poland with the intention of ending Germany's diplomatic isolation. Not long after making this agreement, Hitler assured his General Staff that this agreement was meant not to secure peace but to weaken and mislead Poland and assure the possibility of a future German-Polish assault against the Soviet Union. Hitler further assured his generals that eventually Germany would fight and conquer both countries to ensure Germany got the *Lebensraum* which Hitler had repeatedly claimed Germany needed and to which it was entitled.

In 1935, Hitler announced openly to the world that Germany rejected the disarmament clause of the Treaty of Versailles and was rearming as it saw fit. Hitler instituted a compulsory draft. In the same year, Great Britain and Germany signed the Anglo-German Naval Agreement that set out mutually agreed terms of and limits on warship construction, allowing Germany to develop a navy equal in tonnage to 35 percent of Britain's. This was a greater number than allowed by the Treaty of Versailles. In 1933, the build-up of the German military had taken one percent of all Nazi government expenditures.[17] In 1935, armaments accounted for an astounding 73 percent of government expenditures. Hjalmar Schacht, who was the Economics Minister and Plenipotentiary of War Armaments during the early years of the massive build-up of the Nazi war machine, later admitted during his interrogation on

October 10, 1945 by Lt. Col. M.I. Gurfein during the Nuremburg Trials, that from 1934 to 1938 the Nazi government spent at least 45 billion *Reichsmarks* on rearmament.[18]

Hitler retook the coal-rich Saar region as the French agreed to remove their troops. In 1936 Hitler reoccupied and remilitarized the Rhineland, again in total violation of the Treaty of Versailles. The British and French, the cosignatories on the treaty, did nothing to enforce its terms and conditions. Hitler reportedly admitted: "If the French had invaded the Rhineland, we would have had to retreat in humiliation and shame, since the military resources at our disposal would not at all have been equal to even moderate resistance."[19]

Commenting on the danger of appeasement, Henry Kissinger has noted "I, too have often made the point that in 1936 Hitler could have been stopped by the movement of a single French division."[20]

In 1938, Austrian-born Hitler, along with a Nazi Fifth Column in Austria, succeeded in uniting Austria to Germany, a union known as the *Anschluss*. Many of the highest-ranking SS-officers in the Nazi hierarchy of genocide during the war, senior directors and implementers of the Holocaust such as Adolf Eichmann were born or raised in Austria.

Appeasement and the Betrayal of Czechoslovakia

Czechoslovakia, the nation of Czechs and Slovaks created at the end of the First World War, was a democratic country. It had a strong million-man army along with formidable fortresses positioned along its mountainous, easily defended border with Germany. Its *Skoda* armaments manufacturing conglomerate boasted a worldwide reputation for the quality of its military production of tanks, heavy artillery for land and naval forces, and various other weapons of war. Its size and scope actually exceeded that of Krupp, Germany's largest arms manufacturing concern. The large German-speaking *Volksdeutche*, lived in the Sudetenland, part of Czechoslovakia's mountainous geographic border with Germany.

Using alleged Czech mistreatment of *Volksdeutsche* as his excuse, Hitler demanded that the Sudetenland be ceded to Germany.

Hoping to avoid war in Europe, British Prime Minister Neville Chamberlain, along with French Prime Minister Edouard Daladier, induced the Italian dictator Mussolini to request a meeting with Hitler[21] to take place in Munich on September 28, 1938. Joseph P. Kennedy, American Ambassador to the U.K. and a fervent Nazi sympathizer, reportedly played a major role in organizing this conference, according to the American aviation hero, isolationist and Nazi admirer, Charles Lindbergh.[22] Lindbergh also admitted to frequent meetings with Kennedy and working "very closely with him at the time of the Munich crisis."[23] Lindbergh had toured Europe and its air forces, in particular Germany between 1936 and 1938. At the behest of Ambassador Kennedy he composed a report on the unassailable strength of the Nazi air force, the *Luftwaffe*. Chamberlain had the report in hand by the time he flew to Munich for the meeting on September 30.

In his report, Lindbergh argued that the *Luftwaffe* was the most powerful air force in the world and in the event of war would destroy London and every other great city in England. The report was greatly exaggerated, partly because Lindbergh overlooked the limited nature of the *Luftwaffe* at that time as a tactical, rather than a strategic force. The *Luftwaffe* would not become a threat to England until it got control of the Low Countries in 1940. In any case, Lindbergh's private and public anti-war speeches and warnings to England allegedly frightened the appeasers in the British cabinet. It strengthened the 69-year-old Chamberlain's resolve to sacrifice Czechoslovakia for the sake of preventing a war with Germany by the militarily unprepared Britain, hoping that appeasing the *Führer* would prevent an outbreak of a hot war in Europe.[24] In fact, the report was merely a rehash of the one Lindbergh had written on November 1, 1937, which the American military attaché in Germany, Truman Smith, had forwarded to Washington. Three weeks after the Munich capitulation to Hitler, on October 18, Göring, Commander-in-Chief of the *Luftwaffe*, awarded Lindbergh the second-highest Nazi government award, the Service Cross of the German Eagle, in "recognition of his services to aviation."[25] Perhaps it was not so much for his service to aviation as it was for his collaboration with the Nazi regime in intimidating Britain.

When Jan Masaryk, former President of Czechoslovakia and at the time Czech Minister in London, was informed by Chamberlain that no representative from the Czech government was invited to the meeting that would dismember and destroy Czechoslovakia, Masaryk responded emotionally: "If you have sacrificed my nation to preserve the peace of the world I will be the first to applaud you, but if not, gentlemen, God help your souls."[26]

Winston Churchill was strongly opposed to the policy of appeasing Hitler. On September 11 he wrote a letter to Lord Moyne in which he predicted: "Owing to the neglect of our defences... We seem to be very near the bleak choice between War and Shame. My feeling is that we shall choose Shame, and then have War thrown in a little later on even more adverse terms than at present."[27]

Churchill would go on to repeat the remark in various iterations, reportedly confronting Chamberlain with the words: "You were given the choice between war and dishonor. You chose dishonor and you will have war."[28]

Hitler promised that if the British and French agreed to cede the Sudetenland to him, he would have "no further territorial demands in Europe." Chamberlain and Daladier acceded to Hitler's demands and ordered Benes, Prime Minister of Czechoslovakia, to turn over the Sudetenland to Germany, telling him that he had no backing from Britain nor France and would be on his own if he resisted Hitler's demands and war were to break out.

Prior to flying to Munich, Chamberlain had given the British people a hint of the predetermined outcome of the talks. In a radio broadcast on 27 September, he addressed the nation with the words: "How horrible, fantastic, incredible, it is that we should be digging trenches and trying on gas-masks here because of a quarrel in a faraway country between people of whom we know nothing."

Upon returning to England, Chamberlain stepped off his airplane at the Heston Aerodrome waving the document signed at Munich. Standing on the tarmac outside the plane, Chamberlain announced that he had brought Britain "peace for our time." He spoke again after he arrived at 10 Downing Street, boasting to cheering onlookers that he had brought Britain if not Europe "peace in our time." Chamberlain apparently believed that his official British government policy of appeasement of Hitler had brought peace to Europe. When he returned to Paris, Daladier was besieged at the airport by cheering throngs shouting, *"La paix! La paix!"* or "peace, peace." In contrast to Chamberlain, the exhausted and depressed Daladier was heard to castigate under his breath "the fools" who knew not "what they were cheering."[29]

During the Nuremberg trials in 1945, Hjalmar Schacht retorted to a question by Justice Robert H. Jackson, "I have already told you that Germany did not 'take over Czechoslovakia,' but that it was indeed presented to Germany by the Allies on a silver platter." During his prison interviews with the psychologist Dr. Gustave M. Gilbert at the Nuremberg trials, Göring opined, "Actually, the whole thing was a cut and dried affair. Neither Chamberlain nor Daladier were in the least bit interested in sacrificing or risking anything to save Czechoslovakia...The fate of Czechoslovakia was essentially sealed in three hours."[30]

At the Nuremberg trials, a question was posed to Field Marshal Wilhelm Keitel by the Czech representative to the trial, Colonel Eger, "Would the Reich have attacked Czechoslovakia in 1938 if the Western powers had stood by Prague?" Keitel answered, "Certainly not. We were not strong enough militarily. The object of Munich was to get Russia out of Europe, to gain time, and to complete the German armaments."[31] In November 1938, General Franz Halder, Chief of the *Wehrmacht's* General Staff, warned an American diplomat, Raymond Geist, that the West's appeasement of Hitler would not prevent him from implementing his plans to invade and colonize Eastern Europe and then attack Western Europe. Halder wasn't complaining. He was boasting. He actually shared Hitler's vision of conquest, at least in the East.[32]

Meanwhile, Hitler continued his war against the Jews of Germany. In April 1933, barely a month after taking office, Hitler had ordered a boycott of Jewish businesses in Germany. Jews were barred from all government jobs, including judges, teachers, and civil servants. In 1935, the Nuremberg Laws stripped German Jews of their citizenship. Public bonfire burnings of Jewish-authored or Jewish religious books were staged. On November 9 to 10, 1938 (Night of the Broken Glass), Hitler's storm troopers carried out a massive wave of violent pogroms throughout Germany, Austria and the Sudetenland, snatching Jews from the streets, their homes, their businesses, beating or killing them, destroying 267 synagogues, burning them to the ground as firefighters watched, ordered to not interfere other than to prevent non-Jewish structures from catching fire from the flames engulfing the German Jews' properties.

The Nazis vandalized or destroyed some 7,500 Jewish-owned shops and businesses, looting their wares, and seizing some 30,000 Jewish men, sending them to prisons and concentration camps, such as Dachau, Buchenwald and Sachsenhausen. In their typical *modus vivendi*, the Nazis blamed the Jewish victims for their own suffering and economic ruin, proclaimed that the Jews were responsible for the damages that the Nazi storm troopers and the Hitler Youth had inflicted. The Jewish community, individual Jewish businessmen and ordinary citizens were ordered to pay the German government a fine of one billion *Reichsmarks* (equivalent to approximately 400 million in 1938 U.S. dollars and over seven billion in today's dollars) in compensation for the damages done to *them* by Hitler's own government-employed thugs and murderers. Not wanting the Jewish businessmen who had suffered destruction from the vandalism and fires to collect compensation from the German insurance companies that had insured the destroyed properties, Hitler ordered the companies to pay the compensation directly to the Nazi government's coffers. The uninsured middle- or working-class Jews who had had their homes and small businesses damaged or burned to the ground had to empty their savings accounts to pay for the damages done to themselves. And if they had no money to pay? Well, the state could simply confiscate what was left of their assets.

Barely six months after the Munich Conference in September 1938, Hitler's *Wehrmacht* marched into what remained of Czechoslovakian territory and occupied it without any Czech resistance in March 1939. The Munich Agreement was thus indisputably exposed as a worthless scrap of paper. Hitler was implementing plans for a two-front war quite methodically. His first front, the war against the Jews, was announced in the Nazi Party's "25-point Program" published in 1920, and later openly and widely disseminated in book form in his *Mein Kampf*, and continually rebroadcast in his speeches to the Nazi Party faithfuls and to the German people in mass rallies and over the radio airwaves.

Once he had taken office, Hitler, Göring, Goebbels, Himmler and their underlings implemented the plan in stages via racist laws, violence and unrelenting propaganda instilling in the consciousness of the German population the delusional meme that Jews were some kind of subhuman creatures who needed to be removed from German life and later from Germany itself. As the dictator of Germany, Hitler had had the parliament pass laws that made dehumanizing and deadly persecution of Jews *legal*. In 1933, the first year of the Führer's reign, 522,000 Jews lived in Germany. By the eve of the Second World War, only some 214,000 Jews continued to live in Germany (within its 1937 internationally recognized borders). By May 19, 1943, the Nazis would brag (incorrectly, as it turned out) that Germany was *judenrein* or free of any Jewish inhabitants. The majority of those who had been unable to flee had been sent to concentration camps, though in reality there were hundreds or perhaps thousands of German Jews living in hiding. By the end of the war, only 10 percent of the Jews of Germany in 1939 would be found alive.

Hitler's plans for his second-front war, to extend Germany's borders and rule Poland and the formerly independent nations of Western, Central, Eastern and Southern Europe, were implemented like the chef who dropped one frog after another into a pot of cold water and then turned up the heat gradually enough so that the frogs were too weak to jump out when the water became unbearably hot. Eighteen months after Britain and France capitulated to Hitler in Munich, Lord Lothian, British Ambassador to the United States, opined more diplomatically to his friend, Conservative MP Victor Cazalet, that underlying appeasement "is the natural instinct of every democracy to avoid war if it possibly can, which is the ultimate explanation why Hitler had been able to take them one by one without any of them learning experience from the rest."[33]

Germany and the U.S.S.R. – Partners in Crime

Hitler's penultimate move on his strategic chess board in preparation for the German attack on Poland was to sign an economic treaty with the U.S.S.R. on August 19, 1939. The two dictatorships agreed that German-manufactured products and technical design plans would be exported to the U.S.S.R. in return for Soviet shipments to Germany of raw materials lacking in Germany, such as oil, manganese and massive amounts of grain. The Soviet trains, packed with huge amounts of grain to feed the Germans, would continue to roll until literally the eve of Hitler's attack on the Soviet Union fewer than two years later.

Germany's final move came on the night of August 23, 1939. On that infamous date (actually 2 AM on the 24th local time), Soviet Foreign Minister Vyacheslav Molotov and German Foreign Minister Joachim von Ribbentrop met in Moscow and signed a non-aggression pact which shocked the world when it came to light. For more than 16 years, Hitler had ranted against the Bolsheviks and Soviet Communists, and tarred Jews as enemies because they were allegedly Bolsheviks. Now, the German *Führer* signed a diplomatic agreement with the Communist regime, essentially making the Nazi and Soviet dictators partners.

Members of Communist parties around the world, including in the United States, were shocked by Stalin's sudden and seemingly incomprehensible alliance with Hitler's Nazi regime. But members of the Comintern (Communist International) had no trouble reorienting their loyalty to the new Soviet-German axis. Claiming amongst themselves that "Uncle Joe" must have a very good reason to sign a pact with Hitler, they supported the alliance rather than withdrawing their own ideological alliance with Stalinist U.S.S.R. The secret part of the Molotov-Ribbentrop Pact held that Germany and the U.S.S.R. would have their own spheres of interest in Europe; the U.S.S.R. would annex the Baltic states (Latvia, Lithuania and Estonia) along with Bessarabia, and in concert, Germany and the U.S.S.R. would divide up Poland. Poland was now threatened on three sides: the U.S.S.R. on the east, German-absorbed Czechoslovakia (Bohemia and Moravia) on the south and the German Reich on the west. With the German Queen, Rook and Bishop cornering the Polish King, it was imminently checkmate. Obviously, this meant a war of aggression against Poland. And it was not long in coming.

---

1. Weber pp. 142f.
2. Pool, *Hitler*, chapters 3-5.
3. Miller, Richard p. 45.
4. *Ibid.* p. 46.
5. See: Gross, Jan T. *FEAR*...; Laquer *The Holocaust*....; Zimmerman (see especially chapter 21 by Zvi Gitelman).
6. Watt, p. 361.
7. *Ibid.* pp. 362ff
8. Gross; Laquer, *The Holocaust*...
9. Jansen and Weckbecker, p. 20.
10. Stargardt, p. 41.
11. Mendelsohn, pp. 138f.
12. Dawidowicz, p. 96.

13. "Iran" comes from the Persian word "Aryan". "Aryan" as Hitler used it was a racist, political construction that had no connection to European or Persian philology
14. cited in Hanson, p. 28.
15. Feldgrau
16. Shepherd, p. xviii ff.
17. *Ibid.* p. 7.
18. International Military Tribunal. Imt/nca/nca-06-3727-ps p. 480 accessed on 22 December 2017.
19. Original German source quoted in Ullrich 511, 888 n. 152.
20. Personal letter to this author from Henry A. Kissinger, dated January 28, 1991.
21. Watt, p. 384.
22. Lindbergh, p. 79.
23. Lindbergh, *ibid.* p. 420.
24. Wills, p. 87ff.
25. Hart, p. 170.
26. Wills, p. 82.
27. Gilbert, G.M., p. 1155. See also Taylor, p. 978.
28. Taylor, *idem.*
29. Taylor, *ibid.* p. 59.
30. Sprecher, p. 236.
31. Quote in memoir of former PM of France, Paul Reynaud; cited in Churchill, p. 319.
32. Rossino, p. 4.
33. Hart, p. 174.

9

THE SEPARATION

Abe Comes to the New York World's Fair – Summer, 1939

Sonia's cousin, Zalman Schary, ten years Abe's senior, had been trying for six months to get a visa from the American Consul in Warsaw. His reason, as he informed the Consul, was to visit the New York World's Fair. That may have been true, but his more important reason was that he wanted to visit his brother Ben, who had immigrated to the United States years earlier. After one delay after another, one excuse after another, the Consul was impressed by Zalman's persistence and convinced by his arguments that he would contribute to the American economy as a well-to-do tourist and businessman. He believed that Zalman certainly intended to return to Poland after a few weeks given that he was leaving behind his wife and three children. He finally granted Zalman a tourist visa to travel to the land of many Europeans' dreams.

Sonia and the children had left Warsaw to escape the oppressive summer heat. They were staying at a resort in Otwock, while Abe remained in Warsaw alone. It was a Saturday, July 15, 1939, the same day the Boston Red Sox defeated the Cleveland Indians 9-5 in Cleveland. Abe was at home in his apartment, enjoying his rest from the Sunday to Friday work week. Without advance notice, Zalman rang the doorbell. Abe ushered him in and offered him a piece of cake and a small taste of schnapps. Zalman appreciated the hospitality, but immediately got down to business.

"After six months of pleading with the American Consul, I've finally got a visa to travel to America. And I want you to come with me. We'll go see the World's Fair, I'll have the opportunity to visit my brother, Ben, and his family and you'll be able to visit Sonia's father, Isaac. Look, you've been to other countries in Europe. Why don't you come to America? You'll see your father-in-law and maybe do some business."

Abe was surprised and offered all the reasons why he couldn't accompany Zalman on his excursion. In recounting that day's events, Abe remembered that Zalman *"talked and talked, He was a good salesman and he persuaded me. I am lucky I'm not a girl – I can't say 'no.' I figured I would take two suitcases of products with me, and perhaps I'll be able to do some business in the United States. This won't just be a jaunt to America to see the World's Fair, but I'll see family living in New York City and maybe, just maybe, I will do some business."*

"O.K.," Abe replied. *"Let me discuss this with Sonia."*

"No, no," interjected Zalman. "Don't ask her. She might say 'no'."

Zalman's arguments persuaded Abe to accompany him on the voyage. Now Abe only had to convince the Consul to give him a visa, and unlike Zalman, he didn't have six months to wait; the ship, the *Batory*, was due to sail eight days later, on July 23.

Abe gathered his passport, various assorted financial documents showing that he owned three large properties in Warsaw and also a business that manufactured shoes, with 300 Polish employees relying on him for their livelihoods. Abe needed to persuade the Consul that he had no plans to remain in America as a "destitute immigrant" who might become a burden to an America still recovering from the Great Depression.

Abe got an appointment sometime later in the week at the Embassy Annex of the American Consulate General, which dealt with passports for American citizens living in Poland and visas for Polish nationals. Papers in hand, his confidence intact, Abe drove to the American Consulate and presented his case for getting a visa to Vice Consul Douglas Jenkins Jr., a Charleston, South Carolina native.

During the difficult years of the 1920s and 1930s, with the rise of fascism in Europe and the explosion of murderous antisemitism, a large number of Europeans, Jews in particular, frantically sought to emigrate from what many understood was a coming conflagration and wanted to escape to the United States, or British-administered Palestine, a small piece of territory formerly occupied and ruled for 500 years by the Muslim Ottoman Turks, but promised to the Jewish people as a national home by the British and French victors over the Axis powers in the First World War, or finally, to any country that would take them. In the 1939 *White Paper,* the British government slammed nearly shut Jewish immigration to Palestine.

At the same time, the United States had passed strict immigration quotas preventing large numbers of Jews from entering the country. After the war, researchers discovered that the State Department, under the leadership of Breckinridge Long, Assistant Secretary of State, head of the Immigrant Visa Section, ordered that even the tight quotas for the various European countries were not to be filled by Jewish immigrants.

In a notorious memorandum dated June 26, 1940 sent to State Department officials Adolf Berle and James Dunn, Long revealed his instructions to American Consuls abroad: "We can delay and effectively stop for a temporary period of indefinite length the number of immigrants into the United States. We could do this by simply advising our consuls, to put every obstacle in the way and to require additional evidence and to resort to various administrative devices which would postpone and postpone and postpone the granting of the visas."

So, many spots for immigrants went unfilled even though the spots were available. We know now the fate of those who might have been able to immigrate but were blocked by America's State Department and the British Foreign Office.

After Abe presented his case, Vice Consul Jenkins informed him that the ship, leaving in a few days was likely full and didn't have room for him, so he instructed Abe to go to the shipping line's ticket office to inquire if they had room for him and if they had tickets available. He could then return to the Consulate for further consultation and consideration of his request.

Abe did as he was told and drove to the steamship line's ticket office. But he didn't simply ask if space and tickets were available. After getting an affirmative answer, Abe bought a ticket.

Returning to the Consulate on Saturday, July 22, Abe waved his ticket in front of the irritated Consul who blurted out: "What?!? I didn't tell you to buy a ticket; I told you just to find out if you could get one!"

Vice Consul Jenkins turned to his secretary or assistant and spoke to him in English, a language indecipherable to Abe. Undoubtedly exasperated, and with no further tricks up his sleeve, Jenkins issued Abe a visa to enter as a "temporary visitor." The visa was "granted as Non-Immigrant under Section 3 (Paragraph 2) of the Immigration Act of 1924," which reads: "an alien visiting the United States temporarily as a tourist or temporarily for business or pleasure." Abe paid US $9.25 for the four Foreign Service fee stamps affixed to the visa page of his Polish passport. The equivalent cost in today's dollars would be about $168, a relatively considerable amount of money in 1939. At the then exchange rate of five Złotych to one dollar, the nearly 50 Złotych Abe paid for his visa was equivalent to a tenth or more of the monthly salary of a skilled worker such as an electrician and about half or more of the monthly salary of an unskilled worker in Warsaw.

Prior to the outbreak of the war, an unknown American soldier, likely from the military mission in Warsaw, picked up and brought to the United States a poem he had found in the American Consulate in Warsaw. Which Consular official wrote the ten stanzas is unknown. But here are the first stanza and the last two:

> *The day begins, and the office*
> *Stinks with the crowd of Jews*
> *Of various shapes and sizes,*
> *In cloths of various hues.*
>
> *...*
>
> *I'm sure that St. Peter's duties,*
> *To choose the good from the rest,*
> *Are naught compared with the labor*
> *Of sifting the Jews to go West,*
>
> *It may be someday we'll have comfort,*
> *But one thing I know full well*
> *That if there is a Jew in Heaven,*
> *We'll visa him straight for Hell.*[1]

In the end, Vice Consul Jenkins did give Abe a visa, albeit a temporary one, as Abe had requested. Upon leaving the Consulate, Abe realized he now had to get permission from the other, more important official: Sonia. Abe took a train to the resort in Otwock, where Sonia was staying. With him was a bicycle that he bought for Dadjo. Abe was so happy to see Dadjo's excitement over the gift of a bicycle.

Initially unhappy over Abe's sudden decision to leave Poland for two months, Sonia, ever the flexible wife, was won over by Abe's reassurances. Sonia had total confidence in Abe. He was due to return to Warsaw the second week of September, around the 13th, so he would be gone for only seven weeks. It was unrealistic to think that he could get additional visas for her and the children; after all, leaving behind his business and family was the prime reason the Consul thought that Abe was not immigrating to America, and would return to Poland. In any case, it would not be an easy trip for her with an infant daughter and a four-year-old son. Abe would have the opportunity to see Sonia's father and perhaps half-brothers, so she gave him her blessing.

Abe had a cousin who was a correspondent for the Guardian newspaper in England. When the cousin, named Łang, had bills to pay in Warsaw, Abe would pay the bills on his behalf and the cousin would deposit the equivalent money in Pound Sterling into the Westminster Bank in England in Abe's name. When Abe prepared to set sail for America, he instructed his cousin to transfer the money that was in Abe's British account to a U.S. bank.

Abe had received his visa from Vice Consul Jenkins just in time. The next day, Sunday, July 23, Abe traveled to the Polish port of Gdynia. He and Zalman boarded the Batory, unpacked their valises in their cabin and awaited the ship's sailing.

The Batory, built in Italy in 1935, was the pride of the Polish merchant fleet.[2] It operated in the transatlantic service between Gdynia and Copenhagen, Southampton and New York. This run across the Atlantic was likely one of the last two or three sailings the Batory made in the summer of 1939. On September 1, 1939, the ship would be converted to a troop transport and sailed with the Allies for the duration of the war.

Abe was excited and felt secure. He had prepared about 50 samples of his merchandise to bring to America in the event that he succeeded in obtaining some orders. His bags were packed. All was in order for his seven-week roundtrip.

Little did Abe and Sonia know that their separation would not last seven weeks. Seven years would pass until they saw each other again.

1. Bendersky, pp. 148-150.
2. Cwiklinski, p. 142. Named after a 16th-century Polish king, it displaced 16,000 tons. Boasting 190,000 cubic feet of cargo space, it could accommodate 832 passengers in 302 staterooms. Its engines produced 12,000 horsepower and propelled the ship at a speed of up to 20 knots.

PHOTOGRAPHS

Abe and Sonia vacationing in Otwock, Poland circa
1935

Abe laying the cornerstone of 74 Zelazna

Dadjo playing Polish policeman in Otwock

Sonia with Dadjo and nanny, circa 1939

Children wearing slipper socks, 30 January 1941

Sonia with Lusia and Dadjo 1939. Inscription on reverse reads "My loving husband, we send you this so you can see us together. What is most important is that you can see us and now you don't have to worry about us."

Sonia, Dadjo, Mania and Rachelle

Zalman and Abe shipboard sailing for America, July 1939

Rachelle and Sonia in Belgium post-war

Aufbau ad Persons Searching June 8,1945

Sonia with her hosts, the Blumenfelds, in Belgium

Surrounded by friends and Rachelle, Sonia prepares to
depart for the U.S. Caption on back reads in Polish:
"Goodbye. This distant ship will take you to your
dearest"

Abe (fifth row from bottom, fourth from left) with fellow members of the NY city civil patrol corps, circa 1942 or later

Night school reunion. Sonia front, center

Abe measuring diamond weights

Abe with guest of honor, Eleanor Roosevelt at United
Jewish Appeal fundraiser

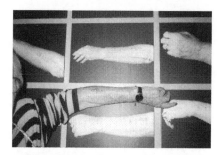

Sonia at the United States Holocaust Memorial
Museum, holding her arm next to its picture on the
museum wall.

Abe with Sarah in Palm Beach, FL, circa 1981

Sonia honored at charity dinner

Rear: Gloria, Sarah, Mark. Front: Ken, David, Sonia,
1989

Sonia and Abe, circa 1983

10

THIS MEANS WAR

Si vis bellum para pacem
Fantasy, Appeasement then War

From July 28, 1914, when Austria-Hungary had declared war on Serbia and the Great War erupted, to November 11, 1918, when an armistice ended the war, casualties of the war totaled, by most estimates, some 37 million people. Nearly ten million military personnel and almost seven million civilians perished, while some 20 million people were wounded or injured. For the United States, out of a population of 92 million, military deaths totaled nearly 117 thousand, and civilian deaths 757, together representing 0.13 percent of the population; over 204 thousand military personnel were wounded, representing 0.22 percent of the population. France alone suffered 1.5 million casualties of the war, killed or wounded.

Even these horrible figures of death and disfigurement were dwarfed by the numbers of the victims of the Spanish Flu, a deadly pandemic that is estimated to have infected 500 million people between January 1918 and December 1920, and killed between 50 to 100 million people, some three to five percent of the world's population. Soldiers on both sides of the conflict were not spared from the deadly flu. At least half of the American military's fatalities in Europe was due to the flu.

Civilians in the Western world must have been overwhelmed by the death toll. Even if they didn't suffer directly from physical or psychological trauma, they were certainly convinced that war was a terrible waste and the World War that had just ended must be the last war, ever.

Politicians who represented their nations' voters, were also in no mood to vote for increases in military spending, believing along with their constituents that "the war to end all wars" had, in fact, ended war as an instrument of national policy, and there would never again be a need for them to send their boys off to war.

To this end, an international organization, the League of Nations, was constituted with the aim of resolving disputes among nations peacefully, according to international law and moral principles. The means of resolving international disputes without war would be via international treaties and moral suasion. The conclusion drawn by the world's powers was *not* that the international community should act in concert to take down dictators and rogue potentates, even if that meant going to war to remove genocidal regimes. Instead, the world's most powerful Western nations, which had just defeated an emperor, a kaiser and a Turkish caliph by force of superior arms and not by worthless treaties, decided that limiting and restricting armaments by signed agreements and treaties would be a successful plan and method for preventing war.

Apparently, it didn't occur to those who came up with this idea, that signed treaties were of value only to the extent that the heads of the signatory states, the parliaments and their *vox populi* were prepared to honor the terms of the treaties. And if there were no mechanism to monitor governments' adherence to the treaties, backed up by the willingness of the Allied victors' governments to use military force to enforce the treaties, then said treaties were worth no more than scraps of paper.

The 17th-century British philosopher, Thomas Hobbes, recognized this with his famous dictum: "...covenants, without the sword, are but words and of no strength to secure a man at all."[1] It may sound contradictory to argue that peace-loving governments need be prepared to use deadly force to ensure adherence to treaties of peace. But the history of our world teaches that this is the case. The ancient Romans are credited with the famous saying: *Si vis pacem para bellum*, "If you desire peace, prepare for war." However, the world's history of the cycles of war proves the truth also of the converse: *Si vis bellum, para pacem*. More recently, Benjamin Franklin, the American ambassador to the court of Louis XVI, warned of this in 1747: "The very Fame of our Strength and Readiness would be a Means of Discouraging our Enemies; for 'tis a wise and true Saying, that One Sword often keeps another in the Scabbard. The Way to secure Peace is to be prepared for War. They that are on their Guard, and appear ready to receive their Adversaries, are in much less Danger of being attack'd, than the supine, secure and negligent."[2]

President Wilson, who had ascended to the American presidency following tenure as President of Princeton University, proposed a millennial delusion of disarmament in the fourth of the Fourteen Points representing his aims in sending American troops to join the fight in Europe. In addition, he ensured that disarmament was enshrined in Article VIII of the Covenant of the League of Nations. Wilson pressured the American Senate to ratify the treaty establishing the League of Nations and to support his goal of disarmament, believing that the alternative was a naval arms race with the European powers and higher taxes on American taxpayers who would pay for America's naval build-up. In the event, the Senate did not respond positively to Wilson's threats and refused to ratify the treaty, keeping the United States out of membership in the League.

The goal of arms control and the reduction of naval forces did not die with the rejection of the League and its Covenant by the Senate. In November 1921, the United States hosted the major naval powers

– Great Britain, Japan, France and Italy – to join in negotiating and signing some seven treaties and twelve resolutions mandating the signatories to refrain from building certain categories of warships. There were additional conferences and meetings among the world powers, whose purpose was to confirm and extend the limitations on naval construction.

In 1928, the United States and France created a document, the General Treaty for the Renunciation of War as an Instrument of National Policy or the Paris Agreement, known more commonly as the Kellogg-Briand Pact, which formally outlawed aggressive or offensive war, as an instrument of national policy. In the minds of the representatives of the 62 nations who signed the Kellogg-Briand Pact on August 27, or at least in the minds of the signatories representing Western, civilized nations, the pact would end wars among states. The pact called on nations to settle disputes peacefully, without resorting to war. Among the first signatories were Italy, Germany and Japan. The U. S. Senate ratified the treaty by a vote of 85 to 1, with the senatorial understanding that the agreement did not limit the right of the United States to self-defense, nor did it require the United States to take any action in the event of violation of the treaty by any of the signatories.

In 1932, the Great Powers met again in Geneva, Switzerland for *the Conference for the Reduction and Limitation of Armaments*, also known as the *World Disarmament Conference*. President Hoover called for a 30 percent reduction in the world's armies and navies and also proposed abolishing offensive instruments of war such as tanks, mobile artillery, chemical weapons and aerial bombardment in the event of war. As late as 1933, President Franklin D. Roosevelt proposed abolishing most offensive weapons. The United States actually sank naval ships and reduced its manpower from the four million-man army of the First World War to 118,000 men.

What was going on in the world when American presidents were pushing unilateral disarmament? In September 1931, after staging an incident at a railroad station in China, Japanese forces invaded

Manchuria, and began their murderous military campaign. When the League of Nations moved to condemn the Japanese aggression in February 1933, the Japanese ambassador to the League spoke in his country's defense and then walked out of the meeting. A few weeks later, Japan gave its formal notice of withdrawal from the League effective March 27, 1933. On December 12, 1937, Japanese naval airplanes bombed the American gunboat, Panay, which had been evacuating Americans from Nanking, then under attack by Japanese forces. The United States took no action other than to demand financial compensation, which was paid by the Japanese in an amount exceeding 2 million dollars. On January 26, 1938, John Allison, the American Consul in Nanking, was struck in the face by a Japanese soldier during the Japanese murderous rampage in the city. Both incidents were acts of war, but they were downplayed by the American government.

In 1935, Italy's Benito Mussolini invaded Abyssinia (today's Ethiopia). His army, with modern weapons of war including armored vehicles, machine guns and airplanes, easily defeated the Abyssinian defenders. Haile Selassie, the emperor of Abyssinia, appeared before the League of Nations to beg for help from the international community to resist the Italian invasion, but to no avail.

In July 1936, shortly after the Spanish Civil War erupted, Nazi Germany sent so-called volunteers from its air force (the Condor Legion) and army to fight on the side of Franco and the Nationalist forces. Mussolini also sent his armed forces to fight on the side of Hitler and Franco. With the assistance of the superior German and Italian forces, Franco emerged victorious over the Spanish Republicans. The *Luftwaffe* and *Wehrmacht* obtained valuable military experience fighting in Spain, learning tactical lessons, in particular the value of air power, which was employed to destroy not only Spanish Republican forces, but entire towns, such as Guernica. Hermann Göring, Commander-in-Chief of the German air force, had urged Hitler to join in the Spanish Civil War not only to fight a Communist takeover of

Spain but to gain valuable tactical experience for his air force. The Germans fielded Messerschmitt Bf 109 fighters, Heinkel He III medium bombers and the Junkers Ju-87 Stuka dive bombers that were to figure extensively in Germany's later wars against Poland and France. Because of the Stuka's steep angle of attack, it was the closest to a precision bombing machine that existed in any of the world's air forces at the time. The shrieking sirens (known as the "Jericho Trumpets") installed on the fairings of the planes' fixed landing gears also instilled terror and panic in the people living in the cities on the ground targeted by the planes' bombs.

More than once, I asked Abe how it was that he didn't realize that war was imminent. Without any irritation, Abe explained that he had no idea, "We had no television news shows. I was busy with my business and family. I wasn't so interested in the political stories in the newspapers. I relied on the leaders in charge to do their jobs. If I thought that Germany was about to launch a war against Poland, don't you think I would have found a way to take Mother and the children and perhaps other members of the family out of Poland to England or South America or someplace far away from Europe, someplace that would let us in?"

The Second World War begins

Sonia and the two children had returned from vacation and were back in their Warsaw apartment by September 1, 1939, the day that German armed forces crossed their international border with Poland and began their aggression against Poland, their destruction of Polish society and their dress rehearsal for the mass murder of Europe's Jewish population.

The invasion of Eastern Europe, *Drang nach Osten* or "drive to the East", had always been one of Hitler's primary goals for two reasons. The first, frequently expressed publicly, was that Germany needed and deserved Lebensraum or "living room" in order for German farmers to have enough agricultural land to feed the German population. This was an idea Hitler had gleaned from a man introduced to him by Heinrich Himmler: Richard Walther Oskar Darré.[3]

Hitler's second goal was to use the Jewish population as a scapegoat for all of Germany's and the world's ills. He wrongly, but conveniently identified Jews with Soviet Bolsheviks because of a very small number of Jews who held prominent positions in the Bolshevik and later Stalinist Communist Party (until most of them were ultimately executed by Stalin or his underlings). If Germans were the Aryans and the superior race, Hitler needed the antithesis. Jews were to become the antithesis to German superiority; they were to be labeled the inferior people, literally *Untermenschen* (subhumans).

Whether Hitler's longstanding antipathy and grotesque hatred of Jews and the Jewish collective was concocted deliberately as a political feint or was the product of psychotic delusions in Hitler's mind has long been discussed. The truth is more likely than not a combination of both. The Nazi ideology of German racial superiority and the racial inferiority of Jews, Gypsies and Slavs permeated the beliefs of all party members. It justified racial and ethnic harassment and persecution especially of the Jews in Germany and ultimately led to the understanding if not underpinning of the willingness of millions of Germans and European collaborators to engage in colossal armed robbery and mass murder, in particular of Jews. There is ample evidence that significant Nazis such as Julius Streicher held psychotic delusions. Streicher edited the Nazi newspaper *Der Sturmer*, an unintended parody of a news publication which specialized in fake stories of lurid sexual and mysterious religious rites allegedly practiced by Jews against Christians. They were designed to incite antisemitic hatred among their unsophisticated readers.[4] At his trial after the war he claimed that his paper was not antisemitic.

Despite the disproportionate contribution of untold numbers of Jews to science, medicine, commerce, philosophy and the arts in Germany, Hungary and throughout Europe and the world, Hitler would irrationally liken ethnic Jews to diseases and pests. He repeated endlessly that the Jews needed to be eradicated from the face of the earth, like diseases and pestilence. The German NSDAP audiences who heard him responded with approval and thunderous applause.

Hitler's ideology demanded that Germany become the pre-eminent military power in Europe in order to fulfill Germany's alleged destiny to dominate Europe if not the world. That required Germany to go to war to conquer neighboring territories. In 1928, Hitler authored a manuscript known as the Second Book (*Zweiter Buch*)[5] that, unlike *Mein Kampf*, was never published – for obvious reasons – as that manuscript laid out Hitler's plans for world domination. It might have been unwise for Hitler to reveal to those who still doubted, his driving ambition to rule the world.

Hitler's success in incorporating Austria as part of the German Reich and occupying Czechoslovakia without a fight did not lead him to try to negotiate seriously with Poland over territory, such as the Polish Corridor, which divided Germany proper from East Prussia. Hitler wanted a war with Poland, an aggressive, annihilationist war with the Poles and with its large Jewish community. He wanted a war against France and Britain, too. But not yet. His General Staff warned against a world war. Hitler misled his own generals, assuring them that he had no interest in a world war and predicted that Britain and France, who had treaties and agreements to come to Poland's aid, would not go to war. He was encouraged in this belief by the reports of anti-war marchers in France chanting "*Mourir pour Dantzig?*"[6] which we can translate as: "We're not dying for Danzig!" Colonel Jozef Beck, Poland's Foreign Minister, also understood the meaning. After the Munich Conference, he lamented to French Ambassador Léon Noël, "We do not forget the press campaigns in France with the slogan 'We shan't fight for the [Polish] Corridor'" [Danzig].[7] On August 22, 1939, when war plans to invade Poland had already been in place since the spring, Hitler spoke to his high-ranking generals at his mountain retreat, the Berghof, and assured them that Britain and

France would not fight for Poland. "A military response can be ruled out... Our enemies are little worms. I saw them at Munich."

Field Marshall Erich von Manstein later recalled that Hitler had declared, "that he would never be so mad as to unleash a two-front war, as German leaders of 1914... Raising his coarse voice, he had explicitly assured his military advisers that he was not idiot enough to bungle his way into a world war for the sake of the City of Danzig or on account of the Polish Corridor."

General Wilhelm Keitel, Chief of the *Wehrmacht* High Command, remonstrated with the Nazi head of the military's supply division, who warned against a world war in August 1939 because of Germany's immature war economy. Keitel chided him, saying that Führer told him (Keitel) that there was no danger of a world war because: "the French were a degenerate pacifist people, the English are much too decadent to render Poland any real help, and America would never again send even one man to Europe in order to fetch England's or Poland's chestnuts out of the fire."[8]

Brutal wars had raged around the world, from Spain to China to Ethiopia. Germany had rearmed and swallowed up Austria and Czechoslovakia. None of this was recognized at the time as a world war. Not until Hitler's *Luftwaffe Stukas* and armored forces began their brutal attack on Poland. It was only then, on the third day of the German invasion, when the British and French governments declared war on Germany was the conflict considered a world war.

Before their invasion on September 1, the Nazis had created a specious cause of war by arranging a phony attack on a German-Polish border radio station in Gleiwitz by alleged Polish soldiers. Hitler had advised his commanders-in-chief in the August 22 speech that he would "give a propagandistic cause for starting the war, never mind whether it is true or not. The victor shall not be asked later on whether he told the truth or not. In starting a war, not the right is what matters, but victory."[9] The attack was fake, and the organizers were actually German SS. This fake attack was the public excuse that the Führer broadcast to justify his invasion.

It was the previous spring, on March 23, 1939, that Hitler had already ordered Walther von Brauchitsch, then Commander-in-Chief of the *Wehrmacht*, to develop an operational plan for the coming war against Poland. Little more than a week later, on April 1, 1939, Hitler gave his famous speech at Wilhelmshaven in honor of the christening of the battleship Terpitz. In his speech he turned truth upside down as he emphasized Germany's "participation in peaceful rivalry with other nations... Germany was for decades the surest guarantor of peace and devoted herself only to her own peaceful business... If people now say that this is the signal for Germany's desire to attack the whole world, then I do not believe they mean it seriously... ...Germany does not dream of attacking other nations... There is no point in bringing about cooperation among nations, until this Jewish fission-fungus of peoples has been removed... we have given great happiness to Central Europe... namely, peace, peace protected by German power... Sieg-Heil! Sieg-Heil! Sieg-Heil!"

In the middle of August, Hitler met with General von Brauchitsch and the head of the General Staff, General Fritz Halder, and informed them that their job in the coming war was *Zerschlagung* or the smashing of Poland. One week later, Hitler elaborated on his order at a conference with the Army Groups commanders, explaining that "the solution to the Eastern Question was a hard and ruthless annihilation of Poland (*Vernichtung Polens*), to proceed with the removal of its vital force since the campaign was not about reaching a certain line, but the annihilation of the enemy."[10]

The historian Alexander B. Rossino[11] labeled Hitler's war against Poland a new kind of war, a *Volkstumskampf*, an ethnic struggle, a war not necessarily for territory but for annihilation. Rossino rightly points out that the Nazi mass murder of political opponents and those defined by the Nazis as racial and biological subhumans – even "useless eaters" – did not begin in 1941, but began with the Nazi invasion of Poland in 1939. Mass murder was planned and initiated by the Nazi government of Germany and carried out by both specialized killing units and by ordinary German soldiers given killing orders by generals and their subordinate officers.

The orders were to kill partisans, saboteurs, bandits, guerillas (*Freischarlers*), snipers (*Franc-tireurs*),[12] "agitators" and "riff-raff." Any civilian who resisted the Nazis was to be killed, along with hostages and innocent bystanders. These orders were to be the criminalization of aggressive resistance to the Nazi invaders and the justification for mass murder. Ultimately, the most important target for murder was the Jewish population of Poland. Contemporaneous admissions by *Wehrmacht* officers and SS commanders revealed that the objects of the above kill orders were not just literal targets for killing, they were also often code words for Jews – who were to be murdered. This wordplay was made explicit by Arthur Nebe, the commander of *Einsatzgruppe B* who remarked during the German invasion of the Soviet Union in 1941 "Where there's a partisan there's a Jew and where there's a Jew there's a partisan."[13] The Greek historian, Thucydides, wrote millennia ago that those who make war on others also make war on language: "Words had to change their ordinary meaning and to take that which was now given them."[14]

Hitler's desire to annihilate the Polish nation was not mere bluster. His order was operationalized by Himmler and Heydrich in a project known as "Operation Tannenberg," named after the city where the the German army had achieved an early battle victory over the Russians during the First World War in August 1914. The goal for the project, as Heydrich revealed to the killing squads to be deployed to Poland after the invasion, was the "liquidation of Poland's nobility, clergy and Jews."[15] Heydrich, in charge of the killings, told the chief of the Order Police, Kurt Daluege, that the Führer had given him an "extraordinary radical... order for the liquidation of various circles of the Polish leadership that ran into the thousands." The mission was to decapitate the Polish *intelligentsia* in the belief that the Polish population would be easier to control without a leadership class.

To this end, the German security services developed *Sonderfahndungslisten* or "special search lists" of Poles that they had compiled from public information and spies. The individuals named on these lists comprised anti-Nazis, significant Polish political figures, university professors, teachers, doctors, lawyers, civil servants and government officials, Communists, uncooperative Catholic clergy and so on. Hans Frank, who was to be appointed Governor of the General Government, would report on a meeting he had with Hitler on October 2, 1940, wherein Hitler raged: "The task of the priest is to keep the Poles quiet, stupid and dull-witted."[16] By the end of the war, about 1.7 million Poles would be forcibly deported to work as slave laborers in Germany.

The names on the *Sonderfahndungslisten* numbered about 61,000. The names had already been accumulated by Germany's security services and the *Abwehr* since 1936. Additional names were acquired from the Polish *Volksdeutsche* who functioned as the German fifth column in Poland and added to the lists. The lists were compiled into books, the *Sonderfahndungsbücher*, which were distributed to the killers in the *Einsatzkommandos* and *Einsatzgruppen* or "special squads" that followed closely behind the *Wehrmacht* into Poland. Between September 1, 1939 and the end of September, about 16,000 to 27,000 civilians, ethnic Poles and Jews had been executed by *Wehrmacht* firing squads. Many thousands more listed or not on the *Sonderfahndungsbücher* were murdered by the *SS Einsatzgruppen*. By the end of December 1939, about 50,000 Poles (among those approximately 15 percent Jews) had been murdered by the *SS* and *Selbstschutz* auxiliaries.[17]

The *Einsatzgruppen* had significant help from the *Volksdeutsche* in Poland in their search for and murder of the Polish *intelligentsia*. The ethnic Germans in Poland had established a self-defense organization known as the *Selbstschutz*, which comprised about 100,000 men. If males over the age of 16 constituted, say, 20 percent of the *Volksdeutsche* population (assuming an average family size of five), nearly all of the men in this population belonged to the self-defense organization.

When Polish troops were retreating from the German onslaught on September 3, they were fired upon by members of the *Selbstschutz* while passing the Polish city of Bydgoszcz (called by Germans Bromberg). The Polish troops returned fire and killed an estimated 100 to 350 men. The German propaganda machine broadcast over the airwaves and in the press that Polish troops had massacred 58,000 innocent ethnic Germans in Bydgoszcz. Since only approximately 10,000 of the 156,000 residents of the city were *Volksdeutsche*,[18] this claim was patently false. They used the term *Bromberger Blutsonnag* or "Blomberg's Bloody Sunday" to inflame the German public at home and to enrage German soldiers and *Einsatzgruppen* killer squads to exact bloody revenge against Polish troops, irregulars and undesirable civilians.[19] Approximately 420,000 Polish troops were captured by the end of the invasion. Of these, some 60,000 were Jews. The vast majority of the Jewish soldiers were not treated by their German captors appropriately, under the rules of war. Half of the Jewish soldiers were shot outright or sent to hard labor camps from which few emerged alive. Of the 25,000 or so released by the Germans, all would end up in ghettos or camps and nearly all would be dead by the end of the war.[20]

Members of the *Selbstschutz*, led by Himmler's personal adjutant, *SS*-Oberführer, Ludolph-Hermann von Alvensleben, collaborated with the German invaders as an essentially separate organization until about March 1940, when they were mostly merged into *SS* units. Ukrainians were also recruited by the *SS* as auxiliaries. By 1942, more than 1,500 of them were assisting the German's mass murder in the East.[21]

Even before German troops entered Warsaw, a meeting was held in Germany that would foretell long before the Wannsee Conference of January 1942 the existence of plans for the murder of all the Jews of Europe. On September 21, 1939, Reinhard Heydrich, head of the Reich's Main Security Office, held a secret conference in Berlin and teletyped the essence of the conference to all the *Einsatzgruppen* commanders, relevant German Ministries and the Army High Command (OKH). Heydrich described a two-stage process leading to the physical annihilation of Europe's Jews.

In the first, short-range stage, Jews were to be assembled and deported to concentration points near rail junctions "so that future measures may be accomplished more easily." The second stage would accomplish the *Endziel* or final goal which would be *"die geplanten Gesamtmassnahmen streng geheim zu halten sind."* In plain English, the final goal was expressed euphemistically as "the planned total measures" which were "to be kept strictly secret."[22] But for now, Poland would need to be brutally subdued, subjugated and pillaged.

By some miracle, Sonia and the children survived the bombings, artillery barrages, the ear-shattering noise, the nervous-system-battering explosions, the terror, the fear and scenes and smells of death. By the third week of the German assault on Warsaw, utility lines had been cut by bombs. There was no running water, no electricity and no gas. It was many weeks before the broken water mains were repaired by German engineers and interrupted electricity power resumed.

The Polish army fought the Nazi invasion courageously. By the end of the September Campaign, 50 percent of German armored vehicles were out of commission from mechanical failure or destroyed by the Polish armed forces, which would force Hitler to postpone his intended attack on France from November 1939 to May 1940.[23] But Poland fought on its own.

France had signed a mutual assistance pact with Poland on February 21, 1921, following the First World War. The pact was strengthened in September 1922 by a formal military alliance between the two countries. The agreement signed by Marshal Foch of France and General Sikorski of Poland stated explicitly that in case of German aggression against either Poland or France, or both, the two nations would aid each other "to the fullest extent." Fearing that war was in the offing, the Polish government asked for and received in May 1939 a guarantee from the French government committing them in the event of the outbreak of war between Germany and Poland, to immediately undertake air action against Germany. It was also agreed that on the third day of French mobilization, its army would launch a diversionary offensive into German territory, which would be followed by a major military offensive of the full French army to take place no later than 15 days after mobilization.

On March 31, 1939, Neville Chamberlain spoke in the House of Commons as follows: "I now have to inform the House that... in the event of any action which clearly threatened Polish independence, and which the Polish Government accordingly considered it vital to resist with their national forces, His Majesty's Government would feel themselves bound at once to lend the Polish Government all support in their power. They have given the Polish Government an assurance to this effect. I may add that the French Government have authorized me to make plain that they stand in the same position in this matter as do His Majesty's Government."

Echoing the words of his radio broadcast of 27 September, 1938, when he had intimated that Britain would not go to war to defend a "faraway country," this time he told the House of Commons on August 24 that if war came, it would not be "for the political future of a faraway city in a foreign land," but would be fought to preserve fundamental principles of the rule of international law.[24]

The British reassured the Poles that in the event of war the Royal Air Force would, in support of the French offensive against Germany, bomb appropriate targets in Germany. This was formalized in the Agreement of Mutual Assistance between the United Kingdom and Poland, signed on the eve of war, August 25, 1939. The British, however, did strongly advise the Poles even at that date not to mobilize its forces in order to not provoke Hitler.

The political leaders of France and Britain were certainly anticipating war yet were apparently surprised by the German attack on Poland on September 1, 1939. Meanwhile, the American people remained mired in the swamp of isolationism that kept President Roosevelt from openly supporting Britain and joining the battle against Hitler and Nazism until the United States was itself surprised by the Japanese attack on Pearl Harbor on December 7, 1941. The West had deluded itself from the end of the First World War until 1939 or 1941. It had pursued unilateral disarmament, destroyed its own war-making ability, signed agreements that outlawed war, all while the despots of the world, Hirohito and Tojo, Franco, Mussolini and Hitler engaged in massive rearmament and began to set the world ablaze with war and genocide.

The French and British, who had signed security pacts with the Polish government did indeed declare war on Germany on September 3, but they offered essentially no military aid to the Poles fighting for their lives and the independence of their country. On September 6, French forces did invade five miles into Germany, capturing 12 abandoned German towns, but then withdrew five days later to their former positions and remained there, sitting in their bases. The British did send bombers over Germany. But it was not bombs that they initially dropped. The British planes dropped propaganda pamphlets on the Germans, asking them to reconsider their war.

The Polish Air Force fought valiantly though outnumbered three to one in fighters. It was destroyed within days, but not within hours as has often been claimed. Polish fighter planes downed at least 126 German planes, about ten percent of the German attackers. Polish groundfire downed an additional several hundred German planes. In addition, Polish planes dropped 200 tons of bombs in 200 sorties on invading German forces.[25] The *Luftwaffe* not only attacked Polish military targets but also carried out terror bombings of Polish cities, including Warsaw, on September 1, with additional major attacks on the eighth and 13th and finally a major terror bombing with explosive and incendiary bombs from September 24 to 27.

The wanton destruction in Poland and the mindset of the destroyers is illustrated by an unwitting testimony of a *Luftwaffe* airman, surreptitiously recorded by British authorities in a Prisoner of War Camp in England. Remarks by Lieutenant Pohl to another airman: "On the second day of the Polish war I had to drop bombs on a station at Posen. Eight of the 16 bombs fell on the town, among the houses. I did not like that. On the third day I did not care a hoot, and on the fourth day I was enjoying it. It was our before breakfast amusement to chase single soldiers over the fields with [machine gun] fire and to leave them lying there with a few bullets in the back. [Civilians] too. We attacked the columns in the streets. I was in the "Kette" [flight of three aircraft]. The leader bombed the street, the two supporting machines the ditches, because there are always ditches there. The machines rock, one behind the other, and now we swerved to the left with all machine guns firing like mad. You should have seen the horses stampede! I was sorry for the horses, but not at all for the people. But I was sorry for the horses up to the last day."[26]

While the Polish government never surrendered to Germany, the commander of the Polish army defending the capital, Warsaw, finally surrendered on September 27. German forces entered Warsaw on September 30 and were in full control by the next day. An estimated 25,000 to 40,000 civilians had been killed in Warsaw alone from the German terror bombings and constant artillery barrages. An estimated 95 percent of buildings in Warsaw had been damaged and at least five percent of them had been totally destroyed. On September 17, notwithstanding the 1932 Polish-Soviet Non-aggression Pact, and in accordance with the Molotov-Ribbentrop Pact, the Soviet army had invaded Poland from the East, putting paid to any chance for Poland to defend itself from the *Wehrmacht*, now that it was under attack on two fronts.

Polish resistance finally collapsed and surviving remnants of the Polish army were ordered by the fleeing government to escape to Romania. Many of the troops later succeeded in fleeing to England where they served with Allied forces during the war. Some of the best pilots in the British Royal Air Force that defended the U.K. during the Battle of Britain were Polish pilots, who, in fact comprised about a third of all Royal Air Force pilots during the war. They initially flew dispersed among British squadrons until their skills in flying and downing German aircraft were recognized and fully Polish squadrons were created.

On October 6, the Nazis divided the occupied Poland into three parts. The western part (to be known as the *Warthegau* [Western District]) was absorbed into the German Reich, the eastern part, absorbed into the Soviet Union, and the middle, the so-called General Government was constituted as a separate administrative area under German control and ruled by the Nazi appointee, Hitler's lawyer, Hans Frank. The General Government was itself subdivided into districts: Krakow, Lublin, Radom, Warsaw and in 1941 (with the invasion of Soviet occupied Poland), additionally Galicia, all ruled by Frank.

Special decrees were issued for Jews. They were not allowed to keep more than 2,000 Złotych in cash, the rest of their money had to go into special bank accounts that were blocked to them; they needed permits to ride special city transport reserved for Jews (or were totally forbidden to do so); Jewish businesses had to be turned over to special Aryan "trustees." Beginning in December 1939, all Polish Jews were ordered to wear armbands or sew into their outer garments a Jewish star. The Germans had little to no respect for the Catholic Poles. Their *intelligentsia* and outspoken anti-Nazis were rounded up and sent to concentration camps or murdered on the spot. The non-Jewish population of Poland was initially not marked for total annihilation, but they were threatened with death if they rendered any aid, including providing food to Jews or hiding Jews from their Nazi executioners (German Proclamation, October 15, 1941). Records document that at least 1,000 ethnic Poles were, in fact, murdered by *Wehrmacht* soldiers or Nazi death squads (e.g. *SS* forces) when discovered to be hiding Polish Jews. Polish saviors, when they were discovered, were often beaten to death or shot on the spot by

Germans or their Ukrainian helpers as an object lesson to other Poles.

With the start of the occupation, the civilian population survived in a state of shock. Shock turned to terror when *Gestapo* agents followed the occupation troops into Warsaw, closed all universities, looted or destroyed libraries and Polish and Jewish cultural treasures. They took possession of all factories. Raw materials and manufactured goods deemed useful as war material were confiscated and shipped back to Germany. Other factories considered important or those that had contracts with the Polish army were harnessed into the German war industry or given to *Kommissarische Leitung* or German managing boards, including the Starachowice Works; Stalowa Wola Steel and Arms Plants; State Engineering Works; Associated Mechanics; State Radio Works; Marconi Radio Company; airplane factories; Cegielski Plants (in Rzeszow) that manufactured heavy tanks and armored trains; State Rifle Works; Rohn, Zielinski Electrical and so on. The Polish Cable Factory (Polskie Fabryki Kabli) in Ozarow near Warsaw was handed over to the German Siemens Corporation. Banks and bank accounts were confiscated. Not only were universities closed, but so were high schools. Polish children were forbidden to attend school past primary school. Germans forbade the teaching of Polish history. Polish monuments were torn down or destroyed. Marshal Piłsudski Square was renamed *Adolf Hitler Platz*.[27] Some Polish museums and libraries had been destroyed by German bombing. Those remaining standing were looted and their treasures shipped back to the Reich for its museums and private collections, such as those from the Ethnographic Museum in Poznan.[28]

One surviving Polish archaeologist recounted after the war: "The Nazi invasion of Poland was a catastrophe without precedent for all branches of the nation's cultural life and archaeology was no exception. One quarter of Polish archaeologists perished on the battlefield or in concentration camps. Others, threatened with arrest and almost certain death, had to live in hiding (as did the doyen of Polish archaeologists, Professor Józef Kostrzewski in

Poznan); the few remaining ones were forbidden to engage in scientific work."[29]

On November 4, 1939, the SS, under the name of the city's military commander, General von Neuman-Neurode, ordered that all Jews were to be concentrated in a certain area of the main Jewish neighborhoods of Warsaw. This necessitated the uprooting and resettlement of over 250 thousand people; half were ethnic Poles who had to evacuate the Jewish quarter, and the other half, Jews who had to find new living accommodations. All were given three days to relocate. Sonia's apartment at 74 Zelazna street was in this first Jewish quarter, which the Jews were forbidden to call a "ghetto" so Sonia was lucky enough to be allowed to remain in place.

The first step taken by the Germans against the Jewish population was to humiliate them and rob them of their valuables. With guile, the Germans led the Jews to believe that they would be subject to oppression – a huge and perhaps unprecedented pogrom, but a pogrom, nonetheless. The Jewish population had survived previous pogroms in Europe and believed that they would survive this one, as well. It never occurred to the vast majority of Polish Jews, certainly in the beginning, that they were to become the victims of a German-perpetrated genocide.

On the heels of the *Wehrmacht* occupation of Warsaw, Sonia was forced to let her two housekeepers go immediately, because Jews were no longer allowed to employ Gentiles. Her governess, Lunia, was Jewish, and therefore was able to stay with Sonia to help her with the children. Professionals such as doctors, dentists, lawyers were forbidden from having Gentiles as patients or clients. Jewish businesses and stores were closed or seized by the German occupiers and sold or awarded to German individual businessmen as *Treuhänders* or Trustees. Business concerns that were deemed useful to the Germans were kept open and were to employ Jews in the ghetto that was to be formed the following year. Abe's brothers, Yitzhak and Moshe, didn't turn in all of the money that the German occupiers demanded. For the next few years, they did what they could to watch over Sonia, Rachelle and the children and to arrange for the purchase or smuggling of food to the family. A photo of Sonia's two children, dated 1941, shows the two wearing slipper socks. The footwear might have remained in a hidden inventory after the Nazi invasion or perhaps were fabricated during the occupation, by Hadebut employees working in secret or for a *Treuhänder*. Two cooperatives for shoe fabrication, employing about 500 workers, had been established in the ghetto, but there is no information about the possibility that Abe's brothers were involved in those enterprises.

The Germans had also developed lists of Jews living in the Jewish neighborhoods in Warsaw and sent police to the apartment buildings to find educated and professional Jews – the Jewish *intelligentsia* – and arrest them. They arrested Jewish doctors and engineers. Sonia witnessed German troops going into her building and arresting a woman dentist. She witnessed uniformed looters going into Jewish factories and stores and emptying them of their contents. Warsaw's "Seventh Avenue," *Gentsche* street, was known for textile factories and stores. She saw them emptied of all their goods. It was open season for criminals wearing German army, police or *SS* uniforms to raid Jewish apartments and steal for the Nazi occupation authorities or to line their own pockets.

On March 27, 1940, the SS ordered Jewish leaders to fund and build a brick wall around the Jewish quarter. The wall was finally completed in early November 1940. It was at that point that Sonia was forced to move, as her apartment was no longer within the confines of the new, closed ghetto area. She, the children and the nanny, Lunia, moved into an apartment with another family of four people. On November 15-16, 1940, the ghetto was declared closed by the German authorities. Entry and exit of Jews without special permission and permits were forbidden. Hundreds of thousands of people were now crammed into two or so square miles. Jewish businessmen and craftsmen (who comprised 80 percent of Warsaw's craftspeople) who depended on trade outside the Jewish quarter now lost their livelihoods and soon their ability to feed their families.

Food became scarce. The Germans allowed food into the ghetto – for which the Jews had to pay inflated prices – through the German-controlled *Transferstelle* ("transit post") on the corner of Stawki and Dzika streets. The food allowed in by the Germans allowed for starvation rations for the approximately 400,000 Jews trapped in the ghetto. Eighty percent of food that was to come into the ghetto was smuggled in, most of it through the city's sewers and much of the goods smuggled in by Jewish children and teens – with the help of Poles or Jews hidden outside the ghetto, on what was called the "Aryan side." By July 1942, at least 100,000 Jews would die from starvation or disease. In the beginning, Germans grabbed Jews off the streets in the ghetto and sent them to hard labor camps. A Jewish administration was set up in the ghetto and was forced by the Germans to select and provide workers for German industries in or near Warsaw and later throughout Poland. Poles were also seized in Warsaw and sent to work as slave labor in Germany, while Jews were not sent to Germany.

Sonia lived in terror, afraid that the Germans might catch and arrest her. In one of her many brave acts, she removed her armband emblazoned with the Jewish star and went out shopping for food. She removed the armband to avoid being identified and beaten or arrested. The Germans grabbed Jews in the streets and forced them to do labor like washing the vehicles of Nazi officers or getting down on their hands and knees to wash the streets. Not because the streets needed cleaning, but as a means of humiliating the Jews. But they didn't give them rags to use in washing the cars; they forced them to use their own clothes, ordering, for example, Sonia's brother-in-law, who had just returned from service in the Polish army, to use his pants. At the end of the day, after washing cars and having been given nothing to eat, he was taken by the Germans into a building, along with others the German soldiers had grabbed off the streets, and forced to undress, after which the German soldiers beat him and the others mercilessly. He came home and could barely sleep at night or sit on a chair, because he was black and blue and in such full-body pain. The soldiers had taken away his passport and ordered him to return to their office the next day. He told Sonia that he was not returning; he would just as soon have the Germans kill him. As a result, the family decided to leave their apartment. They moved to another apartment in the same building, and the Germans did not come looking for the brother-in-law.

The Germans continued their plunder of Polish and Jewish businesses. Sonia recalled, "Every day there was another announcement. Children weren't allowed to go to school, they couldn't play in the park. We were ordered to bring all of our valuables, gold, silver, jewelry and radios to the Germans. The Gestapo rounded up the *intelligentsia*."

Those Poles (mostly) and Jews who were considered society's leaders: journalists, professors, doctors, anyone who might be able to have an influence on large numbers of ordinary Poles and perhaps lead them into noncooperation or even sabotage against the occupying Nazi army, were rounded up. These were people who needed to be liquidated first. And they were. Sonia heard shooting all day long for days. She saw a doctor and the aforementioned dentist whom she knew taken out of the building by gun-toting, German soldiers and never saw them again.

Some Jewish, community leaders were permitted to survive as members of committees that exercised self-rule in the ghettos constructed by the Germans all across Poland and Eastern Europe. These committees, known collectively as *Judenrate*, were supposed to govern the ghettos and serve as the intermediaries between the Jewish residents of the ghettos and the ruling *Wehrmacht* military or German civilian administrators appointed to rule the conquered European countries occupied by Germany. The main job of the *Judenrat* in Warsaw for example, was to fill the demands of the Nazi administrators for "workers." The *Judenrate* were given quotas of Jewish ghetto residents to be sent to alleged labor camps, and it was the job of these governing committees to round up those who were selected by the *Judenrate* to fill the quotas, orders for which were given daily or weekly.

The cooperation of the *Judenrate* with the Nazi occupiers has been the subject of intense and sometimes vicious debate by survivors and historians since the end of the war. Many survivors bitterly criticized the committee members as collaborators who should have refused to assist the Germans. Other survivors and historians have concluded that the *Judenrate* occasionally succeeded in negotiating improved conditions for ghetto residents and often succeeded in postponing various round-ups, keeping Jews who were not deported, alive, while they kept the ghetto from collapsing into chaos. In the event, many *Judenrate* members were themselves sent to camps and killed after their ghettos were liquidated. Others committed suicide either from feelings of guilt over their behavior or to make final statements that they preferred their own deaths over collaborating with the criminal Nazi occupiers in deporting Jews to what they knew by then was violent death.

There are two sides, both sad, to the story of the *Judenrate*. However, in no way can these self-governing bodies in ghettos, which were essentially forced urban prison camps, be compared to the willing collaborators with the Nazis in conquered territories such as France, Holland, Norway, Hungary, Romania, fascist Italy, the Baltic states and unoccupied Arab countries in the Middle East (such as Vichy Syria and Iraq). It is well known that Soviet prisoners of war in German hands were in some cases forced at the point of a gun or compelled in order to avoid starvation to don German army uniforms and assist in mostly labor battalions, German troops fighting the Red Army.

Hitler's willing Helpers

The German High Command succeeded in recruiting hundreds of thousands of men from conquered territories, in particular the Ukraine, Romania and the Baltic states: Lithuania, Latvia and

Estonia. These volunteers, known as *Hilfswillige* (or "*Hiwis*"), literally "willing helpers," fought enthusiastically on the side of the Nazis. It's been estimated that as many as 15 to 20 percent of German troops were auxiliary *Hiwis*. Between June 22, 1941 and the end of 1942, local Lithuanians assisted the *Einsatzgruppen* to murder some 220,000 unarmed Lithuanian Jews. The Lithuanians had little eagerness to fight with the Nazis against armed soldiers of the Red Army, so the Nazis sent some 36,800 Lithuanian men to labor battalions in Germany. Early in 1942, the *Wehrmacht* formed 16,000 Lithuanian volunteers into 15 *Schutzmanschaft* (special auxiliaries) battalions and deployed them to Poland, Byelorussia and the northern Ukraine where they primarily engaged in hunting and murdering Polish Jews and anti-Nazi, Polish resistance fighters. Members of Lithuanian Police Battalion No. 252 served as guards at the Majdanek concentration camp. In Latvia, Viktor Arajs headed a large band of Latvian auxiliary police who murdered 60,000 defenseless Latvian Jews. Some 100,000 Latvian men fought with the Germans, while 20,000 fought with the Red Army. Five percent of the entire population of Estonia fought for Germany against the Soviets: 60,000 out of a population of 1,200,000. In 2004, a monument to the Estonians who had fought in the Waffen-*SS* was erected in the Estonian city, Lagedi.

The *Hiwis* didn't stem just from the East. Franco's Spain sent 47,000 troops (the Blue Division, or the German 250th (Spanish) Infantry Division) to fight with the *Wehrmacht* on the Eastern Front. Sixty-thousand Frenchmen served with the *Wehrmacht* during the war, 25 percent on the Eastern Front, 7,000 of them in the so-called Charlemagne Division. Only about 1,000 survived the Russian attacks on Pomerania and then went on to serve in the defense of Berlin against the Soviets. An additional 3,000 Frenchmen volunteered to fight for Germany in what was called the "Legion of French Volunteers against Bolshevism" comprising the 638th Infantry Regiment of the *Wehrmacht*.[30] The French police in Paris set up a unit known as the *mangeurs des Juifs* ("eaters of Jews"), whose job was to hunt Jews in hiding.[31] Sixteen-thousand Walloon and 22,000 Flemish volunteers from Belgium served in the *Waffen-SS* on the Eastern Front. More than 6,000 Danish volunteers served as *Hiwis* with the Germans, many of them in the *Waffen-SS* or *SS-Totenkopf* ("Deaths Head") Division. One of the large independent formation of foreign auxiliaries fighting for the Germans were 40,000 Dutch who served in the *Waffen-SS*. While they were serving on the Eastern Front, about 20,000 Dutch civilians back home starved to death during the German starvation assault (the *Hongerwinter*) against Holland during the winter of 1944-1945. The Dutch police also set up the Henneicke Column, a unit tasked with tracking down Jews in hiding.[32] Norway bore the distinction of having had the leader of its collaborationist wartime government, "Minister-President" Vidkun Quisling, give his name to our vocabulary, used to describe a collaborator or traitor. As many as 4,500 Norwegians volunteered to fight for the Nazis. The list of nations whose citizens volunteered to fight for the Nazis, including the SS is long.[33] In addition to the countries mentioned above, Albania, Bulgaria, Croatia, Finland, Hungary, India, Ireland, Italy, Serbia and Montenegro also collaborated with the Nazis.

In many cases, it was the *Hiwis* who perpetrated some of the worst atrocities carried out against the ethnic Poles and Jews in Poland and in the East. It was Ukrainians and Latvians who were to lead the Nazi ground forces in April 1943 against the few remaining Jews in the Warsaw ghetto, who had risen up to resist Himmler's order to liquidate the ghetto and deport all the Jews to death camps.

There were many governments in Europe that collaborated with Nazi Germany. Perhaps the most well-known is France. After six weeks of less-than-stellar resistance to the German invasion, the French High Command capitulated in surrender. Marshal Philippe Petain, an elderly general in the First World War who had been called out of retirement to lead the French armed forces against the Nazi invasion of May 1940, was appointed French Prime Minister after he signed the surrender documents.

Petain led what came to be called the Vichy government, because he ruled from Vichy, a city in the South of France, an area unoccupied by the Germans. The Vichy government not only collaborated with the Nazis but also persecuted French Jews on its own initiative. Vichy is remembered, in particular, for one of many atrocities, the round-up by 4,000 French police of over 13,000 Jews, primarily those with foreign passports in occupied Paris on July 16 to 17, 1942. These unfortunates were deported to German death camps. Only some 100 survived. None of the approximately 4,000 children survived.

Non-occupied European countries, such as Romania and Hungary, had fascist and virulently antisemitic governments that allied themselves with Nazi Germany and collaborated with the Nazi genocide of their countries' Jews. Hungary, whose troops fought alongside *Wehrmacht* troops, cooperated with the Germans between March and July 1944 in deporting to their deaths an estimated 500,000 Jews, and on their own initiative murdered at least 70,000 of Budapest's Jews, shooting them into the Danube, which literally ran red with the blood of the Jewish victims;[34] Bulgaria deported to their deaths thousands of non-Bulgarian citizens in the country, while protecting those Jews with Bulgarian citizenship; Romania deported to German death camps or murdered nearly all Romanian Jews, some 300,000 to over 400,000 souls, killing them in the most brutally sadistic fashion. Romanian police and soldiers participated actively in the *Einsatzgruppen* murder squads, largely responsible for the brutal murders of 100,000 Jews in Odessa in the autumn of 1941.

The reputations of countries that remained "neutral" during this war between civilization and the Nazi darkness haven't fared well from the perspective of history. Churchill famously remarked on the "neutrals" in his radio broadcast on January 20, 1940: "Each one hopes that if he feeds the crocodile enough, the crocodile will eat him last. All of them hope that the storm will pass before their time comes to be devoured."[35]

Turkey supplied Nazi Germany's war industries with chromium, a mineral crucial for fabricating steel alloys. It was not until April 20, 1944 that Turkey announced it was halting its export of chromium to Nazi Germany.

Sweden sold high-grade iron ore to Germany, delivering it in Swedish ships. It also sold ball bearings to the German armament factories. These sales led many to claim that without Sweden's exports, the German military would have ground to a halt. Sweden's shipyards built warships for the *Kriegsmarine*. The Swedes allowed German troops to ride the rails and traverse Sweden to reach German-occupied Norway and to travel to battle against the Soviet army. In August 1944, the Swedes finally required the Germans to use their own ships to transport Swedish war material to Germany. It wasn't until the end of 1944, when all except the Führer knew the Nazis were finished, that Sweden ceased selling ball bearings to Germany.[36] In preparation for Germany's invasion of the Soviet Union, Sweden had allowed an entire *Wehrmacht* division to pass through on the way to the front.[37] After the war, it was discovered that Sweden had sold Germany vital components used in the V2 rockets that pounded Britain.[38] Portugal sold wolfram to both Nazi Germany and the Allies.

Spain provided not only men for Hitler's army but also sold wolfram, iron ore, zinc and mercury to be used for Germany's arms production. Switzerland sold arms and ammunition to Nazi Germany, ceasing only on October 1, 1944.[39] It's well known that Switzerland laundered Nazi-plundered gold[40] and labored for decades to avoid returning to surviving Jews or their heirs money and property that Switzerland had stolen from them. During the war, "neutral" Switzerland allowed Italian and German military supply trains to cross its territory. Swiss police were ordered to keep Jews fleeing France from entering the country. At the end of the war, Switzerland opened its borders to fleeing Italian fascists and German Nazis.[41]

Ireland declared its neutrality, but then proceeded to deny the British navy's use of three strategic Atlantic ports which Britain had handed over to the Irish government in 1938 in accordance with the 1921 Anglo-Irish Treaty. This action would cause the destruction of British ships and the deaths of their crews in the early years of the Battle of the Atlantic.[42] When word came of Hitler's death on April 30, 1945, Ireland's Prime Minister, Eamon de Valera, paid a condolence call to the German Legation in Dublin.

His research taught him, says Father Patrick Desbois,[43] "that a mass killer is never alone with his victim, even if he appears to be in an image. It took many pairs of hands – voluntary, requisitioned, or forced – to ensure that the Jews were publicly murdered."

Outside of Europe, the British issued the infamous 1939 White Paper, which drastically limited the immigration of Jews to Palestine, all the while encouraging unlimited Arab immigration from surrounding Arab countries into Palestine. The British governing authority in Palestine had appointed Amin al-Husseini, then the head of the Higher Arab Committee and the highest-ranking Muslim leader in Palestine, the Grand Mufti of Jerusalem, i.e., the supreme Muslim religious leader of the Muslim Arab community in Palestine. The Arab community in Palestine was sympathetic to the Nazis, and their leadership would actively collaborate with the Nazis. In 1929, al-Husseini had incited a murderous, religiously based pogrom against the Jews living in the ancient, Jewish holy city of Hebron. He then launched a rebellion against the British in 1936-1939, put down with great and violent force by the British troops garrisoned in Palestine. Reports found in the files of the German High Command in Flansberg recorded that the funding of the so-called Arab Revolt came from Nazi Germany, "Only through funds made available by Germany to the Grand Mufti of Jerusalem was it possible to carry out the revolt in Palestine."[44] In haste, al-Husseini fled Palestine for Iraq.

During the war (1939-1945), after fleeing from Baghdad, al-Husseini shuttled between Rome and Berlin encouraging the Führer to invade Palestine and massacre the Jewish residents and urging him to annihilate the Jews of Europe and the world. He broadcast propaganda radio programs in Arabic to the Middle East, inciting the population against the Allies, in particular the British, and inciting his listeners to kill Jews wherever and whenever they had the opportunity.

Al-Husseini helped the Nazis recruit and establish a *Hiwi SS* division of 10,000 Bosnian Muslims, the 13th Waffen Mountain Division, later renamed the *Handschar* ("Scimitar") Division, whose record of brutal murder of Jews and Christian Serbs reportedly even pleasantly surprised the commanders of the Nazi regime. A separate, albeit undermanned, Muslim force was created by the *SS*, the 21st *SS Waffen* Mountain Division. Significant numbers of additional Muslims were recruited into both the *Wehrmacht* and the *SS*, playing, according to the historian David Motadel, "a significant role" in the slaughter of Balkan Jews and Orthodox Christians. Motadel believes that Hitler actually had little use for al-Husseini and limited his role primarily to his propaganda broadcasts.

Though likely coincidental, it was only a few hours after a meeting between al-Husseini and Hitler that Hitler tasked Reinhard Heydrich with organizing a conference to plan a more efficient genocide of the Jewish people.[45] Instead of bringing German and Ukrainian executioners to shoot Jews into pits outside the towns and villages across Central and Eastern Europe, the Nazis would now largely transport the doomed Jews to the murderers in centralized locations of mass murder all across Central and Eastern Europe.

Of all the occupied countries of Europe, only Poland did not have a collaborationist government. The German High Command needed to keep some 500,000 troops in occupied Poland to keep the country pacified. These troops were in addition to the thousands of Order Police, *SS*-units and *Hiwis* who were involved in the labor- and death-camps where the murders of political prisoners, Soviet prisoners of war, Roma, homosexuals and the genocide of the Jews took place. *SS* and *Wehrmacht* commanders followed orders from Berlin to make it appear that local gentile neighbors of the Jews in occupied territories carried out pogroms against their Jewish neighbors in revenge for the supposed oppression of the Gentiles by the Jews. While street thugs and delinquents, not to mention genuine antisemites among the Polish Blue Police and citizenry, attacked, beat, robbed and sometimes killed defenseless Jews in Warsaw and other cities and towns, documentation shows that many of the formal gang attacks (pogroms) on innocent Jews in, for example, Warsaw, were permitted or actually incited by local *SS* or *Wehrmacht* officers.

In one instance, the invasion into the ghetto by hundreds of pogromist Polish thugs who beat and robbed defenseless Jews became so intolerable that the Jewish chairman of the *Judenrat*, headed a delegation of prominent Warsaw Jews to *SS–Obersturmführer*, Fritz Arlt, head of the General Government's Interior Ministry. The delegation had the *chutzpah* to threaten to stop all cooperation with Nazi authorities unless the Nazis stopped the assaults. Arlt agreed, picked up a telephone receiver and called underlings in Warsaw. For a time, the mass attacks of the hooligans stopped, proving the relationship between the hooligans and the Nazi officers who incited and encouraged the attacks.[46] With a phone call and an order, the unprovoked attacks could cease. It was clear that the Nazis wanted to torment the Jews, while using them as scapegoats for the violence-prone local thugs to express their anger against the Jews rather than against the occupying Germans.

For propaganda reasons, the Nazis also wanted to create the message that it was the locals who hated their Jewish neighbors, not the allegedly "civilized" German occupiers. In March 1940, about 1,000 "Polish" hoodlums conducted an eight-day violent pogrom against the Jews of Warsaw. Eyewitnesses testified seeing the rioters getting paid by the Nazi organizers. Surviving members of the Polish *intelligentsia* were reportedly outraged by the pogrom, in particular because it was carried out by Poles. But a contemporaneous witness reported that the pogromists beat, tormented and cursed the Jews in German,[47] suggesting that many of the pogromists were likely *Volksdeutsche* who had been imported to Warsaw from the ethnic German territories of Poland to assist the Germans in their persecution of the Poles and Jews.

Besides gangs of young hooligans preying on largely defenseless Jews, there were those who acted alone for personal profit. These were Polish individual blackmailers and extortionists known as *szmalcowniki*. They acted alone or with the cooperation of Polish policemen or even German authorities such as the criminal police or Gestapo agents. They operated primarily outside the walled-in ghetto, on the so-called Aryan side of Warsaw.[48] It is thought that as many as 28,000 Jews hid in the Aryan part of Warsaw, while an estimated 70-90,000 non-Jewish Poles were involved in hiding these Jewish "non-persons." They and those in their care were deathly afraid of the German or Polish police who prowled the streets looking for Jews or their protectors in order to arrest them and more likely than not, execute them. Their other constant fear was being identified by *szmalcowniki* who would threaten to inform on them to the Gestapo unless they paid exorbitant bribes. In the event, the *szmalcowniki* milked their Jewish targets dry of their money and personal possessions and usually informed on them, anyway, often collecting a reward from the German authorities.

The Nazi occupation authorities had not disbanded the Polish civil police forces. But when ordered by *SS* Police leader, Friedrich-Wilhelm Krüger, to report for duty by November 10, 1939, only 35 percent of Polish officers complied. To fill the ranks, the Nazis recruited additional men who had at least a fourth-grade education, could prove their Aryan ancestry and preferably had a command of the German language. *Volksdeutsch* (Austrian) Polish Police Major Vinzenz Edler von Strohe (real name Wincenty Sloma) was appointed head of the newly established police academy in the Krakow district.[49] Known as the Blue Police because of their navy-blue uniforms, the officers were deployed to keep order, enforce curfews and pursue black marketeers, which allowed them to steal from Poles and especially Jews. They were deployed to guard ghettos, help with deportations of Jews to death camps and search for Jews living "illegally" outside the ghettos. Some Blue Police helped Jews smuggle food and goods in and out of ghettos as well as helping Jews escape ghettos to hide in Aryan areas, in return for bribes.[50]

As the war progressed, the Blue Police organized *Judenjagd* or "Jew Hunts" to uncover Jews hiding inside and outside ghettos and in the Polish countryside. This generally ended with the murder of the discovered Jews and those Poles who were hiding them. The ethnic German policeman Kazimierz Nowak, for example, led 80 officers in "hunts" that resulted in the murder of many hundreds of Jews and the Poles protecting them.[51] In November and December 1941, 32 members of the Blue Police under the command of Colonel Aleksander Reszczynski carried out two mass executions in the prison at Gesia street in Warsaw. Many thousands or tens of thousands of Jews were hunted down, robbed and murdered by Blue Policemen all across Poland.[52] Polish resistance fighters regarded many of the Blue Police as collaborators and traitors. In 1942 alone, the fighters were assassinating one Blue Police officer every four days. In one three-month period in 1944, members of Polish resistance organizations killed or wounded 279 policemen.[53] After the war, some 600 Blue Police were prosecuted by the Polish government, convicted by the courts and most sentenced to long prison sentences.[54]

---

1. Hobbes.
2. Franklin.
3. Born in Argentina to German and German/Swedish parents, Darré received his Ph.D. in agriculture from a German university in 1929. Darré promulgated and peddled racist, antisemitic, eugenicist theories of *Blut und Boden* or blood and soil which concluded with the operational plan for the allegedly superior German race to dominate the Eastern European territories by enslaving or killing the native population. In 1930, Darré was appointed by Hitler to head the NSDAP's agrarian sector. A year later, Darré was appointed head of the Nazi Party's Race and Resettlement Office.

4. Streicher's own testimony at his post-war Nuremberg trial strongly suggests he was quite delusional. He was one of the few top Nazis who was sentenced to death and was hanged as a war criminal.
5. Weinberg, *Hitler's...*
6. Frieser, p. 16.
7. Namier, p. 450.
8. Frieser, *op. cit. idem.*
9. Noakes and Pridham Vol. 2, p.743.
10. Jansen and Weckbecker, *ibid* p. 29.
11. Rossino, pp. xivf., 228.
12. "French shooters" – a term derived from the Franco-Prussian war of 1870.
13. Stahel p. 363.
14. Thucydides, pp. 69-85.
15. Westerman, pp. 128ff; Rossino, pp. 58ff.
16. Sprecher *op.cit.* vol. 1 p. 602.
17. Rossino, p. 234.
18. Matthaus et al., p. 51.
19. Jansen and Weckbecker, *op. cit. p.* 27.
20. Krakowski
21. Westerman, p. 156. Note: Jansen and Weckbecker's 100,000 number (p. 35) and Westerman (p. 156) number of 17,000 *Selbstschutz* differ.
22. Ferencz, p. 6.
23. Frieser, *op.cit.* pp. 21f.
24. Overy, *1939*, p. 2.
25. Koskodan, chapter 4.
26. Neitzel and Welzer, p. 45.
27. Chylinski.
28. Jasinski.
29. Pringle, p. 381
30. Stahel, p. 288ff
31. Grabowski, p. 22.
32. Grabowski, *idem*
33. See: Hale. Also: Rolf-Dieter Müller, pp. 180f
34. Ozsvath.
35. Roberts, p. 113.
36. Weinberg, *A World...* p. 396
37. Roberts, *op.cit.* p. 114.
38. Roberts, *idem.*
39. Weinberg, *op.cit.* p. 398
40. Bower; Chesnoff; Taber.
41. Roberts, *op.cit.* p. 113.
42. *ibid.* p. 115.
43. Desbois, *In Broad...* p. 256.
44. The Nation Associates, p. 11.
45. Gensicke, see especially pp. 128f.; Patterson, David, *A Genealogy...* See especially pp. 114-122; Motadel, pp. 43-48.; Rubin, see especially pp. 157-168; See

also stenographic notes of the Führer-Mufti meeting in Fleming, *op.cit.*, pp. 101-105.

46. Gutman, p. 28
47. Gutman, *idem* and p. 29.
48. Paulsson, pp. 20f.
49. Mlynarczyk, pp. 166ff.
50. *Idem.*
51. *Ibid*, p. 176.
52. Grabowski, *op.cit.* pp. 1-33.
53. Mlynarczyk, *op.cit.* pp. 176f.
54. *Ibid.* pp. 179f.

11

THUGS ON A CARRIAGE

In the ghetto, Sonia would say in her typically understated way, *life was miserable.* She was in contact with some of Abe's cousins who lived in a small village, out in the countryside. They urged Sonia to come stay with them where there was no ghetto and where food was available. After the closing of the ghetto in November 1940, it had been forbidden by German decree for Jews to leave the ghetto without special permission. Not only were police stationed at the exit from the ghetto, but *szmalcowniki* also lurked outside the ghetto gate looking for opportunities to catch Jews leaving without passes in order to rob them.

But Sonia didn't hesitate. If caught by German or Polish Blue Police, she could have been arrested and carted off to jail, even shot with her children or shipped to a concentration camp. Nonetheless, Sonia took off the armband – white with a blue Star of David printed on it – and left her apartment. The Germans typically stationed three guards, a Ukrainian or *Volksdeutsche* in a German uniform, a Polish Blue Policeman and a Jewish ghetto policeman at the entrance to the ghetto. Sonia had succeeded in bribing the Jewish policeman in advance to allow her and her two children to leave the ghetto and had also managed to arrange for a horse-drawn carriage to come to the ghetto entrance at the appointed time. It was common for the guards to accept bribes from the imprisoned Jews, and divide the money amongst the three, with the German-uniformed guard getting the majority of the cash.

Sonia exhibited her typical *sangfroid* even if her heart pounded. She caught sight of the ordered carriage and signaled the driver to approach. After lifting up the children and placing them in the carriage, she mounted the carriage and took her seat. Calmly and authoritatively she instructed the driver to go to the train station.

The carriage hadn't gone more than a few dozen yards down the street and around a corner, before two young, Polish *szmalcowniki* waiting outside the ghetto to pounce on people entering or leaving the closed ghetto, jumped on the carriage and screamed at Sonia, while the children looked on in terror, "We know you're Jewish, we saw you come out of the ghetto. Give us all your money and jewelry."

"*What?!*" exclaimed Sonia in her clearly educated and perfectly enunciated Polish. "*I came to visit a Jewish friend who owes me money.*"

Clearly surprised and irritated by Sonia's words, one of the thugs lifted up his hand as if to strike her and with a raised voice, demanded she give them money. Mustering up her courage, Sonia, sitting in a carriage in the middle of the street, who-knows how far from the nearest Nazi patrol, now raised her voice and snapped at the thug who was clearly in charge, "*No, why should I?!*"

At this point, the driver of the carriage flicked his whip and the horses took off with a start, both thugs grabbing on to the carriage to avoid being thrown off.

Sonia knew that the driver wasn't heading to the train station; he was heading to Gestapo headquarters. In a split second, Sonia thought to herself that the driver must be in on the mugging with the two thugs. Their plan must be to take her to Gestapo headquarters and turn her and her children in for the reward the Germans offered for Jews found outside the ghetto, Jews not wearing the required armband on it and Jews hiding money or valuables. She imagined that the driver planned to split the money with the two thugs.

When Sonia recounted this story, she smiled and let out a little laugh, "*I really don't know what got into me. Without any thought, I jumped up and starting shouting at the top of my lungs: Policia, Policia. I was practically jumping up and down holding on to the carriage for dear life, swiveling my head here and there as if looking for a police car to come roaring down the road to my rescue.*"

At that, their faces red, eyes bulging in terror, the two szmalcowniki jumped off the wagon. Legs pumping, their jackets flapping behind them, the two thugs ran off, unlike Lot's wife, without so much as a glance behind.

The driver now looked at Sonia with astonishment. Who is this woman? He must have thought, is she the wife of some Polish Nazi and is she going to denounce me to the Police?

Sonia stared at the driver with fire in her eyes, extended her right arm and pointed her first finger directly at him; it must have been no further than a foot or so from his face, "*Now, you take me to the train station this minute,*" she exclaimed with authority, "*and I mean NOW.*" The driver whipped the horse as if it were the one threatening him. Turning the carriage around, he drove Sonia and the children to the train station posthaste. She arrived in time to board the train, not even a minute late. Jews were not allowed to travel on the trains anymore. But Sonia was traveling as a non-Jewish Pole. And – dangerously – without any identity papers.

I asked her, "How did it occur to you to do something so brilliant and dangerous?"

"*I don't know. I had two little children whom I needed to protect and feed. We had to get out of the ghetto. I didn't think about it. I just acted. Do you know what the Nazis would have done had a police van actually shown up to see what the commotion was all about and discovered I had no papers? Or if the driver had suspected my ruse and driven us to the Gestapo? Do you know what they would have done to us? To me and the children?"*

12

FROM THE COUNTRYSIDE TO THE GHETTO UPRISING

The train ride to the countryside was thankfully uneventful. There were no Gestapo agents walking down the aisle of the train asking all passengers for their papers. At least not on Sonia's trip.

Sonia arrived in the town with the children and was met at the station by Abe's family. They greeted her with hugs and kisses as she let out a sigh of relief. After a short time, Sonia and the children moved into a furnished apartment that the family had rented for them. Sonia felt reasonably safe and secure there. She saw very few Germans at that time and imagined: *Did the Germans even know that this place exists? That Jews are living freely here. We can live here forever – well at least until the war ends and the Germans are driven out of Poland and sent back to Germany.*

Sonia became acquainted with the Jewish *Gemeinder* (self-governing board), and a leader of the local community. After some three months of peaceful life in town, the *Gemeinder* official came to her and revealed news that the Germans were coming to town and were planning to take all the Jews out to the forest to shoot them then and there. He strongly suggested that she go back to Warsaw. At least in Warsaw – so he thought – the Germans weren't willy-nilly shooting the city's Jewish inhabitants. He suggested a plan.

The children didn't boast stereotypically Jewish features. Little Lusia had blue eyes and blonde hair and she and David would blend in with any group of Polish, gentile children. It was arranged that a Polish, Christian woman whom he knew, would take the two children with her on the train to Warsaw, pretending that they were her children. Sonia would take the train – openly as a Jew, if necessary – pretending to be a prisoner of a Polish Blue Policeman from the town who was part of the deception. Everything went as planned. It couldn't have gone more smoothly than a well-directed scene from a Hollywood suspense movie.

They had gone to the countryside in search of life and then fled from the countryside in search of life.

Arriving back in Warsaw, *things were terrible*, according to Sonia, far worse than the situation had been no more than three months earlier, when she had managed to get away. People were dying in the streets. Bodies of men and women, old people, young children were simply lying in the street or on the sidewalk, where they had fallen. They were dying from starvation or disease. There was minimal hygiene; people had no soap, neither to wash themselves nor their clothes. They had no proper diet. There was barely enough food to keep themselves alive. For the community of lice, it was a feast – a carnival and Hitler's birthday party combined. Typhus was rampant while German Police Captain Erich Mehr, a company commander in Reserve Police Battalion 61, "took delight in abusing Jews with his bayonet and randomly shooting them in the Warsaw ghetto."[1]

But Sonia was lucky to be back in Warsaw. As she had been warned, the Nazi *SS* did enter the country town the next day, forced the Jews out of their homes and murdered them all. Sonia and her children had made it out just in time.

For about a year after the German occupation had begun, Sonia had been able to stay in her apartment at 74 Zelazna street. When the ghetto was formally closed and walled, Sonia had been forced to move. She traipsed to 28 Nalewki street, Abe's old shoe store. The space there was already occupied by four strangers, who rapidly became very close acquaintances. Food was rationed and minimal. The Nazis in charge wanted to keep the Jewish population of the Warsaw ghetto weak. If the people, especially the men and more so, teenagers, were weak, there was less chance that anybody would be able to physically resist the Nazi *SS* or soldiers who came into the ghetto. Generally, it was the responsibility of the *Judenrat* to fill the quotas for deportation that the Nazis demanded on a regular basis. And it was the responsibility of the Jewish police to find and drag the latest victims to the train station. The Germans often posted announcements that residents who volunteered to go to labor camps would get a loaf of bread and a jar of jam that they could take with them on the trip. Sonia saw people standing in line by the thousands to go. Keeping the population hungry and even starving made them pliable and more likely to respond to the phony offers of food.

Eventually, not until the summer of 1942 did the starving Jews stop voluntarily lining up, realizing that they wouldn't be given a loaf of bread nor sent to a place where they could work and be fed. At long last, they realized that they weren't going to be sent to labor camps; they were going to be given one-way tickets to their deaths. That is, if they survived the ghetto. Every Jew who died from starvation or disease saved the Reich the cost of a bullet and could be counted among those who died of "natural causes."

The treatment of Jewish civilians in the Warsaw ghetto, as in every other ghetto across Europe, was inhumane. It was *schrecklich* (terrifying"). And it was deliberate. In fact, the Germans had instituted a calculated policy beginning with their invasion of Poland, which they called *Schrecklichkeit* ("terror"). From the black *SS* uniforms designed by the artist Karl Diebitsch and the graphic designer Walter Heck, and manufactured by Hugo Boss, to the sirens installed in the Stuka dive bombers, which shrieked imminent death from the skies, the German plans for total war featured total shock and psychological terror inflicted on the Reich's enemies' armed forces and civilians alike.

Sonia recalled witnessing with her own eyes and ears, a young man, perhaps a teenager, running down her street and all the other streets shouting that the Germans were not taking the Jews to labor camps, they were taking them to places where they were to be murdered. In fact, three young men had escaped from the death camp Treblinka in August 1942: David Nowodworski, Jacob Rabinowitz and 25-year-old Abraham Jacob Krzepicki. It may have been one of these three whom Sonia remembered hearing. Krzepicki had fled Treblinka, hiding in a boxcar full of clothing. Polish civilians helped him return to Warsaw. Krzepicki described the gas chambers and even drew a detailed map of the camp. At first, he was not believed. The listeners dismissed his loud yells, thinking he was crazy, having lost his mind from hunger or due to German savagery.[2]

Even after news came of the liquidation of the Lublin ghetto in March-April 1942, the Jews of Warsaw could not bring themselves to believe this fantastic story. "People gave many reasons to refute the remotest possibility of similar acts of violence, refused to accept the thought that a similar murder could possibly be committed in Poland's capital where 300,000 Jews dwelled. People argued that 'even the Germans would not murder hundreds of thousands of people without any reason whatever, particularly in times when they were in such need of productive power...' A normal human being with normal mental processes was simply unable to conceive that a difference in the colour of eyes or hair or racial origin might be sufficient cause for murder."[3] It took months until the Jews in the ghetto understood that the teenager and the other messengers were correct.

The Germans used guile and stealth from the beginning until the end, to fool the Jews, to keep them docile and to prevent the majority of the victims from resisting their fate. Jews who had not yet been deported from the ghetto received postcards that the

Germans had prepared and often printed up from their relatives who had boarded the trains. The text on the postcards was all the same. Those who sent them only had to put the addresses on the postcards.

As time passed, mail from the relatives stopped. No one was getting postcards anymore. Some of the Gentile Poles who worked in the ghetto or who lived outside and had contact with Jews living within the ghetto warned the Jews that the Germans were not sending those deported to labor camps; they were taking them out and shooting them. The Jews who were voluntarily or forcibly rounded up were being murdered. They told the Jews that the Germans were killing people and putting them in pits and covering them with sand while they were still alive.

The last postcard Abe got from Sonia was, he thought, at the end of 1942, though likely it was 1941, before Hitler declared war on the United States. She was not allowed to write anything on the card, other than to list the names of the family members. At least Abe knew they were alive.

At some point, Sonia decided that she couldn't remain passive; she had to have a plan and needed to act. After a while she and the children began to hide and not go out of the apartment. She was afraid to stand in line for rations, knowing that Nazi *SS* men or soldiers would come and randomly grab people waiting in line, put them on a truck and drive off, or pull them out of line, shoot them and leave them lying in the street.

Sonia had moved with the children from 28 to 34 Nalewki street. Across the street at 31 Nalewki, she and her family built a hiding place in the basement. They cut a hole in the wall of the apartment's basement and dug what they called a "bunker" below the basement to provide a hiding place for the family. They worked on the bunker for months and prepared enough food that they thought would last them a year. They stuffed rags in front of the hole and positioned furniture in front in an attempt to hide the opening in the wall. Her brother-in-law was with her and repeatedly snuck out to try to find food for them.

On a regular basis, the Germans in charge of the ghetto demanded that the *Judenrat* deliver to the collection point known as the *Umschlagplatz*, a certain number of Jews. The number varied but was usually in the thousands. The Jews who arrived at the *Umschlagplatz* voluntarily or were dragged there at the point of a rifle or beaten by a whip or a club, were put on trains for transports to points unknown. The members of the *Judenrat* eventually learned the destinations of the trains and the ghettos' Jews gradually learned as well. The trains were not taking their passengers to "resettlement" in the countryside. They were taking them to brutal slave labor camps or to death camps from which few or none ever returned.

In July 1942, on the eve of Tisha B'Av, the Jewish fast day commemorating the destruction of the two Jewish temples in Jerusalem, what has come to be called the "Great Deportation" commenced. Some 300,000 Jews were deported from the Warsaw ghetto within months. By then most people understood that Jews taken away would end up dead: killed by starvation or beatings or murdered by poison gas.

On one of the frequent roundups, Sonia's mother was found in her apartment, taken out and forced onto one of the trains. Sonia came back to the apartment after spending the day hiding with her children. She discovered her mother gone. She never saw her again.

The Great Deportation passed with little to no resistance by the starved, discouraged and hopeless victims.

By January 1943, the Jews in the ghetto had become aware of the impending German defeat at Stalingrad and the destruction of Field Marshal Friedrich Paulus' 6th Army by the forces of the Soviet Union. Combined with their knowledge of the Allied armies' successes against Rommel's Afrika Korps in North Africa, the Jews' hopes of an ultimate German defeat were buoyed. They might also have learned that on January 3, Polish President Wladyslaw Raczkiewicz requested that Pope Pius XII condemn German atrocities against the Jews. But the Pope issued no such public condemnation of the Nazi atrocities against the Jews nor against the murders of Catholic priests in Poland.[4] By then, the Jews of Warsaw understood that the Germans planned to liquidate all the ghettos. An active resistance against future Nazi deportations began to take shape. On January 18-19, 1943, German officers aided by Ukrainian, Latvian and other Hiwi auxiliaries entered the ghetto with direct orders from Himmler to round up 8,000 Jews. They were shocked to be met by ghetto Jewish teenagers with a few handguns, a handful of hand grenades, iron pipes and some vials of sulfuric acid, who attacked them and their armed irregulars. Only a few of the invaders and most of the Jewish teens were killed. Most of the 8,000 were indeed rounded up. But the shock was so great that the Nazis didn't enter the ghetto for another three months.

The Uprising

The ghetto residents got news that the Germans were planning what they thought would be a surprise invasion by uniformed and armed soldiers in the middle of April. Their mission was to find and seize the Jews still remaining in the ghetto and deport them to one of the camps that the Germans had set up. According to Sonia,

We knew that the Germans didn't need women and children for work; so for us, deportation meant only one thing. We decided to hide. For months we had dug a bunker, that is a cellar deep under another cellar in one of the buildings. We also prepared enough food for a year. Our bunker was at 31 Nalewki street, while all of us lived on 34 Nalewki.

On Sunday evening, April 18, 1943, Avramchik [Abe's sister's husband] came to me and told me that he had heard that the Germans were coming to the ghetto at any time, and he was moving to the bunker. He took his mother, wife and children to the bunker at 31 Nalewki at 11 o'clock that

night. I did not want to go along, because the German curfew forbade anyone to out in the street after 8 PM. I was afraid of being shot and thought it was too dangerous to go out.

This time, Sonia was afraid to go outside. She just had a premonition. Her brother-in-law insisted she go with him. But, uncharacteristically, she refused. She said that she didn't want to take the risk and would wait until early in the morning to follow him to the bunker. Her brother-in-law ran outside and across the street, taking his family into the well-prepared bunker.

I remained with Yitzhak overnight, planning to go to the bunker at 5 AM. Before we could go, thousands of German troops, with Ukrainian and Latvian Nazi auxiliaries in the lead, burst into the ghetto.

The time deliberately chosen by the Germans for their invasion was the eve of Passover, April 19, 1943.

To the apparent surprise of the invading troops, they were met with a blizzard of Molotov cocktails (gasoline fire bombs) hurled at them from rooftops, and a fusillade of bullets fired at them from rooftops, windows and from the street by groups of Jewish teenagers who had organized to resist the Nazis. Using home-made weapons, gasoline bombs and handguns smuggled into the ghetto and bought from members of the underground Polish Home Army on the Aryan side, the teenagers opened fire on the fanatical, trained and well-armed German and Ukrainian soldiers.

When they succeeded in killing soldiers, they ran into the streets and liberated rifles, submachine guns, ammunition and hand grenades from the Nazi wounded or dead bodies. It was an uneven war. On the one side soldiers, armored cars, mortars, flame-throwers. On the other side, small bands of boys and girls, some barely past puberty, none older than their early 20s, fighting with improvised weapons and small arms. The Jewish youths had no illusions. They hardly believed that they would defeat the mighty German army. But, if they were going to die, they would die as combat soldiers, not as victims of a slaughter. And they would kill as many enemy troops as possible. The Nazis would pay with their lives, learning that Jewish blood in Warsaw at that time and place was no longer cheap.

While the Warsaw ghetto uprising was a battle waged by Jewish teens, the adults – if they could – went into hiding, trying to save their own little children and themselves. Many of those left were elderly, sick or otherwise unable to fight. Most were weak from hunger and discouraged if not fatally depressed from the physical and mental torment imposed on the Warsaw Jews by their Nazi captors during the previous three and a half years. All were unarmed.

The Nazis realized that the only way to defeat the Jewish fighters arrayed against them was to attack every building in the ghetto. And the best way to protect the Nazis from the Jews' small arms fire and explosives was to burn each building to the ground. As Sonia recalls,

It was impossible to go to 31 Nalewki. But, at the same time, it was impossible to remain where we were. So, with Yitzhak, Rachelle, Aunt Brutsche and the children, I managed to get to the bunker at 28 Nalewki. Fishek and his family were already hidden on the Aryan side, as were Goldele and Tzirele and her daughter. But Aunt Paula and her husband and Yakov Daiman and their son remained with us in the bunker at 28 Nalewki. Only after I gave the people hiding there the few thousands of Złotych I had, did they let us in. There, I suffered greatly.

There were about 40 people in the bunker. They had enough food and places to sleep, but my children and I had to sleep on the floor and we suffered hunger. Many of the people there were our friends, but nobody gave my children any food. They were afraid they wouldn't have enough for themselves, even though it appeared they had prepared enough food to last a year.

Little Lusia began to cry because she saw a woman with a piece of candy. A man who had been a very good friend of Abe's came over to me and said that if the little girl didn't stop crying, he would choke her or I would need

to do it myself. I was stunned by his words. As the time would pass and I would suffer through Majdanek and Auschwitz, I would learn about the terrible things people would allow themselves to do in order to remain alive for another day. Lusia saw the look on that man's face and heard his tone and immediately stopped crying, holding me tightly and pressing her head into my chest.

The lower bunker had a passageway to the Aryan side. A member of our group went out to see what's what. He came back with the news that 31 Nalewki had been burned down and the Germans had taken away all of the residents who had survived and run out of the burning building. You can't imagine what an experience that was for us. I didn't know if Avramchik had been killed or had survived. I never saw him or his family again. We were all terrified, not knowing when we would be next.

A few days later, a young boy, a messenger, brought us a note from Mother saying that she was in a house on Miska street and she was begging us to come save her. But it was impossible for us to get out, as the passageway had become blocked by large pieces of building masonry that had blown off from burning or exploding buildings. Yitzhak worked for five days and nights clearing the rubble and succeeded finally in making a new passageway out. Unfortunately, as he finished, the Germans discovered us. We were so well-hidden, we had thought we would never be discovered. We complained that a captured Jew must have been forced to give away our hiding place.

In fact, the German troops used trained German Shepherd dogs to sniff out the smell of humans through the smell of gunpowder. They used acoustic devices to hear the sounds of those hiding in the underground bunkers. Often, they seized Jews who fled from burning buildings and pressured them, those who had just come out of hiding, to reveal the locations of the hiding places of others, falsely promising them their lives in exchange for the information. Through one means or another, the troops located Sonia and the others hiding with her. Not knowing whether those in the hiding place were armed, the troops called out to them through an opening that they had made in the basement wall to come out with their hands up or they would be burned out and shot.

Sonia says she was actually somewhat relieved when they were discovered, feeling that she couldn't bear to stay there any longer in the oppressive heat and sweat-drenched fear and trembling. Dying seemed better than living in the bunker. Little did she know that the hot, stinking bunker was paradise compared to what was to come.

A mother and father and three adult children and another family didn't want to leave the bunker, fearful of what the Germans or Ukrainians would do to them. They took poison which they had brought with them into the bunker and the entire family died at their own hands. Sonia saw other women taking poison with their children. The men hiding in the bunker exited first. Many of the men tried to hide in the passageway. The Germans tossed in gas bombs and killed them.

I with the children and Rachelle came out from the bunker. We saw a terrible sight. All the men were already standing against a wall with their hands raised, with their wives and children standing alone, apart from them by a few meters. The men were all shot in front of my eyes. I don't know what happened to Yitzhak.

On May 16, 1943, *SS* Colonel Jurgen Stroop, the German *SS* commander in charge of the suppression of the ghetto uprising, personally detonated the explosive charges that blew up the Great Synagogue of Warsaw on Tlomackie street. It was one of the grandest buildings in all of Poland. Stroop cabled Berlin, *Das ehemalige jüdische Wohnviertel Warschau besteht nicht mehr,* or "The former Jewish quarter of Warsaw no longer exists."[5]

The German and Hiwi thugs in *Wehrmacht* or auxiliary uniforms led the surviving Jews to the station. On the way, little Lusia dropped one of her shoes. Sonia bent down to pick it up, but a soldier pushed her roughly and ordered her to leave the shoe on the ground and keep marching to the *Umschlagplatz*.

Arriving at the train station, Rachelle and Sonia were separated. Sonia and her children, along with perhaps a hundred others, were jammed into a cattle car, an empty wagon without seats. The interior dimensions of the cattle cars were just over 26 feet (eight meters) long, nearly nine feet (2.7 meters) wide and a little over seven feet (2.1-2.2 meters) tall. They were designed to transport cattle humanely, not human beings inhumanely, by the dozens or hundreds. The goal of the Germans was to transport as many Jews as possible as quickly as possible to labor or death camps as efficiently as possible, with no concern for the comfort of the deportees.

The Jews deported from Warsaw, like the Jews deported from all over Europe, had been dehumanized by the Nazis in their propaganda prior to 1933 and by law after Hitler came to power in 1933. By the time the survivors of the Warsaw ghetto uprising were deported from Warsaw to the killing factories; they were seen as so much kindling wood by the soldiers and SS volunteers. And they were observed by the ordinary bystanders who watched the trains fly by their towns, villages and farms. Some of the Polish farmers looked at the faces of the condemned that were pressed to the small, barred-windows and drew their fingers across their throats, apparently in a warning to the human cargo that they were on their way to death.

Conditions were *schrecklich*. So many people were jammed into the cars that it was generally impossible to move and certainly impossible to sit. No food, no water, no toilet facilities other than a bucket – if you could get to it. People died in those cattle cars; but, because they were pressed tightly against each other, the dead remained standing. The smell was unbearable. It wasn't until the train reached its destination and the captives were allowed to exit the cars, that the dead were able to fall to the floor.

Even in those horrible conditions, there were acts of kindness. One woman jammed next to Sonia helped her; she held Lusia while Sonia held David with their heads level with the heads of the adults, so that they could breathe. The survivors of the Warsaw ghetto didn't know where the train was taking them, but many of them understood from the rumors and the warnings that they were not being taken to labor camps, but to camps of death. Scenes from the uprising, hiding in the bunker, witnessing suicides of her friends, and seeing the men murdered, were imprinted in Sonia's mind. The hunger, fatigue, heat and overwhelming stink made her dizzy and often faint. She tried to focus by remembering the happy times with Abe before the war. She whispered encouraging words to little David and Lusia. She didn't know where the train was taking them or how long the suffering on the train would last. She was comforted by the fact that her sister, Rachelle, was on another wagon, and the children were still alive. She was determined to stay conscious and alert as much as she could, in order to encourage the children. She sang to them and told them stories, just like the ones she used to tell them or read to them before bedtime in Warsaw. Many times, she didn't know if they were awake or asleep, but talking to them at least kept her spirits up and, she hoped, helped the children feel safe with her.

We were on the train for two days without food or water. I just waited for my death. I only felt sorry for the children. For my life I just didn't care. It is impossible to describe what we went through on the way. We thought that they were taking us to Treblinka, where the Jews deported before us had been taken and gassed and burned right away. So many Jews jumped through the windows, many of them even with their children. Some of them saved themselves, I think. But most of them were shot. I just don't know how I and Rachelle with the children came out alive.

---

1. Westerman *op.cit.* 12.
2. Kassow, pp. 309-310. Krzepicki later died in the 1943 Warsaw ghetto uprising.
3. Edelman, p. 10.
4. The Holocaust Chronicle, p. 411.
5. *The Stroop Report.* Teletype message to SS-General Krüger, or deputy, dated 16 May 1943.

13

ABE, THE ACCIDENTAL IMMIGRANT

The Rich Polish Relative goes hungry

Abe's sail across the Atlantic was uneventful but momentous. He never in his life imagined the luxury that he would find onboard. He estimated that 75 percent of the passengers fell ill from seasickness, while he experienced each day as nicer and better than the previous. As the ship finally approached landfall, he felt *"wildly crazy with joy."*

Abe was excited to disembark from the Batory, expecting to see all his cousins coming to greet him. The ship docked in New York on August 2, 1939. Abe looked quite the sight, dressed in his fine European suit and spiffy fedora. However, he met disappointment because his entire family had not come to meet the ship. For Abe, family was the most important thing in life. He used to hold up his hand and say to us before we had children, "Gloria, you and Ken, Mark, Mother and I are like the fingers of one hand. The hand needs the fingers and the fingers need the hand." Probably, one of the few criticisms I ever learned Abe express was the line he wrote in one of his essays, "But in America at that time, work was more important than to meet a cousin."

Though Abe was disappointed that the whole family hadn't come to greet him, he was happy to see those who did come: Sam Grossbaum, Uncle Shames and his wife, and Moishe Kahn. Sam owned a furniture store and an automobile, and he packed the family, Abe and his luggage into his car. Abe had gone through customs and immigration and now was headed to the George Washington Hotel at 23 Lexington Avenue. After dropping off his luggage, Sam and Abe drove to the Bronx to see the rest of the family when they came home from work. In the meantime, Sam gave him a brief tour of New York. *Tante Surelleh* ("Aunt Sarah," Surelleh the diminutive of "Sarah" with Polish-Yiddish pronunciation) and her husband, Jacob Hertzberg, had gone to a lodge in the Catskill Mountains for the summer to escape New York's oppressive heat. After a few weeks, Abe took up their offer to stay in their apartment. He checked out of the George Washington Hotel and moved into their apartment on Home street in the Bronx. Moishe and Fanny shared the apartment, sleeping in an alcove big enough only for their bed. Goldie slept in the main bedroom, while Abe slept on a fold-out sleeper sofa.

He was overcome with such calm joy, "so busy with joy and pleasure from being in America," that he inadvertently forgot to write home during his first week in New York. Abe did succeed in going to the World's Fair and looking wondrously with all the other tourists at the latest inventions and creations of the world's leading companies and manufacturers. Though Warsaw was a large, cosmopolitan city, there was only one New York, with its tall skyscrapers and modern department stores filled with luxurious wares. Abe marveled at the stately museums and the bridges and other architectural wonders, the parks and hospitals, the masses of cars and taxis and the hustle and bustle of waves of pedestrians marching down Fifth Avenue. Even in 1939, New York was a marvel to behold.

Abe was proud of his self-made accomplishments in Europe. As the "rich cousin" from Poland, Abe freely spent money "left and right," taking his relatives out to restaurants, buying them gifts and spending money on gifts and souvenirs to take back to Sonia, the children and the rest of the family back home. By August 23, he was hearing talk of war in Europe and considered leaving early, nervous about waiting until his original departure date of September 6.

His excitement over seeing America in person along with family whom he hadn't seen in years waned. On Thursday night, August 31, 1939, Abe was visiting his cousins in their Bronx apartment. He was absent-mindedly thinking about the next day, Friday, when the family would prepare, as usual, for the Sabbath evening meal. Abe was planning to accompany Goldie to the market to pay, as his treat, for the chickens and other delicacies that the family and their guests would consume at the Shabbat dinner. The family typically gathered around the radio in the living room to listen to the evening programs. The programs might have been interrupted by the news broadcast that one and a half million German soldiers had crossed the border and invaded Poland. The time difference between New York and Poland was six hours, so it might have been midnight before listeners in America learned that the *Wehrmacht* had invaded Poland at dawn on Friday.

So Abe was likely asleep when news of the invasion was broadcast to an American audience. Whatever dreams were in Abe's mind when he slept that night, he awoke the next morning to a nightmare. With the German invasion of Poland, Hitler broke his Munich promise to the U.K. and France that he held "no further territorial ambitions in Europe" after the U.K. and France had sacrificed Czechoslovakia's Sudetenland for the sake of peace. The Führer had obviously scuttled the ongoing negotiations in which he was involved with his U.K. and French peace partners regarding the Polish question.

The British and French didn't exactly follow through on their commitments to Poland. The French made a few feeble thrusts at the Germans here and there but rapidly withdrew. The British didn't send in the Royal Air Force until three days later, on September 3, when the British and French declared war on

Germany. The Second World War had begun. While the Royal Air Force didn't fly any missions to bomb German forces for the first three days of the Nazi invasion, they did send planes over Germany – and dropped about 13 tons of an estimated five million anti-Nazi propaganda leaflets.

It is possible that some of those leaflets may have caused paper cuts on German civilians or farm animals, but they didn't lead to a German pullback from Poland. On September 4, British bombers attempted to bomb German warships in the important German naval port, Wilhelmshaven. British Blenheim bombers did accurately hit the battleship Admiral Scheer with four bombs, none of which exploded. The German cruiser Emden was mildly damaged when a British bomber was shot down and the debris hit the ship. Half of the British bombers were hit and never made it home. This was essentially all the help the British and French gave to Poland when it was fighting for its political life and the Polish people who were waiting for their British and French allies to come to their rescue.

By 9 AM on September 1, the *Luftwaffe* was conducting bombing raids over Warsaw. High-ranking Polish officials were, however, safe from danger. They had fled from one Polish town to another, staying one step ahead of the Germans. Ultimately, they managed to escape via Romania to Britain where they formed a government in exile. For the civilians living in Warsaw or those who fled to Warsaw from the countryside, thinking they'd be safer, danger and sudden death literally hovered over them, or more accurately, dive-bombed them.

This was the news that Abe read in the Yiddish-language press on September 1 and the following days. *All day long I was sitting on the sofa and gorging on the news about Poland. I read all the Yiddish language newspapers in New York.* He felt fear and terror that he hadn't ever experienced. Guilt hung over him like a dark fog. Why had he left the family behind? Couldn't he have found a way to bring them with him? Why had he listened to Zalman and made this crazy trip to America? If he were still in Poland, he could watch over Sonia and the children and protect them.

Worrying about Sonia, the children and his whole family were only part of his problems in September 1939. Abe had brought enough money with him for a short stay in America. By September, his money was nearly gone. He had run to the steamship line to see if he could get an earlier sailing to Poland, and if not, to confirm his scheduled departure. But no ships were sailing to the war zone. On September 8, the Jewish Telegraphic Agency reported that the State Department *might* consider issuing refugees and other Europeans temporary visas to remain in the United States for the duration of the war. "However," reported the JTA, "the Department termed as 'speculation' published reports that holders of visitors' permits would be permitted to remain in this country."

Visas to Europeans, understood as primarily European Jews, would not likely to be issued, though, at least not until all American citizens abroad could be evacuated back. Abe was in fact granted a permit to remain in the United States for the duration of the war. Other than that, the government had nothing more to give. His Polish passport was due to expire on January 19, 1940. He would ultimately make five trips to the Polish Consulate in New York City to have his passport expiration extended six months at a time until its ultimate expiration on December 31, 1942.

Tante Surelleh and Jacob returned from their summer bungalow after Labor Day. They understood the situation and invited Abe to stay with them until he could go back to Poland, which they assumed wouldn't take too long. The new sleeping arrangements had Moshe and Fanny in the alcove, Goldie and Tante Surelleh in the sleeper sofa in the living room of the three-and-a-half room apartment, and Jacob and Abe in the bed in the master bedroom. Abe slept on the side of the bed at the very edge, as his uncle didn't like to be touched while he slept.

Do you know how I felt without money, eating and sleeping with my uncle, crying during the night in the dark, swallowing my tears, and worrying about my family? I only knew two English words: "yes" and "no." The minute I had got off the ship, my name was changed to "the greener," the "greenhorn," and everywhere I went I was introduced "this is my cousin the greener." And everyone asked me: "How do you like America?" What could I tell them? "I like America!" But in my mind, I hated everything. I felt with my suffering that America hated me. I came to visit the World's Fair as a millionaire. But I lived like a beggar.

"And so I was hoping from day to day", recalled Abe, *"perhaps today the war would end. Unfortunately, there was no end."* Abe took matters into his own hands and essayed to acquire an affidavit to send to Europe that would allow Sonia and the children to leave Warsaw and come to the United States. According to Gloria's cousin, Henry Jaglom, it is likely that it was his father, Simon, who arranged the affidavit which was sent sometime between September 1939 and the beginning of 1940 to the American Consulate in Warsaw. The affidavit guaranteed that Sonia and her children would not become dependent on the U.S. government for their support and sustenance. Alas, Abe never received a reply from the consulate to his desperate plea.

Day after day, month after month, the war continued and the news reports went from bad to worse to terrible.

American Nazis?

Adding to his dismay over the position in which he found himself, Abe was shocked to discover the existence of a Nazi organization in the United States. Some five months before Abe landed on American shores, the land of the free, the home of the brave, the land of life, liberty and the pursuit of happiness for all, without regard for religion or national origin, a huge pro-Nazi rally was held in New York City's Madison Square Garden on February 20, 1939. The house was packed. Estimates of the crowd inside the Garden varied from 20,000 to 50,000 cheering spectators listening to speeches glorifying Hitler and threatening the Jews. On October 30, 1939, the German American Bund members decked out in Nazi-like uniforms marched in a parade down East 86th street. To the *Goldeneh Medina,* where any man could become rich and successful if only he worked hard, came Abe, who had sailed away from a continent with a long history of antisemitism and pogroms.[1] "They" were here, even in America.

In contrast to Europe, the United States had had essentially little history of antisemitism, no pogroms, and only a few isolated cases of the murder of Jews, *qua* Jews.

But, especially since the Führer had come to power, a pro-Nazi organization, known as the Friends of the New Germany was founded to disseminate pro-Nazi and anti-Jewish propaganda. Sixty percent of its membership comprised German nationals living in the United States. A national leader of the organization was indicted by the Justice Department for not registering as a foreign agent and fled back to Germany. Fearful of jeopardizing relations with the United States, the Nazi-regime banned German nationals from joining the organization and it collapsed. In its place arose the German American Bund based primarily on the East Coast, though it had branches across the country and in California as well. A similar organization known as the Silver Shirts established itself in North Carolina and Los Angeles. Their membership was composed mostly of German immigrants who had come to America after the First World War.

The leader of the Bund, Fritz Kuhn, a wannabe U.S. Führer who had organized the Garden's Nazi fest, was finally put out of business when the U.S. government indicted him for embezzling Bund funds to pay for, among other things, rent and gifts for his New York girlfriend. When the Japanese bombed Pearl Harbor on December 7, 1941, and the Führer declared war on the United States three days later, the U.S. population was no longer in a mood to tolerate pro-Nazis. The Bund disbanded. Some of its members were interned or deported. American boys of German extraction who had no sympathy for the Nazis joined with Jewish and Christian Americans to enlist in the U.S. armed forces.

Beginning on October 5, 1930, a prominent Catholic priest, and virulent antisemite, Father Coughlin, had hosted a radio show on the CBS network where he spewed antisemitic, pro-Nazi rants that could have matched any broadcasts from German Nazi, propaganda radio. Father Coughlin hosted his radio show for years, until the Vatican finally ordered him to cease his radio show in 1942, while he continued to publish his racist, antisemitic newspaper *Social Justice*. A colleague and fellow traveler, Gerald L. K. Smith, a rabidly racist and antisemitic preacher also preached hatred on the radio to an audience of many millions. In 1942, Smith began publication of an antisemitic magazine, *The Cross and the Flag*, which didn't cease publication until December 1977, well after Smith's death.

Until the Japanese attack, the America First Committee had played a prominent role in the country, advocating isolationism and American disinterest in the war in Europe. Its most prominent spokesman was Charles Lindbergh ("Lucky Lindy"), the American aviation hero and major celebrity in the 1930s. In one of his speeches, in a Des Moines auditorium on September 11, 1941, he attacked American Jews, ranting that the Jews were one of the "three most important groups who have been pressing this country toward war." The other two groups were the British and the Roosevelt Administration. Lindbergh echoed Hitler's speech on January 30, 1939 at the *Reichstag* when Lindbergh continued, "The Jewish groups in this country should be opposing it [war]... for they will be among the first to feel its consequences."[2]

Among the America Firsters were U.S. Congressmen such as Senator Gerald Nye, who spoke against any aid to Great Britain and accused Hollywood of making movies such as *Sergeant York*, *Convoy*, and *Escape* as war propaganda to stir up public opinion in favor of another unnecessary war far from America's shores. One of America's most popular columnists of the time, Westbrook Pegler, slammed Nye and his congressional investigation into Hollywood in September 1941, commenting: "The most powerful propaganda against Nazi Germany is to be found in the daily record of events in

Germany since Hitler began to rise... No fictioneer invented the horrors of the concentration camps... The reason [why we have no pro-Nazi films] is that in all the record of Hitlerism there isn't enough favorable material to make a short [film]..."[3]

From Hunger to Riches again

Sometime after Labor Day, no matter how much Abe hoped the war would soon end, reality led him to understand that the end wasn't imminent. In the meantime, since there was no way he could return to Poland, he needed to find a way to make a living and to get his own apartment. He couldn't sleep on the edge of the bed with his uncle, nor live indefinitely on the charity of relatives of modest means.

Obviously, he knew the shoe business and he knew it well. He had no capital and knew only a few English words. He certainly couldn't get a job. Getting a job wasn't on his radar, anyway. Abe was wont to say to us that he preferred to make one dollar working for himself rather than 100 dollars working for someone else. He saw that there were lots of shoemakers in New York, so he thought he might be able to start a business selling supplies to shoemakers. Moshe and Fanny gave him a large suitcase, which he always referred to as "the valise" that he would use to carry his merchandise. He would talk about how grateful he was to Moshe, Fanny and Goldie, as they helped him initially in the hour of his greatest need.

Abe wasn't shy, and he suppressed his pride. He made the rounds of the various shoemakers within a reasonable distance, entered their stores, introduced himself and visited with them. At the appropriate moment he asked them the source of their wholesale leather. The shoemakers he questioned all told him that they bought their leather from a leather retailer, but they didn't know the location of his place of business. Abe spent days looking for the retail store until he discovered that the shoemakers didn't buy their leather from a retailer, they bought it from wholesalers.

Further research yielded the important information that all the wholesalers who sold shoemaker supplies had their establishments on Gold street, near the Brooklyn Bridge. Somehow Abe found a way to travel there. He popped into the store of one of the wholesalers and announced that he would like to buy supplies from them. To his disappointment, he was informed that they couldn't sell to him because he wasn't a member of their organization. Continuing his detective work, Abe asked around and discovered the name of the gentleman in charge of the organization, Max Brazel, whom Abe contacted as soon as he found his address. Max was taken by the brash, young immigrant and told him to go to a meeting of the shoemakers' organization and tell the people there that he was Max Brazel's cousin, but then it was Abe's job to convince the members to make him a member of the organization.

The former Warsaw millionaire, owner of a business with hundreds of employees, now made it his job to attend every meeting of the organization. Swallowing his pride, he understood that his job now was the most important sales job of his life. He had to sell himself. He went to one meeting after another, telling the members about his situation – an immigrant from Poland, his wife and children stuck in German-occupied Poland – crying and imploring them to make him a member. Finally, after a few meetings, either feeling sorry for this refugee, or impressed by his perseverance, sincerity, sense of humor and pleasant personality, the organization took Abe in as a member of the shoe business wholesalers. It wasn't more than a few months later that Abe became a member of the board and was voted in as the chairman of the membership committee. Now, it *was Abe* who would decide who should be allowed to join the wholesalers' organization.

Meanwhile, Abe set to work. He filled up two valises, the one that Fanny and Moshe had given him and another one, well-used, that was donated to him by his cousin, Ben Kirshenbaum. He filled them up with merchandise procured from wholesalers in the morning and then went door to door to shoemakers' stores selling the proprietors supplies: leather, nails, rubber heels, shoelaces, glue, whatever it was that shoemakers needed. It wasn't long before Abe was able to vacate his relatives' "hotel." He rented a one-room apartment on Intervale Avenue in the Bronx. In New York, this was known as a walk-up, because the building had no elevator. In the morning, Abe schlepped his two valises, which felt to him like bags of concrete, down six flights of stairs. Returning home each night with empty valises, he felt relieved, not so much from the absence of weights in his hands, but from the knowledge that he was eking out a living. When he reached the sixth floor, he was happy and his heart light. He had sold all his merchandise and he didn't have to climb any more stairs. Each day more sales. Each day more income. Each day closer to his hoped-for reunion with his family.

At first, he kept his merchandise with him in his room. In this way he could watch over his supplies, the bread and butter of his business, and save the money that it would have cost to rent an office or a store. As he dozed off, he thought back to the days more than a decade past when he slept in his warehouse in Warsaw to protect his merchandise from theft, and two decades earlier when he and his brothers slept in the attic in Kozienice to keep an eye on the family's laundry. He thought back to the time when his father's merchandise was stolen on the way to Russia and his father had to declare bankruptcy. But, with Abe – no more than a young boy – helping, his father had rebuilt the business and Abe had turned it into a phenomenal success. From that memory he took inspiration, talked to himself and convinced himself that with his eye on the goal and hard work, he would once again turn catastrophe into opportunity. He would build a business and rebuild his finances so that he would return to Poland, this time as the rich uncle from America.

As he began to sell a lot of supplies, he was able to have the merchandise delivered to him, rather than having to get up in the middle of the night to travel to the wholesalers and then schlep the merchandise back to his apartment, spending money on a taxi or hired truck. He had few expenses. Monthly rent for his apartment cost 12 dollars.

Abe used to laugh when he reminisced about the "fancy" restaurants he frequented during the war years. At the time, New York boasted a famous eatery that was less than what we would call a cafeteria, the Horn & Hardart Automat. The Automat was for the time some kind of technological marvel. The store was laid out somewhat like a cafeteria. But instead of servers dishing out the "home-made" comfort food, there was a wall of what looked like small postal boxes, row after row of little windows, behind which could be seen sandwiches, hard-boiled eggs, bread, meatloaf, etc. You slid the required coins into the appropriate slots, the little doors popped open and you took out your meal and headed to a table to eat.

Abe's cuisine was simple and modest in cost. In the morning, he bought a bottle of milk and a few pieces of bread. He would drink no more than half the bottle of milk and eat a small piece of bread, saving the rest. For lunch, he purchased a meat sandwich and two extra slices of bread. He combined half of the meat with the extra bread and put another half aside for his supper. His supper was either the leftovers or the same typical meal he had eaten many years earlier in Kozienice: nothing. His stomach may have growled, but it was his heart that ached. He had little problem falling asleep. The sooner that he fell asleep, the sooner he could wake up and make his sales rounds. The sooner he made his rounds, the more shoemakers he could call on. The more shoemakers on whom he called, the more he earned. The more he earned, the more wherewithal he would have when he and Sonia would reunite.

After spending the minimum on personal expenses and necessary business expenses, Abe tried to save every penny that he earned, depositing his earnings on a regular basis into a local bank's savings account.

As time passed, and news from the European theatre revealed ongoing murder and massacre of Jews by German forces, Abe realized that he was not going to be returning to Poland and his successful business in Warsaw. That life was over. In his mind, he was forging a new life in the United States. He developed a one-track mind and motivation. He didn't know how many of his family would survive the war. But he set for himself the mission to establish a successful business so that after the war would end, he could bring what was left of his family to America and help them establish themselves in the new world. He anticipated that they would come with nothing. But he would support them all until they got on their feet.

At some point, Abe was doing so well that he no longer worked out of his own apartment. He found a space in the right location and in it opened his own store that cost him 10 dollars per month in rent. Abe no longer had to call on shoemakers, Now the shoemakers or their employees made the trek to Abe's store to buy their supplies. Eventually, Abe moved to larger quarters costing him 35 dollars a month. By 1946, Abe's business was located in a still larger space that cost him 75 dollars a month. By that time, if not earlier, Abe had two people working for him in the store.

Abe remembered what his father had told him and what he practiced in Warsaw, "If you want to be successful, make your customers your friends." As in Warsaw, so in New York, Abe practiced as he had learned. He made his customers his good friends, and they continued to be his good customers. Although he had a store and didn't need to schlep his merchandise to his customers, he didn't spend his days in the store. Instinctively good businessman that he was, he continued to visit his customers to schmooze and ask about their families and business, and they, in turn, typically knowing his situation, asked about any information he had about his family and commiserated with him over the situation in Europe, as well as discussed the progress of the war on both fronts. Besides maintaining his relationship with his loyal customers, Abe continued to make calls on prospective customers, making friends with them and turning many of them into long-term customers, as well.

The Car

Business became such a success that Abe was able to buy a car, albeit used. He discovered that the car had a door on the passenger side that didn't close properly. He took the car to one of the garages in the Bronx. The mechanic assured him that he could fix the car for a few dollars in three or four days and asked Abe to leave the car. Abe explained that he needed it for his work and couldn't manage without it. The mechanic explained that he could fix the door right then and there but would expect that Abe would still pay him the few dollars they had agreed on as the price of the repair. Abe agreed. He stood aside as the mechanic stuck a three-foot-long piece of two-by-four wood somewhere between the door and the jamb and did something or other, which succeeded in bending or unbending the defective hinge that had been causing the problem. Abe marveled at the cleverness of the mechanic. He paid him the agreed upon sum but asked him, "Why are you charging so much for a job you said could take three or four days to do, when you actually fixed the problem in two minutes." The mechanic replied that Abe wasn't paying him for the time and labor to fix the door. He was paying him for the knowledge that he had that enabled him to fix the car.

This was a story that Abe would later retell more than once. The moral of the story was that we shouldn't begrudge a worker or a professional earning what we might consider a lot of money for something that might take him or her a short amount of time. Abe had a profound respect for people with specialized knowledge and skills. He was never too proud to ask for help for a project beyond his ken. At the same time, he had a tremendous curiosity and was always looking to learn things about the world from experts. Once he had absorbed knowledge, he wasn't afraid to try out solving problems on his own.

When Abe came to America, he didn't speak English. Years later, he joked that he could say "yes" and "no" in every language. When asked to say "yes" in Norwegian, for example, he would nod his head up and down, and everyone would laugh. But in 1939, not speaking English was not a laughing matter. Once Abe understood that he wasn't returning to Poland, he realized that learning English was high priority.

In the first half of the 20th century, the United States hosted so many immigrants from Europe that night schools were set up in New York City in order to teach the newcomers English, the gateway to getting a job doing more than menial labor. Besides teaching English, night schools made it possible for the immigrants to integrate into American society. The schools taught American history, civics, American values and how to manage in everyday activities. Night schools turned the new immigrant greenhorns or "greeners" for short, into Americans. After working all day, schlepping from shoemaker to shoemaker, selling assorted shoemaker supplies, Abe took the subway to his night school, located at that time on the Boston Post Road in the Bronx. During the day, within the walls of Public School ("P.S.") 98, local children learned reading, writing and 'rithmetic. At night, P.S. 98 was the venue for the polyglot adult immigrants from adjoining neighborhoods to learn speaking, reading and writing English, along with lessons on American culture and customs.

On a rainy Thursday, October 15, 1789, American President George Washington had set out from his official residence on Cherry street traveling to Boston along the Boston Post Road to visit constituents. A century and a half later, the temporary resident, Polish national Abe Huberman trekked along the same Boston Post Road through sun and rain, snow and sleet and the dark of night, on his own travels from Polish-Jewish citizen to proud Jewish-American citizen.

At that time, immigration law required an individual with a temporary residence permit to leave the country, get an immigrant visa from an American Consul and then return to the States with the visa in hand. On November 2, 1942, the same day that Field Marshal Erwin Rommel decided to withdraw from North Africa, Abe traveled by train to Montreal, Canada. The same day he received from an American Consul in Montreal the "non-quota" Immigration Visa No. 947 and was admitted to the United States at Rouses Point, New York as a permanent resident by order of U.S. Immigration Inspector John Curley. Abe's one-day round trip to become a permanent U.S. resident came exactly three years and three months from the day he landed on American shores on August 2, 1939. He would become a naturalized American citizen on April 26, 1948. That was the official date. But for many years, Abe had already considered himself a proud, American patriot.

The name Abe had been given in Kozienice was *Avrom*. When he developed a childhood illness, the middle name *Chaim* was added. A not uncommon belief held that if you changed a sick person's name, that might fool and divert the Angel of Death. In addition, *Chaim*, meaning "life," was a good luck talisman that might bring recovery from the illness. Abe arrived in the United States bearing the anglicized name Abrom (or Abram).

When it came time to become an American citizen, Abe changed his name to Abraham. Abe knew by heart the Biblical story of the Patriarch, Abram (Hebrew: *Avrom*), who had been called by God in Aram: "Go forth from your Land, your birthplace, your father's home to the Land that I will show you... I shall make your name great, and you shall be a blessing" (*Genesis* 12:1-2). The voice Abe had heard in Warsaw was that of cousin Zalman's. Abe's assent might have been rather impulsive. But, like his namesake, Abe listened and departed for parts unknown. When the Hebrew Patriarch *Avrom* was settled in Canaan, the Promised Land, God changed his name to "Abraham" (Hebrew: *Avraham*, *Genesis* 17:5). When Abe Huberman settled in America and became an American citizen, in love with the *Goldeneh Medina*, he changed his own name.

---

1. Bailey; Van Ellis.
2. Time Magazine, Vol. 38, Issue 12, September 22, 1941, pp. 13-14.
3. *Ibid.* p. 17.

14

MAJDANEK – THE REAL
CATASTROPHE

Death thus raged in every shape; and
As usually happens at such times,
There was no length to which violence
Did not go
Thucydides: III 69ff

Sonia thought her journey from Warsaw on the cattle car lasted two days. The end of the journey was not Treblinka, where many of the Warsaw ghetto survivors were sent and murdered upon arrival. Sonia's trip ended at Majdanek, a camp near Lublin, built at the end of 1941 to house Soviet prisoners of war to be used as slave labor. None of the prisoners survived and by the end of 1942, the camp was repurposed primarily as a camp to murder Jews.

The Nazi regime had already murdered millions of Jews by means of *Aktions* conducted by the Police Battalions, *SS Einsatzgruppen* or by local Nazi collaborators especially in the Baltic countries. The great extent of the murders by shooting of entire populations of Jews in hundreds or thousands of villages and towns across Nazi-occupied Europe has only come to widespread understanding recently.[1] Desirous of increasing the efficiency of killing every Jew in Europe, the Nazis had set up concentration camps that were primarily industrialized killing centers known as the Reinhard (or more accurately, Globocnik) camps: Treblinka, Sobibor, and Belzec. These were purely extermination camps. Majdanek and Auschwitz were hybrid slave labor reservations and death camps.

Auschwitz was both a killing center and a slave-labor camp, where those deemed physically fit were put to work in a variety of capacities. Auschwitz had 45 subcamps where inmates worked as slave laborers for various German companies such as Krupp, Siemens, I.G. Farben (at Monowitz subcamp). Other camps were used as sources of slave labor for German companies like Bussing (truck manufacturing) and aviation manufacturers whose customer was the *Luftwaffe:* companies like Junkers (which drew slave laborers from Buchenwald), Messerschmidt (Mauthausen and Buchenwald), Heinkel (Sachsenhausen, Oranienburg, Ravensbrück, Mauthausen and the Krakow/Plaszow ghetto), BMW (Dachau) and the battery factory AFA, known after the war as Varta (Neuengamme satellite camp Hanover-Stocken).

In March 1944, Himmler reported that 36,000 camp inmates were working in the aviation industry and he expected to increase that number to at least 90,000. Dozens if not hundreds of German companies benefited from the work of their unpaid slave laborers. They included well-known names such as Telefunken (electronic and radio manufacturer), BMW (jet engines), Daimler Benz, Volkswagen, Auto Union, and the armament and artillery manufacturer Rheinmetall. Rheinmetall survived the war and bid on contracts to manufacture artillery for NATO, winning a bid in 1978 to manufacture 120 mm tank cannons for the U.S. military. Today, Rheinmetall is a giant in the European automotive industry and self-describes as "Europe's foremost supplier of defence and security technology and longstanding partner of the armed forces."

The death camps and most concentration and slave labor camps were constructed and operated in Poland, near railway lines. Estimates of the total number of concentration-, POW-extermination, slave labor-camps and ghettos, large and small plus subcamps created by the Germans reach a staggering 42,500 all across Europe. Majdanek had three subcamps and Auschwitz over 40. These were German camps situated on occupied Polish soil.

Of the 15,000 survivors of the Warsaw ghetto uprising sent to Majdanek, 5,000 were immediately murdered.[2] We don't know why Sonia was sent to Majdanek instead of to her death in Treblinka. Luckily, she and her sister Rachelle were sent to Majdanek and remained alive together, most likely in a barracks in Compound 5.[3]

When we came to the camp, they cut off our hair and gave us torn clothes. The children looked terrible. In the camp it was terrible. We worked very hard. They gave us no food. The children slept on the floor without any blankets. At night it was very cold. Death would have been better than life. Lusia got sick with a cold. I had no food for her except soup made from wild turnips and a piece of black bread. Rachelle and little David were with us. So, I decided to go to work in the field where Polish civilian men worked. For gold we were able to buy a roll. I had hidden in my shoes 200 dollars. They hadn't taken my shoes because they were torn. I brought food every day from work, although it was very dangerous. There was an inspection every day for contraband and unauthorized rolls were considered contraband. But I managed to hide a roll so that they couldn't find it.

For the first two days they had been given no food and were put to work. The children were left with two mothers, while the rest of the women were sent outside to work. Sonia reported that her job was carrying large heavy stones from one part of the camp to another and back again, repeatedly. Why would the Germans put the women to useless work? Sonia's memory was certainly accurate.[4] Make-work was common throughout the camp system. As historian Wolfgang Sofsky has confirmed:

Sisyphean tasks are terror labor in pure and unadulterated form, without any productive secondary purpose. Their sole aim was to harass and deplete the prisoners. For the supervisors, it was a welcome occasion for violence, for the victims, an endless torment, a vivid demonstration that all their efforts were totally worthless, devoid of meaning. There were hardly any limits to inventiveness here. In Dachau, prisoners were forced to push a cart with rubber wheels, the notorious "Moor Express," loaded with heavy stones, back and forth through the deep morass. In other camps, prisoners had to construct stone walls, layer by layer, pull them down the next day, and then rebuild them the following day. Sisyphean tasks destroy the purposeful structure of human labor. The effort had no meaning outside itself.[5]

For hungry women with no nourishment and no strength, the work could easily kill them, which would make way for the next group of "workers." In the meantime, the women were deprived of the strength that they would need to fight to protect their children. With the minimal amount of watery soup or ersatz coffee they were fed under the guise of food, their strength rapidly ebbed.

The children in the women's barracks in Compound 5, were crying. Their mothers had no strength left to cry. Their hearts were heavy from their children's suffering.

Perhaps two weeks of hunger and back-breaking work passed, as far as Sonia remembered – her memory blurred by starvation and the passage of time – when she returned to the barracks after a day of manual, spirit-destroying labor. As she wrote above, Sonia had met some local Polish civilians somewhere along the way to or from the camp, and succeeded (on pain of death for her and the farmers) in buying two rolls from them with the cash or gold that she had managed to smuggle into the camp in her shoes, so old and worn that they had not been seized by the guards. Upon arriving back at the barracks, she looked for the children to bring them the rolls. It was then that she discovered that David and Lusia, along with the rest of the children, were gone.

They took away all the mothers and their children. A thousand people at one time they took to the crematoria. You can't imagine what I went through, then. I wanted to die.

I asked the guard commander to send me where my children were. The guard pointed to the smoke rising from the crematorium, hit me with a club and said with a sadistic smirk, "You'll join them soon; but you are still young and healthy, first you must work for the Reich." And here began my hell. I remained without my children and only thought about death.

In the four years since September 1, 1939, years of suffering and agony, starvation and witnessing her friends and loved ones abused or killed by the Nazis or Ukrainians, Sonia had never once seriously thought of escaping the horror by killing herself. For one thing, she had two children to protect and care for. Sonia was strong. She maintained the hope that the Germans would lose the war, as they had in 1918, she would be reunited with Abe, and they would carry on with their lives.

This time was different. Unable to protect her children, exhausted physically and mentally, Sonia couldn't bear the pain, imagining how frightened her children must have been. Her thought *why didn't I think of a way to save them?* tortured her. Of course, there was no way. There was nothing she could have done to save them.

During the day I worked very hard carrying rocks and sand. Work that was given to people to destroy them. Every day we went through a selection. They selected people that were not fit to work, people too weak. I begged again that they should take me to my death, but the commander wouldn't hear of it.

Fearful that Sonia was serious about suicide, her younger sister, Rachelle, told her what she would remind her repeatedly over the next two years:

All the other women have no hope, even if they live through the war, they will have nothing. You have a husband in America, he is making a life for you. The war will end and you will go to America and have a new life.

Rachelle stayed with Sonia day and night for several days until she was able to calm her to the point where she agreed she wouldn't hurt herself. With faith and hope that she would be reunited with

Abe and a promise to herself to bear witness to what she and other Jews had experienced at the hand of the Nazis, Sonia was determined to live. Dying in the ghettos and camps was easy. Living required work, along with courage and hope.

Two weeks earlier, when she had arrived at the camp with her sister, they had been given old clothes to wear, perhaps belonging to previous prisoners, but which, in any case, looked like rags. Rachelle's garment was uncomfortably tight. Educated, with a Master's degree in Classics, Rachelle told a female, German guard, in perfect German, that the dress given to her was too small. The guard smiled, barked at her, "Come with me," and motioned her to come into another room. When Rachelle came out of the room, she was bleeding and doubled over with pain. She had been beaten up so badly by the guard that Sonia didn't think Rachelle would survive the day. Sonia tore off pieces of her own clothing to make bandages out of them to try to stop the bleeding dripping from Rachelle's wounds.

Now, two weeks later, Rachelle had more or less recovered, and after the murder of Sonia's children, it had become Rachelle's turn to watch over Sonia.

---

1. Wachsmann, pp. 322, 408.
2. Arad, p. 166.
3. Marszalek, pp. 137f.
4. *ibid.* p. 107.
5. Sofsky, p. 190.

15

AUSCHWITZ

Then I decided to go to another camp. Every day they took transports to different camps. So, willingly I put myself on a transport going to a camp known as Auschwitz. - Sonia

Sonia and Rachelle remained in Majdanek approximately six more weeks. On June 24, 1943, *SS* Colonel Gerhard Maurer and Auschwitz doctor, Bruno Kitt, traveled to Majdanek. Auschwitz was in need of additional laborers. As labor deployment chief under Oswald Pohl and head of all *SS* economic enterprises, including all concentration camps, Maurer frequently tried to provide suitable workers for IG Farben and other German corporations located in or near concentration camps such as Auschwitz. He came to Majdanek to look for slaves healthy enough to bring to Auschwitz. He brought along Dr. Kitt to make the medical decision about the adequacy of inmates' health for heavy labor.

Sonia recalled that a German commander had asked the prisoners "who wants to go to Auschwitz to work?" They all knew that Auschwitz was a "terrible, terrible place," presumably because one was worked to death there. Sonia may have known that Auschwitz was a slave-labor camp. She may or may not have been aware that there was a gas chamber in Auschwitz I and an even larger one in Auschwitz II (Birkenau), making Auschwitz both a slave-labor and a death camp. A camp of murder by poison gas followed by incineration of the corpses. She was correct, though, guessing from the rumors she had heard, that the camps worked the inmates to death. That was part of the Nazi plan for the genocide of the Jews and the killing of Soviet prisoners of war, other *Untermenschen* and enemies of the Reich. The Germans had an expression for this: *Vernichtung durch Arbeit* or annihilation through work, a policy ordered by Himmler.

Many mentally and physically handicapped people in Germany had already been murdered[1] beginning with Hitler's euthanasia order of September 1, 1939, until the operation, known as Aktion T4 (named after the location of the euthanasia program's headquarter at 4 Tiergarten street), was ended on August 28, 1941, after 90,000 to 100,000 people had been murdered, initially via lethal injections and later via carbon monoxide pumped from engine exhaust into sealed vans ferrying the victims to their graves. In August 1941, Bishop Clemens August von Galen of Münster publicly denounced the euthanasia program. Many Germans had complained about their relatives' disappearances or sudden deaths. Rumors – true, as it turned out – that disabled veterans of the Great War had been euthanized and wounded soldiers from the current war would likely meet the same fate. Riots by family members had broken out in some instances to prevent buses from picking up their relatives who were patients in hospitals or sanitaria.

Given that the war against the Soviet Union was two months old, Hitler apparently decided he didn't need to antagonize a significant number of German citizens appalled by the T4 program and worried about their family numbers at the fronts. While the killing of newborns with handicaps continued, along with the starvation of disabled elderly, it was at a much reduced rate. Many of the members of the top echelon of the T4 program were reassigned to help organize the coming accelerated murder of all Jews who were or would come under Nazi control. As it turned out, Bishop von

Galen wasn't opposed to murdering innocents; he was merely opposed to murdering disabled Germans. Some weeks later, on September 14, the Bishop issued a pastoral letter endorsing the war against "Judaeo-Bolshevism." Galen wrote: "... for decades the Jewish-Bolshevik rulers from Moscow have been trying to set not just Germany but the whole of Europe in flames."[2] Presumably for Bishop Galen, the *Einsatzgruppen* who at the moment were looting and shooting Jews and Soviet citizens all across Eastern Europe, were doing God's work.

Fazed by the bad publicity attendant to Hitler's signed order to execute the T4 program, Hitler never issued a signed order to Himmler to commit genocide against Europe's Jews. His orders were delivered orally to Himmler and Goring. They passed on oral and written orders to their underlings citing the *Führer's* wishes, which was clearly understood by all to mean an order for the destruction of Jews and other "undesirables."

The first murder camp constructed was in Chelmno, Poland. It began operation on December 8, 1941, the day after the Japanese sneak attack on American naval ships in Pearl Harbor, Hawaii. The Germans went on to construct other concentration camps, the main ones Belzec, Treblinka and Sobibor specifically for the purpose of murdering *en masse* the human beings whom the Nazis considered in their delusional, racial ideology as subhuman.

In order to commit mass murder more efficiently and with less psychological distress to the murderers, the Nazi leaders, in particular Göring, Himmler, Heydrich and Eichmann, organized the system of camps to which gypsies, homosexuals and above all Jews were transported from all corners of occupied Europe. They were all brought to these camps and murdered. At the three *Globocnik* camps (usually referred to as "Reinhard" camps in "honor" of Reinhard after his assassination in May, 1942) the killing method consisted of carbon monoxide pumped by automotive engines into sealed buildings. These camps were known to those who operated them as *Vernichtunglager* or "annihilation camps", i.e., death camps. During the 20 months of their operation, these three camps alone were responsible for the murder of at least two million Jews from all across Europe. During the hyperintense Nazi killing spree carried out during Operation Reinhard in a three-month period in 1942, nearly 25 percent of all Jews killed during the Holocaust were murdered in these three camps.[3]

At Auschwitz and Majdanek, the killing was done primarily through the poison gas, prussic acid (German trade name: *Zyklon* B, provided by the German company Tesch & Stabenow. Initially, corpses were burned in open pits. Later, crematoria were built by the German construction company Topf and Sons for the purpose of turning the corpses of human beings into ash. Sonia couldn't know of the enormous numbers, but between 1941 and November 1944, at least 1.1 million Jews would be murdered at Auschwitz-Birkenau.

Sonia said to her sister that she just couldn't bear to remain in Majdanek, following the death of her children. So, when the announcement was made that volunteers were sought to leave Majdanek to work in Auschwitz, Sonia volunteered herself and Rachelle. *"Then I decided to go to another camp. Every day they took transports to different camps. So, willingly I put myself on a transport going to a camp known as Auschwitz."*

Sonia and Rachelle, in the company of 625 other women and 426 men, had succeeded in being selected by Kitt and Maurer as "fit for extremely hard labor" and approved for transfer to Auschwitz.

They were shipped to Auschwitz on a train, in a coal car, arriving dirty and *"totally black from the coal dust,"* reported Sonia, on June 26, 1943. Official Auschwitz records document the group's arrival: "June 26 1,052 male and female Jews whom SS Second Lieutenant Sell and SS Camp Doctor Kitt considered fit for extremely hard labor are sent from the Lublin (Majdanek) C.C. The 426 men are given Nos. 126377-126802 and 626 women are given Nos. 46797-47422."[4]

Sonia remembered the selection when they arrived at the new camp. In front of them was a girl of about 18 years old, whom the selecting doctor sent to one side. Sonia and Rachelle were motioned to go to the other side. At the time Sonia was terrified, thinking *this is not good. If such a young girl is sent to one line and two older women are sent to the other, perhaps it means death.*

As it turned out, she was to discover that it was the teenager who had been sent to her death. Sonia and Rachelle had been in Majdanek, starved and exhausted from hard manual labor. Incredibly, they still looked healthy enough by Nazi standards for work.

Sonia, along with the others, were stripped naked and given tattered and soiled clothing to put on. The next stop was to a room where a worker tattooed an inverted triangle and a number on her left arm. She would bear for the rest of her life her souvenir from Auschwitz, her number: *47336*. From there they were sent to a room to have their heads shaved and thence to a barracks, where they would sleep – on thin "mattresses" of straw or on bare boards.

They were given very hard labor to do. She felt, accurately enough, that the Germans were working them so hard so that they would all die.

Once a day they were given "soup" consisting of what looked and tasted like dirty water. If you could find a piece of potato in the soup, you would consider yourself very lucky. Every morning at what she thought was 5 or 6 AM, everyone lined up outside for roll call, standing at attention for an hour or longer, until a German officer came to count them. They were sent to work until after dark, which Sonia estimated was around 8 PM. Every morning, while standing at attention, she saw dozens of bodies of women slumped over the electrified wire fences because they could no longer tolerate their suffering. These were women who had lost their husbands, parents, families, and children. And they had lost all hope. They threw themselves onto the electrified barbed wire surrounding the camp and electrocuted themselves.

When Sonia talked about losing hope, Rachelle reminded her that she had a husband in America who was building a new life for her and they had to maintain the hope that the war would end, the Germans would be defeated and Sonia would be reunited with her husband.

Rachelle had smuggled into the camp a 20-dollar gold coin – hidden in her rectum – miraculously not discovered by the Nazis during their usually intrusive, entrance examination. She had heard that one could bribe guards to get an indoor job – in a building with a roof. She found a Jewish *Kapo*, a prisoner functionary, from Czechoslovakia and gave her the coin. In return, the *Kapo* succeeded in getting a German administrator to give the sisters a job in the shoe Kommando. Their job was to process the millions of shoes that the German camp administration stole from the Jews murdered on arrival in the camp, by tearing apart shoes and separating the leather, rubber and other materials. The goal of the Germans was to ship the material to factories, likely in Germany, to be reconstituted as footwear to be distributed to soldiers or sold to civilians. In addition, the shoe Kommandos were to examine the shoes for precious stones or valuable coins that might be hidden in their heels or soles and turn them over to their supervisors to be shipped to the *Reichsbank* (or in many cases to be kept by guards or commanders for themselves, though they were subject to arrest and prosecution if they were caught stealing for themselves by *SS* overseers).

Sonia believed that working in the Kanada Kommando as these indoor jobs sorting victims' belongings were called, saved their lives, because they worked in a barn-like building that had a roof, instead of outdoors in the fields. With next to no food and severe Polish winters, many of the inmates who worked outdoors died of exposure if not overwork and starvation. Lifespan in the outdoors of the work camp was measured in weeks. For some reason, the inmates called these Kommandos Kanada, from some belief that Canada was a wonderful, beautiful, safe, rich country. Working

170

indoors not doing backbreaking work was tantamount to vacationing in Canada.

Sonia recalled a time she found a diamond hidden in a shoe. She reported the find and handed it over to a supervisor, who likely secreted it on his own person, stealing it for himself. He did reward her with a "better" job. That job involved looking for valuables in suitcases that unsuspecting Jewish deportees had brought with them to the "resettlement" or labor camps to which they thought they were going. Working in the suitcase Kommando in Kanada had another big advantage: it provided workers the opportunity to acquire (or "organize" in camp slang) food and clothing they found in luggage, that they could smuggle into the barracks to share with other prisoners. Sonia was returned to her previous job at some point. Perhaps the supervisor hoped that she or her sister would find more treasures for him to steal. The sisters continued to work in the shoe Kommando until the Death Marches of January 1945.

There were additional selections on a regular basis. The women were gathered together on a field, naked, and guards walked row by row looking for women who appeared too weak or sick to work and would then write their numbers down for selection to the gas chambers. Trucks carrying German soldiers then showed up calling out all the numbers on their lists, loaded the women on the trucks and drove them to the gas chambers.

Mornings, when the women lined up for *Appell* (roll call) and Sonia saw the bodies of women lying on the electrified barbed wire fences surrounding the camp, the fleeting thought of doing the same passed through her mind. But the companionship and love of her sister, and the comradeship the women prisoners had established with each other, reinforced her basic will to live. She forced herself to repeat over and over in her mind the mantra that this war will come to an end with the defeat of the Germans and her liberation. News from the outside world certainly made it into the camp. Reports that the Nazis had been driven out of North Africa and that outside the gates of Stalingrad the Nazi 6th Army under the command of Field Marshall Paulus had been annihilated and the remnant surrendered to the Red Army, spread like wildfire in the camp and brought hope to Sonia and Rachelle and to all the other prisoners that the Nazis were going to lose this war.

By 1943/1944, hundreds of thousands of German husbands and sons who had gone to war did not come home on leave because they were in Allied or Soviet mass graves after Stalingrad and the Normandy landings, or in Soviet POW Gulags. When German cities were being destroyed by Allied bombing day and night, German civilians began to think – and some of them, risking Gestapo arrest, began to say out loud, "The deaths of our men, the destruction of our cities – is our punishment for what we have done to the Jews."[5] The Protestant bishop of Württemberg sent a letter to the Reich Chancellery reporting that his parishioners were "feeling that the suffering they were having to endure from the enemy bombing raids was in retribution for what was being done to the Jews." They didn't know how little the Allies cared about the fate of the Jews, let alone how inconceivable it would be that they would carry out bombing raids as punishment for the Nazi crimes against the Jews.

Other Germans were gripped with fear and trembling, knowing what they and their countrymen had wreaked on Europe and in particular the Jewish population. One German soldier who had watched a massacre of Jews in Lithuania in July 1941 openly admitted, "I can only say that the mass shootings in Panerai were quite horrific. At the time I said: 'May God grant us victory, because if they get their revenge, we're in for a hard time.'"[6] A German opinion surveyor overheard two workmen in Spandau-West saying, "We have only ourselves to blame for this war because we treated the Jews so badly. We shouldn't be too surprised if they now do the same thing to us."[7] In April 1945, only a few weeks before Germany surrendered to the Western allies on May 8, a German soldier was traveling among civilians in a train in Berlin and apparently got annoyed hearing the defeatist grumblings of the passengers about the war. He roused himself, shouting to no one in particular,

"Silence... stop whining... We have to win this war... If others win the war, and they do to us only a fraction of what we have done in the occupied territories, there won't be a single German left in a few weeks."[8]

As it turned out, the Americans and British would behave generously to the German civilian population that would come under their administration in 1945. Not so the Soviets. In January 1945, Marshal Georgy Zhukov, who commanded the troops that would capture Berlin, issued an order that included this prediction: "Woe to the land of the murderers. We will get our terrible revenge for everything."[9] And the Soviets would, indeed.

Did these German civilians feel guilt and regret for the genocide that had been committed in their name? Or did they still exaggerate the power of the Jews? And the soldiers who watched or participated in the genocide? They knew. And now they were afraid of the punishment they understood they deserved. They all feared retribution for the terrible crimes committed against the Jews and other occupied peoples in the name of Nazi ideology by the German police, army and their many European collaborators.

But at Auschwitz, the killings, the gassings and the smoke and flames shooting up to the sky continued. Stalin's Red Army and American General Eisenhower's Army Air Corps were nowhere to be seen. Actually, Allied bombers flew overhead from Italy in 1944. On their way to bomb the Buna synthetic rubber factory a short distance from Auschwitz, some bombs were accidently released over Auschwitz and killed some SS men in the camp. But the Allies never sent any planes to bomb the crematoria or even the rail lines or bridges leading to this camp of death and destruction.

---

1. Wittmann, p. 114.
2. Stargardt, *op.cit,* p. 162.
3. Stone
4. Czech, pp. 425, 428.

5. Hastings, p. 470. A Catholic priest in Münster conveyed the same observation (Stargardt, p. 563).
6. Klee, *et al.*, p. 43.
7. Gellately, pp. 253f.
8. Shepherd, *op.cit.* p. 504
9. Gellately, *op.cit.* p. 255.

16

NEW YORK - POLAND

Weeks become Years

New York - The Bronx – Abe Goes to Night School and Volunteers as a sworn "Cop"

Abe was eager to become a "real" American. He had no idea when he would be able to return to Poland. In the beginning, he thought the war wouldn't last too long, and he would return to his home and his business. As time passed and he listened to news of the war on the radio, read about it in the newspapers and saw the newsreels in the movie theatres portraying the horrors of the wars in Europe and then the Pacific, he came to believe that this would be a long war and that in the meantime he needed to make a life for himself in the United States.

His fears for his family grew when he no longer received letters or news about them and when he became aware of the mass murders of Jewish civilians by the Germans and their allies in Europe. He learned about the ghettos into which the Germans had concentrated the Jewish populations as the *Wehrmacht* conquered one after another of Europe's cities. He heard reports of massacres of Jews and hints – which newspapers like the New York Times minimized – of concentration camps where Jews were worked to death or murdered. As time went on, he came to fear that his children would not survive the war, but he always believed that Sonia would survive. He maintained the hope that no matter what, Sonia would somehow, some way survive. This was his main motivation. This is what drove him to live, to work day and night, to save his earnings, so that he would be able to make a life for his wife and family when they would be reunited. Eventually, he would come to understand that he would not return to Poland nor any place in Europe, the graveyard of the Jewish people.

Abe, who had not had any formal education past fourth or fifth grade, was an excellent student. He rose to become President of the NYC 40,000 member night school student body. In that capacity, he was invited to make guest appearances on a New York radio station, where, among other topics he discussed with the host, he made frequent appeals to listeners to buy war bonds. Abe's English language skills apparently had improved to the point that he was able to join a unit of a reserve police force. So many New York police had been drafted, that the city feared for its security.

Thus, in February 1942, Mayor Fiorello La Guardia established the City Civil Patrol Corps. The mission for volunteers was "to assist the Police Department in every practicable way in the protection of life and property in our city." Patrols took place between 4 PM and midnight. One to two four-hour tours per week were required of those who joined. Volunteers were to patrol their beats, protect property, serve as air wardens, prevent crime and be available in times of emergency. Abe wanted to serve his adopted country and aid the war effort; service in the CPC was another way he could take action and feel that he was contributing to the security of the city, in particular, and the United States, in general. He was proud to wear his uniform and devote his time and effort to help protect New York. The City Civil Patrol Corps was formally disbanded and the corpsmen demobilized on September 30, 1945, after a total of 4,500 men and women had served.

Abe saved an essay he wrote as a school assignment and an entry for an essay contest at the suggestion of his teacher Miss Porre, sometime in 1944. The assigned topic was "How I can be a good neighbor in my community." In clear, flowing, beautiful handwriting with his fountain pen, Abe poured out his heart. It's worth reproducing his entire 382-word essay, as he wrote it:

Love your neighbor as yourself. How simple it sounds. Yet how important it is. If all people could realize the meaning of these few words, what a wonderful world we would have.

It is especially important now, more than ever, when millions of people have lost their lives, when so many mothers have lost their children, when so many children have lost their fathers. This is due to one reason: people in one country do not love their neighbors in another country.

Everyone who likes to live in a happy and peaceful world should always keep in mind: I love my neighbors because I like to be loved by them.

For my part, I am trying my best to be a good neighbor. I have given blood ten times to the Red Cross, and I have made an appointment for the 11th time. I hope and pray that my blood will save a few lives.

Last time when I went to the Red Cross, I convinced two of my friends to give blood too. I promised them a free ride downtown and also to take them home by car. How happy I was when they told me that they appreciated my advice and made an appointment for the second time.

Two years ago, Mayor La Guardia appealed for volunteers to serve in our City Patrol Corps. Since that time, I am on duty every Saturday night from 8 PM to midnight.

In 1943, my school collected, in stamps and bonds, about three to four hundred dollars a week. Since October 1944, the sales of stamps and bonds increased to an average of three thousand dollars a week.

Thanks to our wonderful Director, Mr. Schneider, I was able to get the bonds in blank. I have invested three thousand dollars in cash and every Monday night I sell stamps and bonds to our students.

This week our school had a drive for the Red Cross. I collected 42 dollars from friends outside of school. I am very happy that with my help we collected three hundred dollars.

I am always willing to help those who need aid. In 1943, I mailed a letter to an unknown soldier in the Bronx Veterans Hospital. How surprised I was when I received a wonderful letter from Mr. Jennings! I went to the hospital to meet my new friend. How happy I was to meet such a nice friend like Mr. Jennings. When I have time, I visit the wounded soldiers in the hospital.

I pray and I wish that we should not only preach to be a good neighbor, but more important, we should act as good neighbors.

This essay personifies Abe. He truly did want to be a good neighbor no matter what the situation or the cause. During the war years, he wanted to do whatever he could do to help the war effort, to help his neighbors, to help his American family and to prepare a new life for his wife and children when they survived the war. Abe bought 3,000 dollars (equivalent to over 44,000 dollars in today's money) worth of war bonds, with the expectation, but no guarantee, that he would be able to sell them to his fellow night school students, friends, business associates, acquaintances and – what wouldn't be surprising – total strangers.

Abe graduated from night school in 1944. At the graduation ceremony, he was surprised when his name was called as the winner of the annual award given to the outstanding night school student. Let the story be told in his own words:

... two weeks before graduation, the principal of the school asked me to come to his office – a Mr. [Joseph] Koenigsberg, would like to ask me some questions. We met, and I answered his questions. At the graduation ceremonies I was surprised when it was announced that I was to receive the "Diana Koenigsberg Memorial Award." This annual presentation was made by Mr. Koenigsberg and his sisters in memory of their mother who was a graduate of the school. To this day I carry the medal with me at all times, with pride, having had it attached to my pocket watch chain.[1]

The award included a small engraved medal, which Abe first attached to his pocket watch chain and later to the chain of his jeweler's loupe.

The Death List

Poland - Auschwitz

In the winter of 1943-1944, an epidemic broke out in the camp and Sonia fell seriously ill. She came down with what was considered the deadliest camp disease – typhus. Due to the atrocious lack of proper hygiene forced on the inmates by the Nazi commanders, typhus was all too common and dreaded by both inmates and guards. She had a temperature of 104 degrees Fahrenheit and was taken to the Auschwitz hospital. In Auschwitz, the so-called hospital for inmates wasn't really a place to heal the sick. It was a way station, to keep inmates with communicable diseases, such as typhus, away from camp guards and the general population in preparation for sending the afflicted to the gas chambers.

Every day or so, some functionary would walk through the hospital, select people for murder and order those so selected to be carried out to the gas chambers. Aware of the operation of the hospital, Sonia gathered up the little strength she had, wrapped herself in a thin blanket and hurried out of the building with two other girls. They hastened to another block which housed Polish, Catholic women, who immediately screamed at them: "Get out Jews." Sonia pleaded with them to let her hide under the bed until the German guard came, selected women to go to the gas chambers and left. The non-Jewish Poles finally agreed. As Sonia remembered it, after 10 to 20 minutes, she came out from under that bed. She exchanged a slice of bread which she had managed to secrete on her person for a teaspoon of sugar from one of the Polish women, who now saw her as a fellow victim. Rachelle brought her a teaspoon of sugar every day.

There was another occasion when Sonia was warned that a guard was on the way to the hospital to look for people to put on the death list. She didn't know how she drew on remaining reserves of her waning strength, but she succeeded in sitting up, swinging her feet to the floor, dragging herself down the hall, putting one foot in front of the other, and managing to shuffle her way to hide in the latrine until she was notified by another inmate that it was safe to return to the hospital building.

Sonia eventually recovered from typhus with no medicine but a daily teaspoon of sugar. She was in terrible shape. She looked emaciated. Before long, an SS-functionary came through the rows during morning roll call. Sonia tried to push out her stomach to look healthier, but to no avail. The Nazi functionary selected her for the gas chamber, writing down her number in his ledger. Hearing of this, her sister Rachelle burst into tears and cried out, "I won't let you go alone; I'll go with you."

Though wracked with worry, Rachelle steeled herself for another mission. She frantically looked around for someone who might help Sonia.

She used her fluency in German during their incarceration to translate letters between non-Jewish Polish women and German or Eastern European Kapos and guards with whom the women had become involved. Now, Rachelle approached one of these women, a woman from Łódź, whom she had met in the camp, who seemed well connected, and told her that Sonia's number was selected for death. The woman said, "Don't tell anyone that I told you, but there's a woman in the camp by the name of Anna, who had Christian papers, and it turned out that the very German who had selected Sonia for death had taken Anna to be his camp lover." She told Rachelle that Anna had successfully hidden her Jewish identity, but she had a "Jewish heart." She had allegedly saved a lot of people. "Go to Anna," she advised Rachelle, "and tell her: 'My sister has a husband in America and he's very wealthy; after the war, he will pay you a lot of money if you save her'."

Rachelle took off running. She found Anna somewhere in the camp. Unable to control herself, she grabbed Anna's hands with both of her hands and burst into tears. She promised Anna that if she could get her German protector to remove Sonia's name from the death list, Abe would reward her handsomely after the war. Anna steadied Rachelle and calmly said to her, "I'll try."

Anna hurried to her German protector and told him that Sonia worked in her Kommando, and that she was her best worker. She needed her and wanted him to take her name off the death list. As soon as she could, Anna sought out Rachelle and told her to tell Sonia not to worry; her German protector had taken her number off the list and she won't be killed. Sonia later admitted, "*You can't imagine how afraid I was.*"

A female guard came into the block and began to call out numbers for the gas chamber. For seconds that felt like hours, Sonia lay on her bunk, holding her breath, terrified that perhaps her name hadn't been taken off the list after all.

How to imagine the terror she felt as each set of numbers was called out by this female guard, a willing cog in the Nazi machinery of death. Sonia later told Abe, "*If I didn't die of a heart attack at that moment, I knew I would never die of a heart attack, because my heart must be very strong.*"

It wasn't until the guard had finished reading aloud the numbers of the sick and disabled who would now be conveyed to the gas chambers or shot and thrown into open burning pits, that Sonia let out her breath, understanding that her number had not been- and would not be called. The "decent" German boyfriend had kept his word. Given the short life expectancy of prisoners in Auschwitz, there was no guarantee that Sonia would survive another month or even a week. But for now, she was safe. "*Every day was another nightmare. It's hard to imagine that people can survive such torture. But my instinct for life was strong.*"

One thing puzzled Sonia. Why was Anna willing to risk her life for her by asking her German protector for a favor, and why did that German agree to Anna's request to save one of her Jews for another day?

Several years later, after the war, Sonia would learn the answer to her question.

Summer, 1944

From the summer of 1944 on, Sonia noticed that the camp administration didn't bother with selections when trains came in. The Jews were sent directly to the gas chambers and the crematoria. Sonia thought that the Germans kept her and her compatriots alive to help fool the new arrivals into thinking that this was a labor camp where they were coming to work, not to be killed.

That summer, between May 15 and July 9, the Jews of Hungary who had survived until 1944, were deported from Hungary's countryside to Auschwitz and were murdered, as fast as the gas chambers and crematoria could operate. Some 437,000 Hungarian Jews were deported to Auschwitz and nearly all of them were murdered in the gas chambers. *"We would sit in the camp and look at the smoke rising from the crematoria and we would ask, 'where is God? Why is he doing this? Is He going to allow every Jew in Europe to be killed?' The smoke and fire from the burning people went up to the sky."*

Along with the other prisoners, Sonia would look up at the sky to see Allied Air Forces bombers flying overhead on bombing missions to the nearby Buna synthetic rubber plant. They prayed for the planes to bomb the gas chambers and the crematoria. They failed to understand why the Allies stood by and never tried to destroy the killing facilities or, at least, the railway lines leading to the camp.

Catastrophe. The Gunpowder Plot and the Wajcblum Cousins

As Sonia witnessed the trains rumbling into Auschwitz that summer of 1944, so too did the *Sonderkommandos*. It was their job to handle the bodies in the gas chambers and take them to the crematoria. Across all the death camps, it was routine procedure to murder all *Sonderkommandos* after about three months of working. The Nazis didn't want *Sonderkommandos* warning incoming victims. They also feared that surviving *Sonderkommandos* could serve as witnesses to the Nazi crimes if Allied troops liberated the various camps before the camps' staffs could destroy them. Finally, the Nazis wanted to prevent the possibility, no matter how unlikely, that *Sonderkommandos* could organize a revolt against the camps' guards and commanders. And that's exactly what happened.

The *Sonderkommandos* of Auschwitz determined to launch a revolt against their Nazi overseers. Once they learned that there was a small group of young teens who worked at the munitions factory and wanted to help the revolt by smuggling gunpowder to the organizers, the *Sonderkommandos* developed a plan to blow up the crematoria which they determined were softer targets than the gas chambers.

Sonia's cousin, Esther Wajcblum (nicknamed Estusia), had also been shipped to Auschwitz. She was assigned to work in the Union Munitions factory. Sonia didn't know how gunpowder was smuggled out of the factory into the hands of the Sonderkommandos. We now know, because Estusia's older sister, cousin Hanka, described in her own memoir how the girls who worked in the factory were able to do the smuggling.[2] Estusia was a young teenage girl, a ballerina, who was convinced by the 16-year-old Hanka to participate in the plan. Four teenage girls, Ala Gertner, Regina Safirztajn, Roza Robota and Estusia Wajcblum, succeeded, day-by-day, to smuggle gunpowder in small quantities through the gates. They avoided detection during the daily searches at the end of the workday and managed to bring the gunpowder to the *Sonderkommandos*.

An unknown inmate, Kapo or German spy planted amongst the prisoners, informed the camp guards about the plot, forcing the *Sonderkommandos* to put their revolt into action earlier than they intended. On October 7, 1944, the *Sonderkommandos* put to good use the smuggled gunpowder that they had put in shoe polish tins and rigged as explosives. They did succeed in blowing up Crematorium IV, one of the five crematoria in Auschwitz, slowing down the Nazi killing. Instead of having the ability to burn the gassed prisoners' bodies using all the crematoria, the Nazis lost 20 percent of their capacity to dispose of bodies. Their solution was to burn bodies on pyres or in pits, causing an even more terrible smell than usual to waft across the fields and barracks of the camp. But their efficient slaughter was reduced to some degree.

The partial success of the Sonderkommando revolt shocked the Nazis, who feared general uprisings across the entire network of camps. The orders came down from Berlin to treat the known perpetrators harshly. The four girls were quickly identified and tortured cruelly by torture experts who wanted to extract information and names of all the conspirators in the revolt. The *Sonderkommandos* who had blown up crematorium IV had all been caught and shot immediately upon their identification after the first explosion. Fearing additional sabotage, the camp administrators wanted to know the identities of those who could be a future threat to their rule. The only names (or numbers) given out by the girls were those of the Sonderkommandos who were already dead. None of the girls broke under torture (though Hanka writes that Ala, under savage beatings and brutal torture, revealed the names of Roza and Estusia). According to witnesses, their bodies had literally been broken under torture. Regina had not been involved with the smuggling, but she was the girls' supervisor and therefore suffered the same fate as they did. For revenge, and as a warning to the camp's population, all the inmates – Sonia among them – were lined up for *Appell* and forced to watch the murder by hanging of these four young girls on January 5, 1945 – barely two weeks before Soviet soldiers entered and liberated Auschwitz.

Hanka suffered symptoms of guilt after liberation, because she was the one who had convinced her sister, Estusia, to participate in the gunpowder smuggling. Hanka survived, met and married Joshua. They moved to Canada, raised two daughters and lived to enjoy grandchildren. Hanka overcame the trauma of the Holocaust and worked as an award-winning social worker.

The Death Marches

In November 1944, the order had come down to the Auschwitz commandant to prepare to evacuate the camp.[3] Evacuations began in December, and on January 18, 1945, the main evacuation took place. Sonia was among one of those groups of prisoners evacuated from the camp. Inmates heard shooting and exploding artillery shells. Sonia remembered "it was like music to our ears." They didn't go to work, because the German guards were afraid to take them, fearing that Russian forces were not far off. When Russian troops were approaching only a few kilometers from the camp, German guards came and ordered all prisoners to get out. One of Sonia's friends said she wasn't going, "The Russians are coming, I'm not going." The Germans didn't search the camp, and some of the prisoners who stayed behind were liberated on January 27, 1945, when Russian troops entered the camp.

Six years earlier, the Red Army had invaded eastern Poland as political allies of the Nazis and had begun their own persecution of the Polish population. Fewer than two years later, the Soviets were violently thrown out of the eastern Polish territory that they had invaded and illegally incorporated into the U.S.S.R. Now the powerful and victorious Soviet armies returned to Poland, crushing the *Wehrmacht,* liberating concentration camps and witnessing the human remains of death camps. However, they were to become brutal occupiers of Poland, not to leave until the collapse of the Soviet empire more than 40 years later.

Sonia had not attempted to hide in the camp to avoid the new exodus. She was taken – destination unknown – along with some 26,000 other Auschwitz prisoners on one of what came to be known as the "Death Marches", so called because so many of those on the marches did not survive the brutal treks. The *Führerbefehl* or "Führer order" had come down to the camps: no living prisoner was to fall into the hands of the advancing Allied armies. The Führer and Himmler didn't want witnesses to their monstrous crimes testifying about them to the Allied victors. In the event, Himmler did not order the murder of all prisoners in the camps. For one thing, logistically, it was impossible to dispose of hundreds of thousands of new corpses. Finding the newly killed bodies might have enraged the Soviet and Allied soldiers who would enter the camp, making the guilt of Himmler so much more prominent. In addition, Himmler may have thought of using the surviving prisoners as hostages to be traded to the Allies as a sign of his humanity. As for the prisoners who died on the marches, they could be said to have died of "natural" causes during their evacuations to "safety."

Those on the march who were so starved and exhausted, or suffered from frozen and frostbitten feet that they could no longer walk, stumbled onto the road or tumbled into the snowbanks. They were promptly shot and killed where they lay by their Nazi guards, who often acted on their own initiative. Some of the marchers succeeded in running away at night and going into hiding. The Germans were terrified of the Russian armies behind them and didn't want to spend time searching for escapees, so a few succeeded in escaping, some finding food and lodging with sympathetic, local Polish families. Seven thousand inmates who had succeeded in remaining behind were shot and killed by their Nazi captors before the camp was liberated by the Red Army.

Sonia thinks she and Rachelle walked some three to ten days until they all were forced to board a train for Germany. The first stop was Bergen-Belsen. But the camp commandant didn't want them;

apparently there was no room at the "inn." The prisoners were ordered to lie down on the ground. For sure, they finally were to meet their death at the hands of their guards. But that was not to be. Instead, exhausted and starving, the prisoners again boarded a train which took them to Ravensbrück, the sole camp the Nazis had built to house women only.

Among the prisoners was British Special Operations Executive agent Odette Sansom Churchill (no relation to Winston), New York Mayor Fiorello La Guardia's sister, Gemma, and two other surviving British spies, women of the SOE. Sonia must have been among the 7,000 women transferred from Auschwitz to Ravensbrück. Of the over 50,000 Auschwitz prisoners who set out on the marches, at least 15,000 fell dead or were murdered. Of those who ended up in Bergen-Belsen, Ravensbrück, Neuengamme, Mauthausen, Flossenburg, Buchenwald, Mittelbau-Dora or Gross-Rosen or other destinations, additional hundreds or thousands perished. Many were murdered, and many died from abuse and starvation. Working in the shoe Kommando assuredly contributed greatly to Sonia's and Rachelle's survival on their Death March. Survivors have commented that those who marched through the snow barefoot in wooden clogs or feet wrapped in rags often suffered severe frostbite, became unable to walk and ended up freezing to death or shot by the *SS* guards as they stumbled or fell. Before leaving Auschwitz, Sonia succeeded in finding for herself and Rachelle leather shoes or boots and some coats that kept them alive during the brutal march. Sonia and Rachelle remained in Ravensbrück for three weeks.

The war was coming to an end. The commandant of Ravensbrück, Fritz Suhren, was ordered to clear out the camp of prisoners who could march and to kill those who were sick or unable to walk. Selections were made daily and the unfortunate ones were either murdered by poison gas in Ravensbrück's one or possibly two gas chambers or mobile gassing vans, were shot to death, poisoned, deliberately starved or forced to stand outside naked or nearly so in order to freeze to death. Their bodies were burned in the crematorium or on pyres to hide the evidence of their murder. So, too, were camp records and documents burned and the gas chamber dismantled after the last gassing on April 24 or 25. Barracks and other buildings were destroyed, and small trees or saplings were planted to cover up their prior existence. It wouldn't do for the approaching Red Army or American troops to find evidence and witnesses of the crimes committed in the Nazi archipelago of camps.

Between January and March, some 2,000 women were transported from Ravensbrück to Buchenwald subcamps and others to Dachau, Flossenburg and Neustadt-Glewe, Mecklenburg.[4] Sonia and Rachelle were among those sent in February to Neustadt-Glewe, a subcamp of Ravensbrück. Between February and April 1945, author Sarah Helm estimates some 6,000 women were marched into the woods around Ravensbrück and murdered.

Having been selected to work at Neustadt-Glewe saved Sonia and Rachelle from death. They worked at the Dornier Works aircraft facility that had been relocated to Neustadt-Glewe in September 1944. In April 1945, Germany's new high-altitude fighter plane, the fastest piston-driven German plane, began to fly out of Neustadt-Glewe. It seems that Sonia and Rachelle were used as slave labor in producing or repairing airfoils for aircraft or in the assembly of aircraft engines or undercarriages.[5]

They didn't have much food. Even the Germans at that point didn't have food. They were not beaten, but the living conditions were terrible. The women were crowded into storage rooms, factory halls and barracks with no heat and inadequate toileting facilities.[6] Sonia actually said that there were Germans who *were kind to us.* By that point in the war, about half of all German guards at concentration and labor camps were older *Wehrmacht* reservists, mostly in their 40s and 50s,[7] who were considered unfit for combat. Sonia couldn't forget that one man wearing a Nazi uniform seemed distant from the prisoners when he was with other guards, but when he was alone with them, he would say to them *langsam, langsam* or "take it easy" or "slowly." She called him "*a good German.*"[8]

We didn't have the strength to work. And the good German who didn't force us past exhaustion, saved us from death.

Sonia and the others heard the whine and explosions of bombs or artillery rounds falling and exploding around them. The women were hoping that the bombs wouldn't kill them but felt that if they were killed by American bombs, that would be preferable to being killed by the Germans.

Rescue, but not yet true liberation

Sonia worked in slave labor in Neustadt-Glewe for about two and a half months. One morning they woke up and there was no *Appell.* And no guards. All the Germans and Baltic or Ukrainian guards had fled. The prisoners were apparently by themselves. Alone for two days, Sonia recalled many people going to the storehouses of food that had fed the German guards to find some food to satisfy their desperate hunger. Many of them, simply trying to survive after years of hunger and near death, ate more than their system could absorb. Their bodies couldn't tolerate the amount of food on which they gorged, and many of them died. These victims of Nazi brutality had survived beatings, torture, exhaustion and starvation. On what should have been the days of their liberation from brutal captivity, they died from their first opportunity to eat freely.

Sonia and Rachelle were liberated on May 2, 1945, the same day that Berlin fell to the Red Army, barely two days after Hitler's suicide. Russian soldiers, marching west, were the first to arrive at Neustadt-Glewe. The survivors were actually suspicious and afraid of the Russians. They were happy to see them as liberators, but the women, most of them half-dead, looking like skeletons, were nonetheless afraid they would be raped by their liberators. Many women lay on the ground in Neustadt-Glewe pretending to be near death – certainly looking the part.

Sonia, a Russian-speaker, sought out a Russian officer whom she saw sitting tall and straight on a horse, looking like a warrior-savior. She told him that she had a husband in America. What was the best way to find Abe? To go back to Poland or someplace else? The murderous attacks against returning Jews that would take place in Rzeszow on June 11 and in Krakow on August 11 had obviously not yet occurred. Rumors swirled that in a dozen Polish towns Jews had been killed by Polish Home Army partisans.[9] But it was unlikely that Sonia had heard these rumors. Well-informed about the brutal Soviet reoccupation of Poland, or perhaps knowledgeable about the chaos and danger to returning Jewish Poles, the Russian officer said, "I am a Jew, too. Go to another country in Western Europe, like Italy or Belgium, do not go back to Poland."

A short time later, elements of the American 7th Army that had met up with Soviet army troops in Schwerin rolled into Neustadt-Glewe, a half-hour drive away. The survivors were filled with joy at the sight of American troops. They had no fear at all of the American soldiers. The arrival of the Americans likely prevented the mass rapes of the camp survivors by Red Army troops who are known to have committed such atrocities in camps that they liberated.

The Americans who came in were wonderful. They took care of us. They gave us food; they sent the sick ones to hospital.

Upon her liberation, Sonia weighed somewhere between 80 and 90 pounds and Rachelle was probably in similar shape. After surviving the Death March and further work at the aircraft facility, one may wonder how they had the presence of mind to make decisions about what to do and where to go. Sonia didn't want to go to a nearby hospital; she wanted to get out of Germany.

Acting upon the Russian officer's advice, she and Rachelle attached themselves to a group of Belgian girls who were being transported to a hospital in a displaced persons camp in Brussels, Belgium. The Joint Distribution committee (JDC), a Jewish charitable organization operating in Belgium took them under its wing. After a month or so in the hospital, nursed back to health, fed small portions of food gradually increased over time, Sonia and Rachelle looked increasingly like normal human beings. They were given clothes, food, a small amount of money and moved to a hotel. After a short time, they were transferred to a private home where an older, childless couple, the Blumenfelds, hosted them.

When she had gained some weight and recovered some strength, Sonia approached the Jewish organization, Hebrew Immigrant Aid Society (HIAS) for help in finding Abe. They said to her, "Give us his name and the town where he's living, and we'll find him." All she knew was that Abe had relatives in the Bronx and that's where he must be living.

HIAS put ads in five newspapers, including a German language, Jewish newspaper, the *Aufbau* ("Development") published in New York City at 67 West 44th Street.

From 1944 through 1946, the *Aufbau* had been publishing the names of survivors looking for relatives in the United States. On June 8, 1945, on page 27, the ad for Sonia and Rachelle Huberman looking for Abraham Huberman made it to print. Not long afterwards, someone from HIAS informed Sonia that they had found her husband. Sonia was tearful and ecstatic and momentarily pushed from her mind all that she had gone through, just looking forward to her reunion with Abe.

Abe contacted her by telegram. He was able to send Sonia and her sister money and packages of food and clothing. He initially wired Sonia 500 dollars, a significant amount of money at the time. He continued to send Sonia money and packages until the time when arrangements could be made for her travel to the U.S. The greatest gift that Abe ultimately sent Sonia was an affidavit that would allow her to immigrate to the United States.

After connecting with Abe, Sonia wrote him a letter in Yiddish describing what she had been through in the previous seven years. At the urging of a friend, Abe brought her letter and another one that Hanka had written, to a Yiddish language newspaper in New York, *Der Tag* ("The Day"), which went on to publish Sonia's letter on December 31, 1945. It may have been one of the earliest first-person accounts of a survivor's experience to be published in the U.S. press. Sonia began her letter:

My dearest, most beloved husband in the whole world, I received your first letter today. I am so ecstatic that I wasn't able to sleep at night. I am the luckiest person in the world that I still have you. Everything else I have lost. I survived much, but when I think of you, then I still want to live. In the camps, many of the girls committed suicide. It wasn't hard for them. Every day, another one went to the electric wires. Many times, I also wanted to do it, because life was so hard. We suffered hunger and cold. They used vicious dogs to chase us to work. Life was very hard. Every day, girls went to the electric wires, and every morning fifty to sixty were found dead, draped across the barbed wire. So death was better than such a life. But when I wanted to do it, Rachelle would tell me, "Sister, you have to live for your husband." And that is what saved me from death.

She concluded her letter with these words:

So, willingly, I put myself on a transport... [to] Auschwitz. What I lived through there, I will write to you in my next letter.

Of Sonia's next letter to Abe, we have found no trace. Abe, who saved all his important letters and documents, apparently didn't save that letter. We can only imagine why.

---

1. Huberman
2. Heilman
3. Blatman, pp. 79-126 (especially p. 97)
4. This is confirmed by Anna Heilman in her memoir, p. 72. Also, for recent scholarship on Ravensbrück see: Helm, Sarah.
5. Encyclopedia of Camps and Ghettos, 1933-1945, pp. 1216f.

6. *Idem.*
7. Shepard, *op.cit.* p. 475.
8. Survivors did refer to *Anständige Männer* or "decent men," who might have been called in 1940s slang "stand-up guys," or today: "upstanders." The term is relative in that environment.
9. Department of State.

17

THE REST OF THE STORY

*Life is lived forward
and understood backward.*
Holman W. Jenkins Jr.[1]

What if France had upheld its defense agreement with Poland?

Had the French with their superior numbers, and in some cases more advanced armaments (e.g. the Char tank)[2], attacked Germany by September 3, 1939, they would have decimated the German forces arrayed against them. The Polish armies could then have squeezed the German forces retreating west to protect their homeland, while the French and British forces attacked East. This would more likely than not have forestalled the Soviets from invading Poland entirely. The German generals, who had opposed the Nazi war against Poland, in concert with Colonel Hans Oster's group that had been planning a coup to depose Hitler, would likely have arrested Hitler and Himmler and taken down the whole Nazi regime.

Chief of Staff from 1944 to 1945, Lieutenant General Siegfried Westphal, said it plainly in an essay after the war: "The West Wall, or Siegfried line as it was known abroad, was still unfinished and very far from being 'unassailable;' during the Polish campaign it had been manned by a mere 35 German divisions, the great majority of which were ill-trained reserve or home-defense units. The French Field Army consisted of 65 active and 45 reserve divisions. If this Army had launched a major offensive on a broad front against the German security forces manning the frontier... there is little doubt that they could have broken through... Such an attack, launched before any considerable elements of the German army could be brought across from Poland would almost certainly have carried the French to the Rhine with little trouble, and might well have seen them across the river." Westphal added drily: "The subsequent course of the war would then have been very different."[3]

Preventing Disbelief

Even after the war ended and concentration camps were uncovered or liberated by American and British troops, there were still those who disbelieved the reports of mass murder and genocide. For this reason, Supreme Allied Commander, General Dwight D. Eisenhower ("Ike"), after visiting the Ohrdruf Camp, cabled Chief of General Staff, George Marshall, requesting him to bring over to Europe as quickly as practicable, congressmen and journalists to visit "one of these places where the evidence of brutality and cruelty is so overpowering as to leave no doubts in their minds about the normal practices of the Germans in these camps." Eisenhower predicted that in the future there would be those who would deny that these things ever happened. Ike wanted unquestionably reliable witnesses from America to report on what they would see. On April 22, 1945, six senators and six members of the House of Representatives left Washington, D.C. for Europe. The next day, 18 journalists left for Europe. Joseph Pulitzer, the prominent publisher of the *St. Louis Post Dispatch* didn't take long to change from skeptic to witness: "I came here in a suspicious frame of mind, feeling that I would find that many of the terrible reports that have been printed in the U.S. before I left were exaggerations, and largely propaganda, comparable to reports of crucifixions and amputations of hands which followed the last war, and which subsequently proved to be untrue. It is my grim duty to report that the descriptions of the horrors of the camp, one of many which have been, and which will be uncovered by the Allied armies have given less than the whole truth. They have been understatements."[4]

The horrors of Ohrdruf witnessed by Pulitzer, and those of Bergen-Belsen, opened by British troops, as horrible as they were, paled in comparison to the industrial death factories of Chelmno, Belzec, Treblinka, Sobibor, Majdanek and Auschwitz-Birkenau/Monowitz.

Those were not ordinary Tears

When Sonia had got back some strength, she began to search for surviving family or friends. One of the people she hoped to find was Anna from Lublin. Anna was the Jewish woman with false papers, imprisoned in Auschwitz, who succeeded in getting her German protector to take Sonia's name off the list for immediate murder by gas.

Sonia asked everyone she ran into if they knew of Anna from Lublin and if so, did they know whether or not she had survived and where could she be found. By chance, she did eventually locate Anna. They hugged and kissed. Sonia finally had the opportunity to ask her why she had stuck her neck out to ask her German protector to take her name off the death list. Anna took Sonia's hand in her two hands, holding them tightly together:

"Sonia, when your sister came to me to ask me for assistance in saving you, I hesitated, because I was afraid for myself. Your sister, Rachelle, grabbed my hand, as I am holding your hand today and squeezed it tightly. She broke down. Her whole body trembled and tears poured out of her eyes and rolled down her face. They dripped onto my hands. I swear to you, what I saw then was that these were not normal tears, I saw tears of blood dripping from her eyes, the red drops spilling down her face and like heavy drops of bloody rain falling on my hands. I understood that this was a sign from God – I must do what I can to save you. I told my German protector what had happened and that you were a good worker and you were strong. You would recover from your illness and you would return to work. He agreed to strike your name from the list. But I don't think that he did it because I told him you were a good worker. He had been a religious man before the war and I think he felt some guilt over what the Nazis were doing. After the destruction of the German army at Stalingrad, everyone, even most of the Nazis, knew that the war was lost. He was afraid that he would have to pay for participating in the Nazi crimes against the Jews. He, too, thought that your sister's tears of blood were a sign from God, and for that reason he agreed to save you."

Sonia thanked her profusely and the two hugged for the last time.

Volunteering for Auschwitz saved Sonia's and Rachelle's lives

Majdanek was one of the 15 camps in the area of Lublin, Poland. It served as a labor, transit and extermination camp. With the destruction of the Warsaw ghetto, some 40,000 Warsaw Jews were deported to the Lublin camps, with 16,000 sent to Majdanek at the end of April and the beginning of May 1943. Those not killed immediately were used for hard labor in construction, trades[5] or make-work around the camp. That's what Sonia was doing when she was carrying stones from one part of the camp to another. In response to the Auschwitz commander's request for labor, 5,000 prisoners in Majdanek were sent to Auschwitz in five transports from May to July 1943. As we know, Sonia and Rachelle volunteered to be on one of those transports in June.[6]

It is difficult to read about what was happening in Majdanek. Recruited into the *SS*, Germans along with *Hiwis*, primarily from Central and Eastern Europe such as Ukrainians and Lithuanians, were given uniforms, clubs, whips and were dispatched to concentration camps like Majdanek as sentries or guards, allowed to discipline prisoners according to superiors' orders. That Sonia and Rachelle survived the few weeks they were in Majdanek is simply miraculous.

But the end for the Jews in Majdanek came early in November 1943. Himmler had been shocked by the Warsaw and Bialystok ghetto uprisings, and the rebellions and escapes from the death camps Sobibor and Treblinka. In response, on October 14, 1943, he ordered the "liquidation" of the Jews in the Lublin camps. On November 3, a hundred *SS* men entered the camp. Approximately 18,000 Jews in Majdanek and another 24,000 from surrounding camps were shot to death on that one day. Called by non-Jewish survivors of the massacre, "bloody Wednesday," the *Aktion* had been given by the Germans the code name *Erntefest* (Harvest Festival).[7] Had Sonia not volunteered in June for the labor battalion to Auschwitz, dragging her sister along with her, it is very unlikely that either one would have survived at the latest, past November 3, 1943.

The Nanny

Lunia, the nanny, somehow survived the war. She succeeded in immigrating to Israel, where Sonia and Abe visited her in the 1950s. They helped her financially and remained in contact until her passing.

The Woman on the transport

In April 1983, Sonia attended the first Holocaust reunion for survivors, held in Washington, D.C. While walking about a ballroom or lobby, Sonia and Chana (first name unclear but may be "Chuma" or "Ruchla") Siekierka recognized each other and fell into each other's arms. The woman who had helped Sonia hold the children in the cattle car deportation from Warsaw to Majdanek had also survived the war. And now, the two fell into a spirited and happy conversation about their lives since that time.

The Brother-in-Law

Sonia's cousin, Zalman, who had been responsible for persuading Abe to come to America for the World's Fair in 1939, lost his wife and three children in the Holocaust. He became a successful businessman in the United States. After the war, he married a Jewish-Polish woman, Ola, who had survived by pretending to be Catholic. She worked as a housekeeper for a non-Jewish Pole on the Aryan side of Warsaw. Zalman and Ola had one child, Helen, one of Gloria's few and closest cousins.

74 Zelazna Street, Warsaw

In the *Wehrmacht* assault against Poland in September 1939, at least five percent of Warsaw's buildings were destroyed and 40 percent heavily damaged by the bombing and shelling of the city. Because Abe's building was situated outside the ghetto, it survived the German assault and razing of the Jewish ghetto in April-May 1943. By the time of the failed Polish uprising against the German and Hiwi forces in Warsaw in August 1944, an estimated 90 percent of all of Warsaw's buildings had been cumulatively destroyed since September 1, 1939. The German commander, Erich von dem Bach Zelewski, followed his orders from Berlin: "The city must completely disappear from the surface of the earth and serve only as a transport station for the Wehrmacht. No stone can remain standing. Every building must be razed to its foundation."

Demolition squads using flamethrowers and explosives went from building to building, destroying nearly every remaining structure in the city.

Abe's building at 74 Zelazna street remained standing. One-third of the building ("one wing") had been wrecked by German fire, but two-thirds remained intact. After the war, the building was repaired by the Soviet puppet government in Poland. On April 19, 1949, six years to the day after the Nazis invaded the ghetto to liquidate it, the Communist government of Poland seized and nationalized 74 Zelazna as state property.

The State Department

On January 13, 1944, after the vast majority of the Jews of Europe had already been slaughtered, the "Report to the Secretary on the Acquiescence of This Government in the Murder of the Jews" was submitted to Secretary of the Treasury Henry Morgenthau Jr. by Treasury officials Josiah E. DuBois, Randolph Paul and John Pehle. In his introduction, DuBois wrote: "One of the greatest crimes in history, the slaughter of the Jewish people in Europe is continuing unabated. This Government has for a long time maintained that its policy is to work out programs to serve those Jews of Europe who could be saved. I am convinced on the basis of the information which is available to me that certain officials in our State Department, which is charged with carrying out this policy, have been guilty not only of gross procrastination and willful failure to act, but even of willful attempts to prevent action from being taken to rescue Jews from Hitler. I fully recognize the graveness of this statement and I make it only after having most carefully weighed the shocking facts which have come to my attention during the last several months."[8]

Days after the document was given to President Roosevelt by Morgenthau, Roosevelt created, six years after the stillborn Evian Conference, the War Refugee Board, an agency whose mission was to aid the civilian victims of the Axis powers.

The Nazis

Jurgen Stroop, the *SS* commander who had crushed the Warsaw ghetto uprising, destroying the ghetto, killing thousands of Jews and sending the survivors to concentration camps, was caught after the war and tried by a U.S. military tribunal for his murder of nine American airmen who had been shot down during the war.

Condemned to death, he was nonetheless turned over to a Polish court for a second trial. He was convicted of mass murder and again sentenced to death on July 23, 1951. He was hanged at Mokotow Prison in Warsaw on March 6, 1952. And Jurgen Stroop, one might note in his previous own words, *besteht nicht mehr* ("was no more.")

Sonia would survive Stroop by 50 years.

Rudolph Höss, the longest serving commandant of Auschwitz was captured by British forces in March 1946 and stood trial in Nuremberg. He was turned over to a Polish court which condemned him to death on April 2, 1947. The executioners brought him to Auschwitz. At the site of the former Gestapo office on the grounds of the former camp, Höss was hanged on April 16, 1947, six weeks after Sonia had given birth to her first American child, Mark.

Sonia would survive Höss by 55 years.

Hermann Florstedt, the third of five Majdanek commandants, was the *SS* commandant of Majdanek during Sonia's incarceration and the murderer of her children. He was arrested and executed on April 15, 1945 by fellow *SS* officers for the crime of stealing for himself gold and valuables from Jewish victims instead of turning the stolen loot over to the Reich's coffers.

Sonia would survive Florstedt by 57 years.

Dr. Bruno Kitt sent Jewish arrivals at Auschwitz to either hard labor or death. He was the gatekeeper who had chosen Sonia and Rachelle at Majdanek to come to Auschwitz and sentenced them by the flick of his swagger stick to hard labor, sparing them from the gas chambers. He was tried by the British at the Neuengamme war crimes trial as an accessory to war crimes and murder committed at the Neuengamme concentration camp. His death sentence was carried out on October 8, 1946.

Sonia would survive Kitt by 56 years.

Fritz Suhren, commander of Ravensbrück when Sonia arrived, was ultimately found in his hiding place in Bavaria and tried by a French military tribunal in 1949. He was executed on June 12, 1950. Sonia's second American child, Gloria, was 13 months old at the time.

Sonia would survive Suhren by 52 years.

---

1. Mr. Jenkins' felicitous turn of phrase derives from Danish philosopher Soren Kierkegaard: Journals IV A 164 (1843) who credits the phrase to: "as the philosophers say."
2. On May 17, 1940 during the Nazi invasion of France, a Char took 25 German antitank gun hits before the 26th hit disabled it. On the 16th a single Char B had attacked a Panzer column and destroyed 13 Panzers and two antitank guns, surviving 140 antitank hits without a single penetration. Frieser, p. 39.
3. Richardson & Freidlin, p. 3.
4. Van Pelt, p. 133
5. Marszalek, op.cit. pp. 103ff.
6. ibid. p. 70.
7. Ibid. pp. 130-134.
8. Medoff, p. 40.

18

THE REUNION

As time passed, Abe abandoned his optimism about the survival of his extended family and children, but he clung to his belief that Sonia would survive He had brought photographs of the family with him on his trip to the United States and continued to receive some photos from Sonia until postal service between the United States and Germany was terminated. Abe kept a picture of Sonia attached to the dashboard of his car. He spoke to that picture as if he were talking to Sonia. He dreamed of her and talked to her as if she were present in his daily life. After Victory in Europe Day in May 1945, his cousins finally started to say to him, "How can you think your wife is alive? Hitler has killed all the Jews. You have no hope, they're all dead, face it. It's nearly a month after liberation and you haven't heard from her, she's dead." Abe responded in his slow, firm voice, "No, she is alive." When Abe got an idea in his head in which he truly believed, there was no dissuading him. He would not allow himself to think that Sonia had not survived.

In the second week of June 1945, one of Abe's customers came into his store and showed him the ad that HIAS had placed in the *Aufbau*, and said, "Abe, is this your wife and sister? They're looking for an Abraham Huberman." Rachelle wasn't his sister but his sister-in-law. And it was, indeed, his beloved Sonia. His heart leapt with joy. There were tears. Many tears. Tears of joy mixed with tears of sadness. But mostly tears of gratitude, happiness and hope.

Abe sent Sonia money and packages of food and clothing. With the money he sent, Sonia was able to leave the home of the older couple that had hosted her and Rachelle in Belgium, and rented an apartment with Rachelle and their cousin, Hanka.

Sonia was initially angry with Abe for not having come to Europe immediately after liberation to see her. Abe also regretted that he hadn't gone to Belgium to see Sonia; but he kept thinking that she would be arriving soon, and also felt that he had a business to run and didn't feel he could just pick up and leave. It is likely that it was all to the good for Sonia to remain in Europe for a year. She was surrounded by survivors, especially her sister, in a relatively familiar European environment, in a sense, debriefing with Rachelle and others with similar experiences. It is more than likely that this post-war year gave her the opportunity to heal and recover. Had she "parachuted" into the United States before any physical or psychological healing, without the company of other newly liberated survivors, she might not have fared so well. There are many reports of the suffering of survivors who came to the United States after the war wanting to talk about their experiences and hearing from family denial and refusal to listen to their stories.

In the interim, Abe asked a relative, Manya Grossbaum, whose husband, Sam, was the owner of the furniture store, to help him furnish the apartment that he had rented for himself and Sonia. He wanted Sonia to be able to walk into a fully furnished and stocked apartment, so she would not want for anything when she arrived in her new home.

It took 11 months before Sonia was able to come to the United States. First, she was recuperating in Belgium from the physical and psychological effects of the war. Second, Abe had to secure an immigration visa for Sonia. Third, Sonia had to find passage on a ship. Not so easy a task, as U.S. troops coming home filled up most of the ships sailing from Europe.

As the former president of the New York night schools' student body, Abe was able to get members of the New York Board of Education to write a letter to the American Consul in Brussels to request that he issue a visa to Sonia at the earliest possible time. Abe had apparently also learned how to behave as a genuine American. He made an appointment to visit Congressman Bloom in his New York office, and gave him a "nice" campaign donation, then got down to business and asked him to write a letter to the American Consul requesting him to grant Sonia a visa as soon as possible. The congressman was happy to oblige.

Finally, Sonia was able to get a berth along with only 11 other passengers on a freighter, the USS Henry W Longfellow, Liberty ship #0185. Examining the ship's passenger manifest reveals that one of the other passengers, Lucienne, who was listed on the ship's manifest as ten years of age, didn't know her family name, where she was born nor what her last permanent address was. She must have been one of the many Holocaust orphans. On that ship's manifest, Sonia had listed her last permanent address as Auschwitz.

The Longfellow set sail from Antwerp and landed in Charleston, South Carolina on April 29, 1946. Abe traveled by train from New York to Charleston to meet her. In one of the many coincidences of their lives, a local military chaplain, Rabbi Goldfarb, also met the ship when it docked in Charleston. It turned out that Rabbi Goldfarb would later serve as the Rabbi of Temple Israel in Long Beach, New York, the city to which Abe and his family moved in 1949.

For Sonia, April was never the month of April Fools, for her it was always a month of remembrance and celebration. Sonia would later write that she was so happy to come to America, "such a wonderful country," adding, "I am proud to be an American."

Rachelle was not so lucky in getting early passage to the United States. Though Abe worked to get her a visa, it took another year or so until he was able to get a visa for her to come to America. During her stay in Belgium, Rachelle met a charming and brilliant German-Jewish, polyglot refugee from Germany, Henry ("Hans") Lax, and the two of them married and later had one child, Peter.

Henry, himself, had a dramatic story of wartime survival. He spent the entire war living in Berlin, Germany. He was hidden by German Gentiles in a below-ground space in the garage of their moving company. After a while, when it became clear that Henry was a talented polyglot, his employers recommended him for a different job. A German, Gentile woman who must go down in history as one of the bravest individuals, took Henry into her home, where he lived in some kind of crawl space. Even more incredibly, she got him a job in the office in which she worked: the Bureau for the Purification of the German Language. The irony was not lost on Henry. If not for the danger, the circumstances of his life working in that office and living in the home of the German secretary to the SS-man who ran the office, would have led Henry to walk around with a perpetual smile on his face. In the event, his life always hung in the balance. He had no official identity papers. Had he been stopped by a member of any police agency, it would have been the end for him.

Henry used to say that when he could not bear to be cooped up in his hiding places, he ventured out and attended an unending series of movies and stage plays, just to stay off the streets. He always was the last to get on a bus or trolley in order to ensure that there were no Gestapo officers on board. One time he thought he was the last to get on a trolley and made himself comfortable in a seat. Suddenly, two obvious Gestapo officers jumped onto the trolley and began to walk down the aisle asking everyone for his papers. Henry appeared calm enough, reading his German newspaper, while his pulse raced. His thought was *the jig is up*. Then he began to cough. He grasped his handkerchief and pressed it to his mouth, gasping and coughing as if trying to bring up phlegm from the bottom of his feet. The Gestapo agents walked briskly past him and got off the trolley, having asked all the passengers for their papers while ignoring Henry. He later reported to his son, Peter, that the Nazis must have feared getting close to this German civilian who they thought must have been suffering from tuberculosis or some other communicable disease.

After the war ended, Henry was recruited as a civilian employee by the American army to translate documents from German and French into English to aid the Americans in their search for Nazi war criminals.

Abe ultimately learned of an apartment coming vacant in the apartment building in which he was living in the Bronx, so he rented it for Rachelle and Henry, paying the rent himself for the six months it was vacant until Rachelle and Henry arrived in the United States and moved in.

Abe knew a few of the details of Sonia's ordeal from the letters she had sent him from Belgium. He was wise enough to decide that he would ask Sonia nothing. No questioning. No asking of details. He was patient and controlled himself to simply be with Sonia and listen to her when she wanted to talk. Initially, Sonia said that she couldn't speak of the horrors she had endured. Eventually it all came out. She was not one of the survivors who couldn't or wouldn't speak of her experiences in the ghetto and in the camps. *"At first, I couldn't talk. And my husband was wonderful. He never asked. But I decided I would tell my family everything."*

Over a hundred members of their families were murdered in the Holocaust. Abe's mother had six sisters and they all had husbands and children, cousins, aunts and uncles. Of those who had remained in Europe when war broke out, nobody survived except Sonia and her sister, Rachelle, and the aunt and uncle who had already immigrated to the United States. On Sonia's side, her cousins, Hanka and Saba, survived. Many of the Jaglom side of the family had escaped prior to the war and were safe in the United States, the UK, Belgium and Israel.

On the train ride home to New York, Abe told Sonia the story of his life in America during the previous seven years. He minimized *his* suffering but told Sonia how he had struggled to establish himself, to build a business, studying in night school, so that he too, now had successfully completed higher education. Never for one moment, he told her, did he stop thinking and worrying about her. They cried together over the children, promising each other that they would have children again – if possible.

Abe told Sonia about Julius Solomon, his night school principal, with whom he had become good friends. Abe also told her that he had been faithful to her for the entire seven years they had been separated. And he had had offers. One of the night school teachers, an attractive woman, had fallen in love with him and wanted a romantic relationship. But, related Abe, "I told her I was a married man and was waiting for my wife to join me in America. I couldn't possibly have an intimate relationship with her." Upon hearing this, Sonia said, matter of factly, "Abe, it would have been OK with me. After all, you're a man and seven years is a long time. It would have been alright."

Settling in

Sonia asked Abe if he had an apartment rented for them or if he lived in a room with relatives. Ever the kidder, he told her he had a one-room apartment. She asked if the apartment at least had an indoor toilet. Abe so wanted to surprise Sonia with the lovely apartment that he had provided for her, to see the smile on her face, that he lowered her expectations. "Yes, there was an indoor toilet," he said, "but it was down the hall and was shared by all the people on the floor." Compared to the latrines in Auschwitz and the other camps, a real toilet down the hall was fine. Whatever Abe had available for them would suffice.

They arrived at Grand Central Station and took a cab to 908 Freeman Street in the Bronx. Abe brought Sonia to the four-room apartment, complete with indoor plumbing and a modern bathroom, totally furnished, with drapes, tableware, lamps, everything new and as fine as Abe could find. That evening, they were alone together for the first time in seven years.

Abe wanted Sonia to understand that her life in America would be as beautiful as it had been in Warsaw. She would want for nothing. He went to his desk and took out from a drawer five bank savings books, each from a different bank, which he brought over to show Sonia. He explained to her that each bank book showed a balance of 10,000 dollars, the maximum amount, then, that was insured by the Federal Government. Two days later he took her to each of the banks to add her name to the accounts. In buying power, Abe's 50,000 dollars in 1946 would be equivalent to over 664,000 dollars in today's dollars. Abe, the penniless immigrant, really had saved nearly every penny he had earned between September 1939 and April 1946.

Sonia and Abe moved her father, then aged 78, into the apartment with them. He moved with them when they moved to Long Beach (Lido Beach) on Long Island and lived with them for another four years until he passed away.

19

A NEW LIFE IN AMERICA. FREE AT LAST

They shall live in peace of mind,
with no one to alarm them. - Ezekiel 34:28

In the aftermath of the war and suffering both Sonia and Abe had endured, the most important task they set for themselves was to create a new life in the United States.

Sonia got to know the Bronx and Manhattan. She visited with family. She, too, attended night school to learn English and the civics lessons that would turn her into an American. She graduated from night school in June 1948 and would become a naturalized American citizen on February 19, 1952.

Eleven months after setting foot in the United States, Sonia gave birth to Mark. Two years later, she welcomed the arrival of their daughter, Gloria (born six years to the day after the German commander Jurgen Stroop had blown up Warsaw's main Jewish synagogue and declared that the Jewish ghetto "was no more"). Sonia now could raise her children in the land of the free, without worries about war or noticeable antisemitism.

Abe continued to run his business and enjoy his family. He and Sonia settled into their routine of work and play and raising children. Abe and Sonia also became active in supporting charitable organizations in New York.

Four years after Abe's 1944 night-school essay, he came back to his night school, invited to deliver an address to that year's graduating class of students, which I believe included Sonia. We have three pages of his speech that seems to end rather abruptly and it's not clear if that's the entire speech or if, more than likely, additional pages went missing. It's more sophisticated than the 1944 essay, but reveals the same warmth and kindness, love of America and love of mankind that Abe always felt and exhibited:

Miss Ball, Honored guests, Teacher, Happy Graduates, and Fellow Students.

Tonight, we are all gathered here to celebrate graduation eve.

It reminds me just a few years ago, when I was a student at this school, and how happy I was to be one of the graduates.

Most of my fellow students are of different nationalities. Some of us didn't have the privilege or the opportunity to attend school. But in our new adopted home where we can say "justice and liberty for all," life begins again, and thanks to our free evening schools we are able to learn the American way of life. This is the only country in the whole world where we have free school for adults – free school for everyone who likes to learn.

But I wonder if you all know to whom the credit belongs that 40,000 adults are able to attend free evening classes.

It is sure the credit belongs to our government, as you all know our government is called "by the people, and for the people." The credit belongs to the Board of Education. The credit belongs to our teachers in charge like Miss Ball, who is devoting most of her time to improve adult education. The credit belongs to our wonderful teachers who are so kind in helping us to be good Americans.

There was another man to whom the credit belongs. This man is no more with us. His name was Perry L. Schneider.

Perry L. Schneider, an immigrant child himself, loved America warmly, richly, and deeply. He dedicated his life to sharing his love of country with the foreign born. Perry was a true friend of everyone, young and old. He didn't know the difference between color, creed, or nationality. To him, the whole world was his family.

Perry L. Schneider began teaching adults while he was a student at college. After a whole day of hard work, he devoted his evenings to adult education.

Perry's contribution to the foreign born was recognized all over the country, and gradually he reached a position as Assistant Director of Adult Education.

On April 24, 1948, as always, Perry was sitting at his desk working on problems to improve adult education. In the middle of his work, he remained silent forever.

By 1951, Abe was working long hours in his business. Sonia appreciated his dedication to support the family, but she hated to see how hard he worked. She saw how successful Zalman and his brother Ben were in the diamond business and with a much easier life. She knew how capable Abe was and thought that he could certainly learn the diamond business. He would have a more secure income and would have a much easier life, not having to work six days a week.

Sonia arranged a meeting with her cousin, Ben, and asked him if he could and would teach Abe the diamond business. She said, *"He's working very hard and I think he should change how he makes a living."* Ben agreed and answered, "With pleasure."

Sonia then spoke to Abe about her thoughts on his changing his business and work life. Abe thought it over and said he would consider it. Perhaps he would speak to Zalman or Ben and then he and Sonia would discuss it.

"*Well,*" said Sonia, "*I've already spoken to Ben and he's happy to teach you everything you need to know about buying and selling diamonds.*"

Abe thought to himself, *I asked her to talk to the cousin about the business, and she's already done it!*

At the age of 47, Abe changed careers. In order to work in the wholesale diamond business, Abe needed to become a member of the Diamond Club. At first, when he tried to join, they refused to let him in. His cousin called the Club Board and spoke with them about Abe's character and his flair for business, arguing that there was enough business to go around and the Board should have some consideration for what Abe and Sonia had gone through. After much thought and some delay, the Board finally agreed to allow Abe to become a member of the club. Abe studied with Ben, learning all about diamonds, their shape, color, quality and so on. Abe was a quick learner and apparently had a good eye. He passed all of Ben's informal tests.

Ben bought three diamonds from a diamond cutter and gave them to Abe, telling him to go to diamond dealers door to door in the diamond center at 47th Street and Fifth Avenue and sell the diamonds. Abe sold them in no time and made a 75-dollar profit. He thought that this was wonderful. To earn 75 dollars a day in the shoe business was good; here he made 75 dollars in one hour. Shortly thereafter, Abe closed his shoe supply business and began to work full-time in the diamond business. Not much later, he met a gentleman in the diamond business, Bernard Klapper. They hit it off and became partners. In their division of labor, Bernard bought the diamonds in Belgium or Israel and Abe wholesaled them to the diamond and jewelry trade in New York City. They opened a small office at 580 Fifth Avenue at 47th Street and remained partners and successful businessmen until sometime in the 1970s.

In November 1949, Abe had moved the family to Lido Beach, New York. Lido Beach was a small beach community next to Long Beach, on an island south of Long Island. It was a narrow strip of land bounded on the south side by the ocean and the north by the bay separating the island from Long Island. In the winter there were no more than 30,000 permanent residents, but in the summer the population soared to some 100,000 residents and summer vacationers. Abe and Sonia had visited friends in Lido and Long Beach and thought that this would be a wonderful place to raise children. Mark was almost three years old and Gloria about six months old, when they made the move. They lived in a small house on Fairway Road. Sonia and the children enjoyed the ocean air and the many friends they made. The location was ideal. They lived in a quiet neighborhood only a few blocks from the ocean, far away from the hustle and bustle of New York City and the Bronx. Most wonderful were the 17 fruit-bearing trees in the backyard. Abe cared for the trees, so Sonia never had to buy fruit from the supermarket. It must have been these trees that gave Mark and Gloria their lifelong love of fresh fruit. Every day, Abe drove to the Long Beach train station, while carpooling with him were his two neighbors, Mr. Al Miller and Mr. Irving Kaye. They took the 7:39 AM Long Island Railroad train to Penn Station, from which Abe walked to his office. Every evening, he took the 5:01 PM train back to Long Beach and drove home in the car that had been left at the Long Beach train station in the morning.

Rachelle and Henry also bought a house in Long Beach and lived there until they moved to California years later, when Henry took a job as an engineer. Zalman bought a weekend home in Lido Beach, too. The three families were together, again.

20

THE BRAIN TUMOR

Abe and Sonia, like those called "greeners" in general, used to say when the appropriate occasion arose, "As long as you're healthy..." *(Du zolst nor zeyn gezundt)*. Corny as it sounds, the elders were right. You can have all the money in the world, the fanciest home, the coolest car, the greatest job; but, if you lose your health, you can't enjoy your success and your material goods. When you get sick, the only thing you crave is to feel good, to have an appetite and a good night's sleep.

Abe's business and family life were bright and happy. Life was good in the early 1950s. Except for one thing.

Abe started to get headaches. Not one to complain, and like most men, not eager to go to the doctor, Abe tried to ignore the headaches. He treated them with aspirin. When his vision in one eye began to get blurry, he finally revealed to Sonia his symptoms. He went to his family doctor who referred him to a neurosurgeon. After diagnosing Abe with a brain tumor, he was scheduled for surgery.

Abe and Sonia experienced tremendous anxiety during the weeks and days leading up to the surgery. After all they had weathered in their lives and then making a wonderful, new life in America, who knew what would come after the surgery? What disability would he carry with him as a result of this surgery? Would he be able to work and support the family? Would Sonia have to become his caretaker at the same time she was taking care of the children? Or might he not survive the surgery at all? Abe didn't show fear to Sonia. But he did ensure that the family's financial paperwork was in order.

There were dangers in all surgeries then, perhaps even particularly in brain surgery. There were no CT scans, MRIs or PET scans. Brain surgery was literally cut-and-hope-to-miss important brain tissue.

Two weeks before the scheduled surgery, Abe and Sonia, needing some diversion, went to a dinner. One of the guests was Abe's good friend, Julius Solomon, Abe's night school principal. Hearing Abe's story he was adamant: "Abe, you don't undergo brain surgery in a community hospital, not even Westchester Community." He gave Abe the name of a neurologist he knew, urging Abe to postpone or even cancel the surgery. "You don't schedule surgery without a second opinion," he advised Abe.

The week before the as-yet-uncanceled surgery, Abe was ushered into the office of the neurologist to whom Mr. Solomon had referred him, a well-known and respected doctor at a major hospital. Abe underwent the doctor's neurological exam, heard the diagnosis and headed for home.

Sonia hadn't gone to the doctor with Abe; she had stayed home with the children, occupying herself with worry, but keeping the hope alive that the neurosurgeon had made some kind of error, or else this new doctor would refer Abe to a specialist in Manhattan for the delicate surgery.

Abe soon drove up the driveway and parked. He opened the front door and walked in, planting a kiss on Sonia's cheek. "Well," she asked, "what's the news?"

Abe smiled his well-known pixie smile and repeated the words the specialist had said to him: "Mr. Huberman, you don't have a brain tumor; the one who has the brain tumor is the neurosurgeon. Cancel the surgery as soon as you get home."

It wasn't a brain tumor. But because Abe had been misdiagnosed, it was too late to treat the glaucoma in his right eye. Within a short time, Abe was totally blind in that eye.

Because of the blindness, Abe no longer had any depth perception. Despite his disability, he had a long and successful career buying and selling diamonds. He was able to evaluate diamonds and gems with one eye and no depth perception. Not only did his eye no longer have sight, but it also clouded over and moved close to the bridge of his nose, something that was immediately noticeable when you looked at Abe's face. Yes, it could be seen, but because of his personality and his big smile, the better you knew Abe, the less you noticed his disabled eye.

21

LIFE OUT OF THE ASHES

With their European accents, Sonia and Abe could have passed for any one of the hundreds of thousands of European, Jewish couples who immigrated to the United States between 1900 and the late 1940s. If not for the number tattooed on Sonia's arm, she and Abe would not have stood out from any of the other immigrants. Sonia was not one of the Holocaust survivors who wouldn't or couldn't talk about her terrible experiences during the war. But Sonia was not obsessed with her suffering.

Abe's business flourished. He and Sonia were blessed with their two children, Mark and Gloria. Both of them were brilliant students. Mark was a handful at home – not pleased that he was dethroned by the birth of his younger sister. But at school Mark was an angel and a superior student. Gloria was an all-A student from the first grade through the 12th. Mark played tennis and Gloria showed off her considerable talents as co-captain of the Long Beach High School majorettes. Both of them scored nearly perfect scores on their SAT's and the highest scores on their AP exams. Mark got his undergraduate degree *Summa cum laude* from Swarthmore and his Ph.D. in Physics from Cornell. Gloria, her BA

Magna cum laude from Brandeis and her Ph.D. in Psychology from the State University of New York at Stony Brook.

Abe and Sonia busied themselves raising their children and involving themselves in charitable activities. Sonia's main charitable activism involved raising money for Hadassah, the women's organization that raised money for Israel's medical institutions and services in Israel. The first hospital, the Rothschild, was founded under Ottoman-occupied Israel in 1888. The Hadassah women's organization was founded formally in 1912 and the cornerstone for what would become the world-class Hadassah hospital was laid in 1934 in Jerusalem's *Ein Kerem* neighborhood. Medical and dental schools and a full range of medical and health services were established later. Hadassah, like all hospitals in Israel, employs both Jewish and Arab doctors and treats patients regardless of background or religion.

Abe's main charitable activity was with his synagogue, Beth Shalom, led by Rabbi Miller. Abe sat on the Board and took on the role of *Gabbai* with another congregant. In that position, they were the ones on Shabbat and holiday services who handed out the honors of participating in the services to various members of the congregation.

Abe gave himself the honor of chanting the entire book of *Jonah* during the afternoon service on Yom Kippur, the most solemn holy day of the Jewish calendar. His voice, strong and sure, chanting the traditional melodies, carried throughout the large sanctuary the rhythms and cantorial sounds he had learned in his childhood from the modest cantors of Kozienice to the great cantors of Warsaw. Abe's chanting was an annual tradition in Lido Beach for many years, as were the donations he gave to the synagogue. Later, he left the Conservative Beth Shalom synagogue and helped establish an Orthodox synagogue, the Lido Beach Synagogue. The Bnai Brith organization, Anti-Defamation League and United Jewish Appeal also benefited from Abe's activism.

Sometime in the mid-1950s, Abe read in the newspaper that New York State's Great Parks Commissioner, Robert Moses, was to cap his career with the construction of a bridge between Brooklyn and Staten Island.

Abe used to say in a phrase I thought he had invented, "They aren't manufacturing land." His business was good, and he was looking for a way to invest his profits. Reading about the proposed bridge, he reasoned that land in the backwater Staten Island would likely go up in value after the bridge was built. So, he set about buying real estate parcels of raw land in Staten Island. Typically, Abe wanted to share his idea. He brought in friends and a relative, buying separate parcels with each of them, as partnerships. In 1959, construction on the bridge began, and in 1964 the Verrazano Narrows Bridge was completed. At the time, this bridge was the longest bridge in the world, keeping that title until the 1981 completion of the Humber Bridge. Abe began to sell the parcels in the late 1960s and 70s. With his profits, he bought an apartment building in the Bronx with his partner in the diamond business, Mr. Klapper. He moved his relatives of modest means, such as the ones who had helped him in 1939, into the building to ensure that they would have rents they could afford for the rest of their lives.

Abe was smart enough and had the foresight to set up an income stream for himself. He retired from full-time work at the age of 68 and gave up his 47th Street office. Not surprisingly, he was bored, despite his charitable activities. He went back to work two years later, part-time, by referral only. He ultimately bought out his partner's interest in the building and invested his profits in the stock market. He lived on stock market dividends and Treasury Bill interest after his total retirement and the sale of his building. Abe was a "value investor." He used to say, "If you find a diamond on the ground, pick it up." I don't remember Abe ever losing money in the market. He bought stock in what he thought were excellent companies that were undervalued. When he made what he thought was a reasonable profit, he sold. I once remonstrated with him for having sold too soon his position in the toy company Coleco, which he had bought just before it started marketing the Cabbage Patch dolls. He had bought at 8 dollars per share and sold at 13, after which the stock soared. Abe had no regrets over his sale. His philosophy was, "*I made money, now let someone else make money.*" Abe reminded me of the American financier and advisor to Presidents, Bernard Baruch, who was once asked how he had become so rich. He echoed Baron Edmund de Rothschild in his answer, "I always sold too early."

Abe's philosophy was modest. He was not avaricious, nor materialistic, and he never looked back. He was a living example of the Rabbinical saying, "Who is rich? He who is happy with what he has."[1] As it turned out, he had been smart to sell Coleco. After rising to over 100 dollars per share, Coleco stock sank to zero as the company went into bankruptcy.

Abe had decided he had no interest in returning to Soviet-occupied Poland even for a visit. But he always wondered what had happened to the real estate he owned in Warsaw. He had submitted a claim for his property under U.S. law, Title II of the War Claims Act of 1948 as amended by Public Law 87-846. Because he had not been a national of the United States at the time of his losses in Warsaw, he was deemed ineligible for standing and his claim was denied. He then learned that the United States and Poland were to negotiate a deal to compensate American citizens who had had property in Poland confiscated by the Communist rulers of Poland and were soliciting claims from American citizens.

On July 16, 1960, the United States and Poland concluded a Polish Claims Agreement, formally known as the "Agreement with the Government of the Polish People's Republic Regarding Claims of Nationals of the United States." The agreement covered property in Poland that had been owned by American citizens and seized by the Polish Communist government prior to July 16, 1960.

We have seen above that Abe's building at 74 Zelazna street was seized on April 19, 1949. The land at 65 Nowolipki street was taken on October 19, 1948, and the land at 36 Nizka street on February 20, 1964. Abe had submitted a claim with the Foreign Claims Settlement Commission for 890,000 dollars, which was the value

Abe calculated his property was worth in 1960. But the Commission made their calculations based on what the properties had been worth at the time of their seizure, minus mortgages owed. On that basis, the Commission approved an award of 87,915.08 dollars plus 59,636.30 dollars interest, all to be paid over the course of 20 years. However, 7,000 American citizens had submitted approved claims to the Commission, totaling 101 million dollars. The 40 million dollars that the Polish government had agreed to pay to compensate for the properties they had seized was inadequate to compensate all of the approved claims. As a result, none of the interest was paid. Each approved claimant was awarded 1,000 dollars and only about one-third of the approved principal amounts were paid out over the course of 20 years.

Abe's property at 36 Nizka street was not included in the settlement, as it was not taken until 1964. To date, nothing has come from that claim. By coincidence, Abe's property at 65 Nowolipki street was across the way from 68 Nowolipki. On August 3, 1942, during the German *Grossaktion* to deport 300,000 Jews from the Warsaw ghetto to Treblinka, Israel Lichtenstein had buried in a large milk can the first cache of the Jewish archives organized and written by Emanuel Ringelblum under the building at 68 Nowolipki. Recovered after the war, this archive has provided the most complete historical record of Jewish life in Warsaw during the war as viewed by the historian Emanuel Ringelblum and his colleagues.[2]

The Communist Polish government did well, essentially "buying" Jewish private property at bargain basement prices. On the other hand, Poland was a poor country, its industry and businesses having been wrecked by the German occupation and its top businessmen and *intelligentsia* murdered. And now, Poland was occupied by the brutal and economically illiterate Soviets. At least Poland made an attempt to make things right, paying out a small portion of the value of what their Jewish and non-Jewish citizens had owned. In contrast, neither the Baltic states, incorporated into the U.S.S.R., nor the Soviet Union itself, took any responsibility for the businesses, factories and riches that the Soviets had moved into the Soviet Union proper before the Nazis invaded in 1941.

The Soviet Union has never paid any compensation to American citizens and Jewish refugees, who had owned valuable property or businesses in the Baltic states or the U.S.S.R. My father's family (the Zwillings) had owned the second largest foundry in Lithuania along with a factory that manufactured farm equipment. As far as we know, after Stalin's Red Army took over the Baltic nations in accordance with Stalin's agreement with the Führer in August 1939, the steel mill and factory were dismantled and moved to the interior of the Soviet Union, east of the Urals. Perhaps those two factories participated in the manufacture of the U.S.S.R.'s tens of thousands of T-34 tanks and some 85,000 fighter planes and bombers that the Soviet forces used to destroy the *Wehrmacht* and *Luftwaffe* on the Eastern Front.

After visiting friends in Palm Beach, Florida, Abe allowed Sonia to persuade him to buy in 1976 a one-bedroom apartment in a condo development on South Ocean Boulevard, right on the beach. During the winter they lived in Palm Beach, and the rest of the year in the family home in Lido.

Abe had become friendly with Simon Jaglom, Sonia's first cousin. Simon and his brothers had made their considerable fortune in a variety of businesses in Europe. Simon Jaglom was once described as the "richest man in Danzig." After the Nazis came to power in Germany, they planned one way or another to get control of the Polish Corridor, a sliver of land given to Poland in the peace treaty that ended the First World War, and its seaport and main urban center, Danzig. The corridor gave Poland a route to the sea but divided Germany between east and west Prussia. Simon, who had been in charge of all trade in the free city of Danzig in the Polish corridor, had been, probably, the most important businessman in Poland and found himself in a position where he couldn't avoid frequent contact with Nazi officials and businessmen.

As the Nazis increased their railing against and persecution of

Germany's Jews, they feared that wealthy and influential Jews like Simon might depart the continent. Although this would suit their racist ideology, it would also likely damage the German economy severely. When it became known that Simon was planning to leave Danzig for good, the Nazi hierarchy offered to make him an *Ehrenarier* or Honorary Aryan. Despite their hatred of Jews as a subhuman racial group, the highest officials in the Führer's office, including Hitler, himself, when it suited their purpose, issued to hundreds of Jews or Germans with Jewish ancestry (the so-called *Mischlinge* or "racially mixed") certificates of Aryanhood (*Ariernachweis*) or certificates of German Blood (*Deutschblutigkeitserklärung*), which would presumably protect them from the fate of the rest of the Jews of Europe.[3]

At that point in 1937 Simon concluded that it was time to get out of continental Europe and the Nazi grasp. "I was practically running the economy of Danzig, arranging all the trade permits with Poland, issuing import licenses, running the Rice Syndicate, everything else, but I saw what was coming, I saw that someday they wouldn't need me: if they attacked Poland, what would they need trade permits for? But nonetheless they thought they needed me, the Germans... Anyway, for me it was absolutely clear: when they want to make you an Honorary Aryan, then it's time to go, no matter what your position."[4] He took his wife and son, Michael, leaving his office, business, home and all possessions behind and traveled to England. After his second son, Henry, was born, he moved his family and business from London to the United States.

The 1950s flew by, the 1960s, the 1970s. Ah, but 1969. That's when I first met Abe and Sonia on a trip I made to see my girlfriend, Gloria, in the summer of 1969. The country back then was on fire with riots and marches. But I was on fire with something else: burning love for Gloria. I suppose you could say, as Johnny Cash famously sang, I "fell into a ring of fire, and the flames, they burned higher."

---

1. *Babylonian Talmud*: Tractate: *Pirkei Avoth* – generally translated as: "Ethics of the Fathers" IV:1
2. Miller, Peter. See also Kassow and Ringelblum.
3. Rigg, pp. 31ff.
4. Jaglom.

22

THE RING

Gloria and I met during our junior year in college at Brandeis University. I was a serious Psychology major, looking forward to graduate school and an academic career. Gloria was a Psychology major as well, though she could have succeeded with any major. She blasted through advanced math classes, as well as American History with Professor Ray Ginger (the real-life model for Richard Burton's character in *Who's Afraid of Virginia Wolf?*) and European History with Professor Norman Cantor. As a Freshman, she was writing term papers in French, analyzing 19th-century French authors. We discovered that we had both taken courses in Near Eastern and Judaic Studies with the master teacher, Nahum Sarna. We also learned that, without knowing each other, we had taken many art history courses at the same time, with Robert Berger and Gerald Bernstein.

We discovered that since we were born in the United States, we were both first-generation Americans (usually called second generation; or second-generation survivors). Like Gloria, my parents grew up in Europe. Gloria's ancestors, had lived in Poland for generations, my parents' ancestors had lived in Lithuania for generations, as well. My parents were lucky. They survived the Holocaust because they had been able to flee Europe in 1937. Most of the family, who hadn't succeeded in leaving or didn't see the coming disaster, were killed.

Lithuania has the distinction of having had the highest percentage of any country's Jewish citizens murdered during the Holocaust – over 90 to 95 percent. The Lithuanians' shame is that a large number of Jews were murdered by Lithuanian citizens, so-called partisans, Jews' own Lithuanian neighbors, customers and employees, who beat them to death in the streets with axes and crowbars, incited by members of the *Einsatzgruppe* assigned to Lithuania. One of these so-called partisans was Klimaitis who began a pogrom on June 25-26, 1941 in Kovna ("in such a way that no German order or German instigation was noticed from the outside"), which resulted in the gruesome murders over several nights of more than 2,300 Jews, the destruction of synagogues and many neighborhoods of residential homes.

I knew by our third date that I was going to marry Gloria. It took me just two years to help her realize that she was going to marry me.

Having sufficient AP credits, Gloria graduated a semester early. Having enough AP credits, I spent my last semester of my senior year working on my Senior Honors Thesis (a research study on stress ulcers), while Gloria moved into a house in Cambridge with other girlfriends and after six months left the country for an adventure. After spending nine months touring and visiting friends and relatives throughout Europe and Israel, Gloria returned home in March 1971. On April 15, we got engaged. On June 20, we were scheduled to be married at Temple Beth Shalom in Lido Beach.

But first, I needed an engagement ring. Obviously, I couldn't buy a diamond from Tiffany & Co. nor any other retail store.

As someone who had read a sufficient number of novels and seen enough romantic movies, I believed that I, as a gentleman, needed to talk to Abe. I started the conversation with Abe by asking him if I could have his daughter's hand in marriage. True to form, he replied with a laugh and a twinkle in his good eye, *"Why are you asking me? Ask Gloria."*

We both knew that I already had her answer. With that settled, my future father-in-law asked me how much I had to spend on a diamond ring. I was an impecunious graduate student and proudly revealed that I had 500 dollars to spend on a ring. *"Perfect,"* Abe said. *"I have a wonderful stone for you."*

We sat down at the dining room table in their Lido house on Blackheath Road and Abe pulled out a small package of glossy tissue paper and unwrapped it, showing me a dozen or so diamonds of different sizes and, apparently, different quality. I couldn't tell the differences among the various stones, not with Abe's loupe nor by naked eye – well, maybe I could see the color, and, with the loupe, imperfections. With one working eye, Abe could judge any diamond, like an experienced miner or archaeologist – or diamond dealer. He knew what Gloria wanted. He took out a pair of tweezers and plucked a sparkling 1.5 carat marquise diamond out of the bunch and showed it to me. I told him I thought it was fine. I gave him five one-hundred-dollar bills and he told me he would have the diamond set in an engagement ring.

Many years later, after Abe had passed away, and Gloria and I had been married for several decades, Sonia revealed to Gloria that the diamond I had bought from Abe for 500 dollars had actually cost him 2,000 dollars. That was his diamond-dealer cost.

Had I bought the ring at a jewelry store at a retail price, it would have cost between 6,000 and 9,000 dollars, an amount I could have never afforded at that time, given that my annual income as a graduate student wasn't much over 6,000 dollars. While it's certainly true that Abe may have wanted Gloria to have a proper diamond engagement ring befitting the daughter of a diamond dealer, nonetheless, it was a heck of a wedding present.

Abe never told me what he had done. He didn't want to embarrass me.

23

DENOUEMENT

We spent many happy years as a family. When we lived on Long Island's North Shore while we went to graduate school, we spent many Friday nights in Lido Beach having dinner in Gloria's childhood home together with her parents and their closest friends, Henno and Rosie Zuker. Abe drank tea the traditional Russian way, *Prikusku* – with a cube of sugar or hard candy in his mouth filtering each sip of tea. Abe and Henno were great story and joke tellers. I had soaked up my father's sense of humor and his cornucopia of Jewish jokes and stories and I held my own in the Friday night "dinner-and-shows" when we men traded jokes in English, Yiddish and Hebrew, regaling ourselves and our wives, who were kind enough to laugh out loud though they had all already heard the jokes hundreds if not thousands of times.

Abe's office on 47th Street was not far from Simon Jaglom's office. Frequently Abe walked to Simon's office, where the two men visited and discussed family, politics and business. His son, Henry tells the story that once when he was a young actor and writer in New York, he rushed to his father's office to discuss an important matter with him. Abe had been sitting in Simon's waiting room and had struck up a conversation with another gentleman, a Mr. Salinger, who was sitting in the waiting room, also waiting to meet with Simon. Learning that this fellow had a son who was a writer, Abe said, *"Mr. Jaglom's son is also a writer."*

Abe not only loved to meet and learn about people but also liked to help people in any way he could, even if only to connect them with other people he knew, which might benefit both of them. So, when Henry came running into the waiting room telling the secretary that he needed to see his father as soon as possible, Abe interrupted him, telling him that this gentleman's son was also a writer and this fellow would be happy to introduce Henry to him. Henry apologized, saying that he was in a big hurry and didn't have time to chat. He rushed into his father's office and waved goodbye as he rushed out. Henry told us with a hearty laugh that one of his literary idols was J.D. Salinger. Had he been in less of a hurry, he would have had the opportunity for Abe to introduce him to Mr. Sol Salinger, who would have been happy to introduce Henry to his son, J.D.

Gloria and I had never met Simon and Marie, Michael and Henry. In 1975, we were preparing to move to Dallas to take jobs at the University of Texas Southwestern Medical School. Gloria decided that it was time to meet the Jagloms, about whom she had heard so much. Her mother was always reminding Abe that she was a Jaglom – and that was some *yichus!* Gloria got the phone number and called. Marie was so friendly on the phone and invited Gloria and me to dinner at their apartment. It wasn't long before we drove from Stony Brook, Long Island to the City. We took the private elevator to the apartment and were greeted warmly by the whole family, Michael and Henry having been invited to join their parents for dinner. The apartment was softly lit and elegantly furnished. Gloria admired one small table and learned that it had been bought in London after Simon and Marie had fled to England. It had a twin, which resided in Buckingham Palace. Gloria and I admired the paintings hanging on all the beautiful wood-paneled walls. Now, we looked around and studied dozens of Impressionist paintings that we had seen in our Brandeis art history classes only as slides projected on a screen. Renoir, Manet, Monet, Pissarro, etc. This was an Impressionist collection that surpassed collections at most museums outside of the Metropolitan Museum of Art in New York and the Louvre in Paris. The dinner that we shared was superb. We spent hours at the dinner table and later in the study in conversation about family and the state of the world. Mostly, our hosts took a great interest in us, peppering us with questions about ourselves, our families and our work. One conversation I remember clearly. I had not long before finished my Ph.D. dissertation and was working at a Veterans Administration Hospital in Northport, New York. Henry took a special interest in my work. I described my various research projects and publications. My clearest memory is of Henry, already an accomplished film director, asking me insightful questions about my dissertation research on migraine headaches. He knew nothing about the subject, but asked questions in depth, as good as or better than those I had been asked at my dissertation defense by the professors on my dissertation committee. I was greatly impressed and took away my impression that Henry was brilliant. And why not? As Sonia might have said, "He's a Jaglom."

Years later, after Marie and Simon passed away, Henry and Michael donated the art collection on extended loan to the Tel Aviv Museum of Art. A building was constructed to house the collection, which can be seen today in the museum's Simon and Marie Jaglom Pavilion of Impressionist Art in Tel Aviv.

After we moved to Texas on December 30, 1975 we vacationed with Abe and Sonia yearly, in Palm Beach in December and in Lido Beach in the summer. Our frequent evening activity was playing the card game Gin Rummy. We played with partners keeping score of points won and lost. My recollection is that Sonia won 90 percent or more of her games, regardless of whether her partner was Abe, Gloria or I. She paid attention to and remembered all the cards thrown, which kept her from giving her opponent the cards from her hand that he or she needed. She also was able to change her strategy as she played, for which cards in her dealt hand to use to make gin, hence which cards to keep and which cards to discard. We took other vacations together, to the Catskill resort Kutscher's and to Israel. As my parents had moved to North Miami Beach in 1975, out trips to Florida gave us, and later on, our children, opportunities to spend time with both sets of grandparents.

I remember one event that typifies Abe's fearlessness and eagerness to experience new things. We were all lying on chaises on the condo building's common deck facing the ocean, talking or reading. I stopped reading and looked up when I heard a commotion around the swimming pool. I leapt out of my chair when I saw Gloria running to the pool. Abe, who had never had a single swim lesson, knew no strokes and could not swim at all, had jumped into the pool and was swiveling his arms as he imagined a swimmer would. Before I could jump in to grab him, Abe surfaced from beneath the water in the shallow end, stood up, wiped the chlorinated water from his eyes and calmly climbed the steps out of the pool. Drying himself with a towel, he explained that he had watched everyone swimming and thought that it didn't look very hard. He decided he would jump into the pool and simply imitate the swimmers he had seen. He took a calculated risk. After all, he had taught himself to ride a bicycle in Lido Beach when he was in his sixties – and ride he did. So, why not teach himself to swim in Palm Beach in his seventies?

The greatest events in our lives and the greatest gifts we gave our parents were the births of our two children, Sarah and David, whom they loved. Abe and Sonia became parents for the second time later in life, and grandparents even later in life. The war had stolen not just things from Abe and Sonia, but also their families and friends, and irreplaceable time from their lives. They adored their grandchildren and their grandchildren adored them.

While we traveled to Florida and New York frequently, the grandparents traveled to Dallas on a regular basis. Especially on Passover, both sets of parents made a point of coming to Dallas to celebrate the holiday with us and our friends.

Passover of 1943 is when the Nazi hierarchy had decided to liquidate the Warsaw ghetto, and when the Jewish teenagers in the ghetto rose up to attack the Ukrainian troops who led the way into the ghetto intending to round up the remaining Jewish residents. During our annual Passover *Seders* (much like the Greek *symposia* on which they were likely modeled), we and our guests read from the *Haggadah*, a collection of prayers and excerpts from the Bible and Talmudic commentaries. The point of the Seder is to remember and to teach our children about the Israelite Exodus from Egypt and journey to the land of Canaan, which would become the land of Israel. At our Seders, discussion was usually the order of the evening. I or one of our guests would pose a question about the text or about the meaning to us today of Passover and freedom from slavery, and our guests, often numbering between 14 and 30, would contribute to the discussion.

One line that we would read aloud, became increasingly meaningful to us as we grew older, "In every generation there arise those who wish to annihilate us; but the Holy One, blessed be He, saves us from their murderous hands." At that point, it was common for someone to point out that the generation of Jews that lived in Europe in the 1930s and 1940s was nearly annihilated by the German Nazi-regime and its collaborating governments in countries all across Europe and the Holy One blessed be He did not save us. A hush would fall over all of us as we turned to look at Sonia, and without any prompting, Sonia would tell her story. She talked about her experiences in Warsaw, the suffering in the ghetto, the uprising, the methodical German murders of the men and boys, and her transport to Majdanek.

Gloria or I would light a *yahrzeit* (memorial) candle in memory of the relatives who were murdered in the ghettos, the camps or the forests – the places and dates mostly unknown to us. We and our guests often sat in our seats with tears in our eyes, but Sonia told her story in a strong voice, matter-of-factly retelling, as she had many times, the trials she had undergone. The Seders ended with a fabulous meal cooked by Gloria with her mother's help and the contributions of our guests who brought various dishes to the Seder, followed by singing and laughing and hopes for good health and happiness in the coming year.

Early in our marriage, Gloria and I and later with the children, traveled to New York and still later to Florida to celebrate the Passover Seder. Abe would conduct the Seder singing the prayers with the traditional melodies that he had learned in his childhood. Although he had had to drop out of school early in elementary school, he was a lifelong student. He could read Hebrew, Aramaic, and Yiddish as well as English (and of course, Polish) – and sing in all of them.

The only time I ever saw or heard Sonia and Abe argue was when Abe wanted to invite more people to the Seder than Sonia felt she could accommodate because of space and the work involved in preparing a meal for 15 to 20 people. Sonia would say something like, "*It's enough to invite our family; what do I need strangers for?*" And Abe would argue, "*I don't ask for much, all I ask is that we invite our friends and neighbors to the Seder*". Abe usually won the argument. Sonia conceded. But, more often than not, Abe would involve Gloria in the discussion. Gloria helped clinch the deal by volunteering to fly up to New York or Florida prior to the Seder, to help with the preparations. And I, of course, helped set the table. When it became too difficult for Abe and Sonia to prepare the Passover Seders, they came to us in Dallas.

Abe and Sonia were not spared the ravages of aging. In his 60s, Abe went to the doctor for a minor complaint and the doctor discovered Abe's colon cancer. Post-surgery, cancer of the colon would never recur. But in his late 70s, Abe was hit with a diagnosis of lymphoma. Radiation appeared to chase that cancer away. When it appeared that the cancer had returned, Abe checked into one of the pre-eminent cancer hospitals in New York City. After a few days, Abe called us, calm but to our ears worried, to tell us that a doctor had come by to see him and told him that there was nothing more they could do for him. We were still living on Long Island at the time. We quickly drove into the City and hurried up to his hospital room. A medical resident had apparently seen him and given him the bad news. I introduced myself to the nurses on duty as Mr. Huberman's son-in-law and a doctor, and asked to see Abe's hospital chart. I read the chart and told Gloria, "We've got to get Dad out of here, before they scare him to death or kill him." We got Abe dressed, signed him out and drove him home. Abe's lymphoma had not come back and he was not dying.

Abe's view of life is illustrated by a letter he wrote to us on July 8, 1980 (when granddaughter Sarah was not yet three years old):

Dear Gloria, Ken and Surelleh,

What does Sarah say when she answers the telephone: I LOVE YOU VERY MUCH. After talking to you last night, listening to your problems, I said to myself Gloria is learning about life now, the same way I started 45 years ago. You are starting a new chapter. Life is not a straight road. It is hilly. Up and down. And it has curves. This is normal. I pray and hope that God should protect you and watch over all of you. And your problems should be: getting better babysitting help for Sarah or getting a better school for her; should you take your vacation five days earlier or five days later. I know it disturbs your mind when it happens all at once. But a few hours later it is much easier. And a few days later it disappears... I had bigger problems to solve. But they say time is the best teacher. Time passed and my problems passed. When I had a tough problem, I turned it around in my mind and I started to think about my wonderful family and I thought about less fortunate families, and all my problems disappeared... And I always say, "Dear God, if you want to punish me, please punish me financially." At present, I have a problem. I can't get tomorrow's newspaper today. If I could solve this problem, I would make a lot of money. Your reservation in the Huberman's hotel was approved. The tomatoes and cucumbers are waiting for Sarah to pick them. We are looking forward to seeing you at our home. Love Father.

Dear Sarah, Papa is lonely. Please come to visit us, we will take you to the merry-go-round. I love you very much.

Papa Abe and Baba Sonia.

Only a few years later, in 1981, Abe and Sonia came to Dallas to celebrate the birth of our second child, David. The day before they were due to go back to Florida, Abe complained of dizziness and vision problems in his good eye. We took him to the office of his Dallas doctor, our good friend, Neal Sklaver. After a brief exam, Neal told us that Abe and Sonia were not going back to Florida. Abe was going to the hospital for an endarterectomy, as one carotid artery bringing blood to his brain was 99.9 percent blocked. Two weeks later, Abe had another endarterectomy on the other carotid artery, which also showed a major blockage. David's birth had saved Abe from an imminent stroke. Well, that and Neal's quick and accurate diagnosis. While resting in bed in his hospital room at Dallas' Baylor University Medical Center, Abe wrote a page of his reminiscences of his childhood. He ended his short essay:

God bless America. Thank you, God, for saving me and taking me out from a land of persecution and misery and bringing me to this land of freedom and opportunity.

His fierce love for America was a recurrent theme for Abe since the war. Two years before his Baylor hospitalization, he had also penned a similar note:

There is no one in this wonderful country who can appreciate [America] as much as we Europeans who lived through the Second World War, who are the surviving witnesses of the Holocaust, who saw our loved ones, relatives, parents and children taken away and led to the gas chambers.

In 1989, Abe was admitted into the hospital in Dallas again for tests related to a possible diagnosis of lymphoma and while hospitalized suffered a stroke. It wasn't too bad and after a while he returned with Sonia to New York. He took a turn for the worse in October and Gloria flew up to New York to accompany her parents back to Dallas. Witnessing how sick Abe was, and ever the practical daughter, Gloria spoke to her father on the airplane and asked him if he was OK being buried in Dallas, where we lived in the event he would die. Despite his precarious physical condition, Abe's cognitive ability and sense of humor apparently remained relatively intact. Abe answered Gloria in the affirmative, adding with a weak smile, "*I've always wanted to own real estate in Dallas.*"

I picked them up from the airport on a Saturday. That Sunday, Abe passed away. It was remarkable how composed Sonia was at home, at the funeral and for the week after that she spent with us in our home. She actually comforted us.

Sonia continued to live most of the year in Lido Beach, New York, and winters in Palm Beach, Florida. We were concerned about her living alone in the two-story house in Lido. But Sonia was fine. She was independent and had friends and activities. Gloria flew up frequently to visit and reported that all was well. Sonia traveled to Dallas not just for Passover, but at other times such as the children's school graduations. One year, Sonia took us and the children on a Royal Caribbean cruise to the Southern Caribbean during Christmas vacation. During that cruise, Sonia and our son David played cruise bingo, along with hundreds of other passengers. Sonia bought two bingo cards for nine-year-old David and another two for herself.

Gloria and I had finished our shipboard activity and joined the two in the ship's theatre just in time to see David jump up and, with his grandmother, yell "bingo." This wasn't Las Vegas and we were in international waters, so the Master of Ceremonies had no trouble handing over eight, crisp hundred-dollar bills to David while the shipboard photographer snapped David's picture. Gloria, always a believer in doing the right thing, turned to me and suggested that since Sonia had paid for the winning bingo ticket, we ought to turn the winnings over to her. With a twinkle in my eye, I replied "OK, let's give Mother 10 *dollars* to reimburse her the cost of the ticket."

Before I could get Gloria's response, Gloria had already approached Sonia and told her that the 800-dollar winnings were due to her. "*Absolutely not,*" came the answer. Sonia was adamant that she had bought David the bingo tickets as a gift, and she wanted him to have the money. We should put the winnings with the rest of the money we were saving for David's college only ten years hence. I knew that Sonia would want David to keep "his" winnings, but, as usual, I admired Gloria for not taking Sonia for granted and giving her the respect she deserved. David's big bingo win was further proof to him of the truth of what we repeatedly told him, that he was born under a lucky star.

In truth, Gloria and I always felt that our whole family was lucky. If my parents hadn't been able to flee Lithuania for America in 1937, if Abe hadn't come to America in June 1939, and if Sonia hadn't had or taken one lucky break after another, neither Gloria nor I would be here, nor would our children, grandchildren and future generations exist now, or in the future.

I believed Sonia must have had some kind of sixth sense, or at least an amazing capacity of observation and quick decision-making. After the death of her beloved husband, most assuredly the CEO of our family, Sonia decided to avoid disrupting her life and kept to her routine. Sonia informed us that she would continue to stay in the Palm Beach condo during the winter months and go back to Lido for the rest of the year. Gloria and I were concerned about Sonia living alone in her house in Lido, which had twice been burglarized, but we didn't argue with Sonia. At the age of 74, she was physically strong and mentally as sharp as ever. She had even recovered on her own from a nasty fall. She had been riding her adult tricycle on the sidewalks of Lido and while crossing a street, her trike tripped over a curb and tumbled her to the concrete, causing her to break her arm. We didn't hear about it until Sonia returned home from the hospital, sporting a cast on her arm.

If Sonia could learn to write cheques to pay her bills, as she did after Abe's passing, to call workmen for the usual household repairs and to drive herself (or catch a ride with friends) to Hadassah lunches, and wasn't afraid to sleep alone in her large home, we just had to learn to trust her ability to function independently.

Sonia continued her active life, participating in charitable lunches and dinners, visiting with friends with whom she loved to play Canasta, and popping down to Dallas for her grandchildren's life milestones. Gloria and I assumed that Sonia's life revolved around us and our children, but, in truth, Sonia lived an independent life.

I've often heard the saying that in life, "timing is everything." I know that that's certainly true in love, finance and war. I suppose in most of life. Getting to the airport late and missing the plane that later crashed. Leaving work early and getting hit on the driver's side by that car that ran the red light at 50 miles per hour. I always thought that Sonia had an expert sense of timing.

So, when Sonia decided to sell the house in Lido in 1992, we didn't argue. Even though we thought the house would continue to appreciate in value, we understood that Sonia believed that shuttling between Lido and Palm Beach was too much for her and it was time to let Lido go. Leaving the Lido house unoccupied was out of the question. But renting it out and managing it, maintaining it and overseeing repairs long-distance would be too great a burden for Gloria and me, let alone Sonia. So, Sonia put the house on the market and sold it to a young couple, because she liked the couple and wanted her house in which she and Abe had lived for decades and in which they had raised Mark and Gloria to go to a buyer who she thought would benefit from the home's warm and loving ambience. In the years after the sale, the house did appreciate significantly. But Sonia never looked back. What was done, was done. Besides, it would turn out that none of us would have to deal with the house during the storms that swept Long Beach and Lido in August 2014, which flooded the dry land as the Bay and the Ocean met, forming one body of water across most of Lido and Long Beach.

The sale of the Lido house revealed an important clue to how Sonia was able to cope as well as she did with the traumatic events she experienced during the Holocaust. The young couple who ultimately bought the house offered less than the market-value price that Sonia was asking, explaining that while they loved the house, they couldn't afford the asking price. Sonia agreed to sell them the house at the price they said they could afford.

Gloria had flown up to New York to help her mother with the sale and to help pack up the house in the event it sold. She was present during Sonia's discussion with the buyers (it could hardly be called a negotiation). Gloria took Sonia aside out of earshot and said to her, "Mom, I think they're trying to take advantage of you."

Sonia quickly replied, "No. This young couple wouldn't do that. They're very nice. I have never met bad people."

Gloria's eyes widened and her jaw dropped. "Mom, how can you say that?! After what you went through...?!"

"Oh that," explained Sonia, *"that was different."*

For Sonia, the Holocaust did not define her worldview. Her approach to life was to assume the best in people, until proven otherwise. After Sonia sold Lido, she lived full-time in her condo in Palm Beach, Florida for six years. She enjoyed Florida's sunshine and kept a busy life with the friends she had made in her building and in other buildings on South Ocean Boulevard. She remained independent. When not visiting with friends or attending charity events, she exercised, walked along the ocean and read one book after another.

In 1998, Sonia made another momentous decision – to move to Dallas to be near us. We were happy to hear her decision which meant we would have Sonia nearby. Actually, Sonia reasoned that she was going to move to Dallas eventually, anyway. As she aged and developed medical issues, she would be forced to move near us, and would be totally dependent on us for company. She wisely made the decision to move while she was "young" and healthy enough to have an independent life in Dallas. We helped her find a lovely building that had originally been built as a condo development. The development had failed, and Hyatt bought the building and turned it into senior independent living residences.

The building was gorgeous and looked like a hotel, with a beautiful lobby, nice, spacious apartments, group rooms and a dining hall where fine restaurant food was served.

After the birth of our second child in 1981, Gloria had stopped working to become a full-time mother and CEO of our household. By the time our daughter was in college and our son starting high school, we decided that Gloria would return to work outside the home. By that time, however, managed healthcare had entered the delivery of mental health services and, for better or worse, decimated many independent psychologists' practices, including my own, as I was determined to not join any managed care panels.

Despite her Ph.D. in Clinical Psychology Gloria decided to make a career change. For the good of the family, she would venture into the business world. She took a job as a mortgage consultant. After a year working for a small mortgage company, she moved to a larger, private company that had been started by Roseanna McGill and was by then considered one of the top mortgage companies in Texas. Gloria was asked if she wanted to be salaried or on commission. Recalling one of Abe's famous sayings, she chose commission only. Today, celebrating over 24 years in the business, Gloria remains as she started in the top tier of her company's mortgage consultants. She was recently ranked in a national mortgage magazine as the 125th top consultant/broker in the United States out of some 80,000 brokers.

Gloria went back to work and started her new career at the age of 47, the same age as Abe had been when he began his new career in the diamond business. We both always had time to spend with Sonia and to tend to her needs. For Gloria, her mother and our children always came first.

Sonia's health deteriorated. She had to give up her apartment and full-time, wonderful caretaker, to move first to a nursing home, from which we rescued her after a month, moving her to a lovely private home that had been converted to an assisted living/nursing home for six residents and two staff, owned by a married couple, both of whom were registered nurses. Best of all, the house was literally a five-minute walk from our house.

By the age of 89, Sonia's physical health had begun to fail significantly, following her hip fracture and hip replacement. Mentally, the fog of old age, technically known as dementia, clouded her memory and changed her personality. She was no longer the tall, strong, independent, happy woman who had always been able to offer (when asked) wise and useful advice about life. Now, she was weak and fragile. Worst of all, she was sad. In her 70s she was still riding her bike, now I or her caretakers wheeled her around in a wheelchair. She began to say to us, "*Why is God punishing me? Why won't He let me die?*" This is what hurt us the most. We hated to see her suffer – aches and pains, total loss of independence, cognitive decline and now, sadness and depression. The brave, strong, defiant, iron-willed woman who had survived trauma and lived life with a passion, serving as a role model for her children and grandchildren, now longed for God to take her from this life and relieve her of her suffering. And then came the cruelest blow...

Gloria's brother, Mark, years after he had received his Ph.D. in Physics, had gone back to school to get a Master's degree in Biostatistics. He was working at the medical school associated with the University of Southern California, doing research with his medical colleagues studying the epidemiology of black lung disease and making important contributions to the research. Mark was diagnosed with kidney cancer on February 14, 2001 and in a twist of fate began treatment in the same hospital where he had been doing his research. Our son, David, after his sophomore year at the University of Pennsylvania, found a summer job at a bank in Los Angeles in order to spend the summer with his Uncle Mark, to keep him company and help him in numerous ways during the last summer of his life

David spoke about his time with Uncle Mark in this excerpt from the eulogy he later delivered in Dallas:

"Mark really cherished his time with people and was so happy that his friends would bring him dinner every night and spend time to talk with him. When I would ask Mark how he was doing each day, he would tell me that he was doing "OK" and was "taking it day by day." I would have to prod him with further questions just for him to hint to me that he was experiencing some pain. He would keep his pain and suffering to himself and never complained to me. He would rather hear about my day and smile at my jokes. To the very end, my uncle was exceptionally strong in battling his cancer and fought hard for so long. Towards the end, Mark and I didn't talk very much, because he had much difficulty breathing and was too weak to talk. When I would come home from work, I would heat up some dinner and sit with my uncle at the table, holding his hand and telling him about my day. Then I would finish talking and eat. With my hand pressed tightly into his, I felt that I was becoming closer to my uncle than I had ever been before.

Not needing to engage in conversation, I cherished just being there with Mark, just being with him and feeling his love. In the silence of the room, his hand gave me as much strength and support as mine did to him. The night before he died, I visited him briefly in the hospital, seeing him for the last time. He had an oxygen mask on but could still speak softly through it. I wanted to stay in the room longer with him, but he insisted that I go home because it was getting late and he didn't want me to get home too late. I remember thinking about how weak and thin he was, how much he must have been suffering, and even then, he was thinking about me and telling me to go home to get some rest. He took off his mask and kissed me and told me that he loved me. I gave him a kiss and told him that I loved him, too."

Earlier that summer, cousin Helen had flown in from afar to visit with Mark for a week. Gloria was booked on a flight to visit Mark one more time on Saturday, August 11, 2001. In the middle of the night, just a few hours before the alarm was due to wake us to leave for the airport, we were awakened by a phone call from Mark's closest friend, Paige, who was with Mark in the hospital. Gloria didn't need to fly to Los Angeles. Mark had died and we would be flying his body to Dallas, to lay him to rest next to his father at the Shearith Israel Cemetery in Dallas.

What should we tell Sonia? Wasn't it enough that Sonia had had to bear the horror of having her two young children murdered by the Nazis? Must she now have to bear the news that her third child had died too young? We considered not telling Sonia. We could make up an excuse. Perhaps we would tell Sonia that Mark had had to fly to Japan for a post-doc and wasn't able to call her on the phone? It didn't take long for Gloria to decide that she had never kept secrets from her mother, and she wasn't going to start now. Sonia would have to be told. But what to do about the funeral? Certainly, we wouldn't bring her to the funeral – wheeling her across the ground in her wheelchair, forcing her to sit through the service and eulogies, the custom of the mourners throwing shovels of dirt onto the casket. Even her Dallas doctor, our close friend, Neal, advised us to not bring her to the cemetery – it would be too upsetting. Gloria spoke to her friends; she and I talked and discussed.

The next day, we brought Sonia to our home for lunch. As we sat around the kitchen table, Gloria gave her mother the news. She took it better than we expected and asked about the funeral. We told her that her doctor didn't think she should go to the funeral, because going to the funeral would be too upsetting, making her sad. She replied, "*Of course, it will be upsetting. Of course, I'll be sad. Mark was my son.*"

Sonia's response was in character and Gloria's instinct was solid. We brought Sonia to the funeral. She was naturally grieved. All of our friends, dozens and dozens of them, almost all of whom knew Sonia, even those who had never met Mark, were there. Our friends came to our house to spend time with us during the next seven days of *Shiva*, the traditional mourning period.

To this day, I remain amazed at how brave and stoic Sonia was after Mark's death. But she continued to deteriorate physically and mentally. For the first time, Gloria heard her mother wake up and call out something in Polish, which Gloria didn't understand. For the first time ever, Gloria saw her mother frightened. Sonia was obviously having memories of her wartime experiences. In dementia, our short-term memories disappear. But old memories, well established in the brain's memory centers, generally remain to various degrees intact. Now, Sonia was plagued with memories of her suffering, which must have appeared to her as happening then and there – flashbacks. Luckily, Gloria was by her mother's side most evenings, and would wake her up when she began to get agitated and reassure her that she had been dreaming and having nightmares.

On January 26, 2002, we got the phone call. Sonia had died peacefully in her sleep, a little more than five months after Mark had died. She was buried next to her beloved husband, just a few rows away from Mark's grave.

Our daughter, Sarah, Sonia's first grandchild, gave one of the three eulogies at Sonia's funeral:

"I think Baba Sonia would want to thank you all for coming. We loved Baba Sonia and we know that Baba appreciated our love. Each time I called her, Baba would end our conversation, 'Thank you so much for calling. You made my day a very happy one.' So, I think Baba would want to thank her friends for being here and for loving her throughout her life.

The center, the pulse of life for Baba was family. During the war, Baba's will to live was fueled by the knowledge that she had a husband waiting for her in America. Throughout her entire Holocaust experience, from the Warsaw ghetto to Majdanek to Auschwitz to liberation, Baba managed to stay with her younger sister, Rachelle. They were called 'the good sisters,' because they shared, and when one was sick, even though they were both starving, the other would give her food portion to her sister. We are used to hearing Baba talk proudly about her family. 'I have a wonderful family,' she would say. 'I had 54 happy years with my husband, Abe. I have wonderful children and I have good grandchildren who are close to each other.' A few months ago, sitting in her wheelchair, struggling to keep her eyes open, Baba looked at me and smiled. 'I am a happy woman.'

So, I'd like to talk about Baba's family and what I've seen these past months. After a long day at work, before eating dinner, before stopping home, my mom would go to visit my grandmother at the home where Baba was being taken care of, around the corner from us. It didn't matter whether my mom was tired or whether she was missing any social event or even if she had to go back to the office; my mom would consistently head straight to Baba's. Even when Baba started forgetting, when Baba would not remember that Mom had been to visit her the day before, Mom would continue to go, saying, 'If it makes Baba happy for the moment, it's worth it.' And Mom wouldn't go empty-handed, either. She would bring Baba a roast beef sandwich on rye, because that was Baba's favorite. Or she would bring Baba a new outfit in pink, Baba's color. Or she might bring a photo album to page through with Baba. Most importantly, she would bring Baba dignity. My mom would treat her mother as the Sonia Jaglom, from a family of *yichus*, that my grandmother was so proud to be. When Papa Abe died, he left a note asking my mom to take care of Baba. Boy, would Papa Abe be proud.

And then there's my brother, David. Like a magician, David would search for the trick that would bring Baba Sonia joy, despite her suffering. Once, on a particularly difficult day for Baba, David, pulling a Yiddish song out of thin, Internet air, brought Baba headphones, and we all watched unbelievingly as she smiled and swayed to the music she recognized. David would shower Baba with kisses, according to Baba's taste. 'Would you like a strawberry kiss?' David would ask, 'or a blueberry one?'

My mother and brother not only demonstrate the values that Baba Sonia taught us – to love, to give, to appreciate, to make our own happiness, to be optimistic, to never give up – but they are living creations of Baba's miracle of survival.

Last month, Baba Sonia held my hand and left me with words of comfort, 'Sarah, I love you. And even in death, I will love you.' And I want to tell Baba, my Miracle Woman, 'I love you. And even in death, you live. Because your strength and your will to live produced my family and all our future descendants. And I know, as I have always known, that I owe my life to you.'"

AFTERWORD

*It is easy to see that life is the cumulative
effect of a handful of significant shocks.*
Nassim Nicholas Taleb, *The Black Swan*

The love story of Abe and Sonia has come to an end, as all human stories do. But what a story it has been. What a wild ride. From modest beginnings, Abe pulled himself up metaphorically – but almost literally – by his boots to become a 30-year-old millionaire businessman and real estate developer in Warsaw.

Abe had an entrepreneurial personality before the word was common. Like other immigrants to America who became self-made businessmen, Abe didn't spend his time focusing on what he could have or should have done; he set for himself goals to assimilate into America. What kept him going, putting one foot in front of the other, was hope and working diligently towards the goals he set for himself.

Sonia had been thrust into a world of suffering for herself and her young children. When it appeared that things couldn't get worse, they did.

Sonia explained her survival saying that she had *"a strong instinct to live."* Like other camp prisoners she tried to maintain the hope that the United States and the Soviets would crush the Nazi-war machine. As news filtered in first of the German defeats in North Africa and Stalingrad and later the *Wehrmacht's* retreat from the Soviet battlefields and the Allied successes in Italy, followed by the Normandy landings, it became easier to maintain the hope of survival

It was the close relationship with her sister, Rachelle, that kept both of them from feeling totally abandoned and bereft. As the "good sisters," so called by the other women in their barracks, they helped each other when one or the other was mentally distraught or physically sick. Sonia also had an instinct that led her to take or refrain from taking chances that helped keep her alive.

The symptoms following the experience of traumatic stressors are generally normal responses. They are our understandable interpretations and adaptations to dangerous environments, learning, often unconsciously, to identify danger while our bodies respond to it with physiological arousal and a response of fighting or fleeing. Nearly every living organism learns from trauma to be alert to stimuli that resemble those that accompanied their previous experience(s) of danger(s) or trauma(s).

Obviously, the reason for living things to be vigilant to stimuli that remind them of previous, memory-documented danger is to prepare them to take action to confront or avoid the new danger. Post-traumatic Stress Disorder describes the condition where new situations perceived as life-threatening actually pose little to no danger at all. The individual is overly vigilant ("hypervigilant") to perceived danger, a vigilance that is no longer realistic nor adaptive. Constantly being in a state of alertness to imminent, minimal or objectively non-existent danger takes a toll on, at least for humans, our mental and physical state. A researcher once likened this state to that of an automobile whose engine is running while the transmission is kept in neutral and the gas pedal is pushed to the floor for long and repetitive periods of time.

The core characteristic of the sequelae of trauma and the major component of PTSD is disturbing memories of the traumatic event(s) that keep popping up in the minds of the traumatized. They can appear seemingly out of the blue or triggered by a visual or auditory cue in their outer or inner environment. Of the hundreds of military veterans I have evaluated, those who suffered the greatest unrelenting, troubling memories from combat were the medics. This has been noted by others across many wars. It is not necessarily the carnage they witnessed, although that alone can and has caused PTSD in many medics. What becomes clear from talking to the medics is that they feel profound guilt for not having been able to save fellow soldiers, the majority of whom had such severe injuries that resurrection would not have been within the power of these ministering medics. It is not the hundreds or more war-wounded that the individual medics remember treating and having saved from death. It is those they didn't save – and felt that they should have, that they remember, often in great detail.

People recover from trauma at different rhythms and periods of time. The main road to recovery from the psychological sequelae of trauma is to keep the brain occupied with new experiences and thus to layer new memories on top of (and sometimes in place of) the old ones. Memories are understood now as far from immutable. From laboratory studies of eyewitness testimony, we know that recollections of events are influenced by many factors, including the situational aspects of the event(s) and personal characteristics of the witness. Memories of events are also influenced, if not transformed, by experiences of the witness (or participant) post-event. Changing one's interpretation or understanding of the traumatic event – sometimes even using humor – can also affect its impact. Later in life, Sonia showed very high levels of cholesterol (over 300 mg/dl) but no coronary artery disease. Once, after receiving her lab results, Sonia told us with a smile and perhaps a

251

big dose of humor that maybe starving in the camps had been good for her coronary arteries.

Sonia told us that after she was reunited with Abe, she rarely suffered from symptoms understood as hallmarks of Post-traumatic Stress Disorder. I have no doubt that Sonia remembered many details of her six-plus years in Nazi-occupied Europe. Her traumas had been chronic, essentially daily. But the memories she related to us and to interviewers were of significant, discrete events (episodic memories, in psychological parlance). As the author Nassim Nicholas Taleb has called them, a number of "significant shocks." Sonia was lucky not to be one of the dozen or so individuals in the world found to have Hyperthymesia, also known as Superior Autobiographical Memory. People with this unique ability – or curse – remember the events of every day of their lives. When asked about a traumatic or common event, they can recall it in great detail, including the date and time of occurrence. The big problem with this is that the recall of the traumatic event recreates as well the negative emotions experienced at the time, as it does in PTSD. Sonia was lucky to have a psychological constitution devoid of obsessive compulsiveness. Quite the opposite, she never sweated the small stuff.

As people age, the ability to recall recent events fades, while old memories in long-term storage generally remain accessible. In the last year of her life, when Sonia experienced some dementia, she began to suffer from nightmares. When Gloria was with her, she gently awakened Sonia when she seemed to be having a nightmare. Sonia woke agitated and began speaking in Polish. Gloria comforted Sonia and reminded her to speak English, the language Gloria understood. Apparently, Sonia's memories that had dimmed earlier in her life, were now coming to the fore.

Psychiatrist Viktor Frankl, himself an Auschwitz survivor, developed a theory and technique of what he called Logotherapy. It held that one way to cope with trauma is to find meaning in suffering or a reason to live in the midst of tragedy or trauma. Even if there is no intrinsic or obvious meaning in one's suffering, if you can create meaning, explained Frankl, you can live a satisfactory, if not happy life. For Sonia, her missions were to stay alive, reunite with Abe and start a new family. For many of the American soldiers who were imprisoned in the Nazi concentration camp, Berga, after capture during the Battle of the Bulge, their mission was to survive and get revenge against the Nazis who had imprisoned and tortured them.

Experiencing trauma in childhood is believed to be a factor in chronic emotional distress, while trauma in later life, after personality is formed, is thought to be more manageable. Trauma in childhood, such as emotional, physical or sexual abuse appears to make an individual less resilient and more likely to develop PTSD in response to later trauma in adulthood. Experiencing abuse in childhood is more likely to condition the child to what's called "learned helplessness,"[1] itself a frequent precursor of and concomitant to depression. Sonia's childhood and pre-war life were happy and fulfilling and her peacetime personality well formed.

Two common themes expressed by survivors are that having family, friends and social support lessened the effects of trauma, while isolation increased emotional distress in reaction to traumatic events. Many testimonies of Holocaust survivors reflect their beliefs that they survived primarily because of their social ties with family members or friends in the ghettos, camps, or forests. Their relationships reflected the help they gave each other in terms of stealing or smuggling food for each other, intervening on each other's behalf with authority figures, helping each other in work groups or escape planning. But most important for their survival, as they testified, was the emotional and spiritual support they lent each other, encouraging each other to maintain their will to live, to never give in to despair even in the depths of emotional and physical starvation and torture, and to nurse and nurture their hope for future life at the end of the war. This was certainly the case with Sonia and Rachelle.

In his short, classic book on Auschwitz, Otto Friedrich observed, "Most of those who survived Auschwitz did so because of a powerful faith in something outside themselves – family, friendship, patriotism, religion – and nobody survived without help. Those who lived alone died alone." Sociologist Nechama Tec agreed, "... most inmates concur that membership in a group of some sort had the power to keep them from giving up on life... Not belonging moved them closer to death." She continued, "The prisoners who had a predisposition to keep to themselves or who for any reason were alone had a particularly hard time withstanding camp pressures... under conditions of extreme cruelty and degradation; mutual support and solidarity improve the quality of life and may even aid survival." Based on her research, Tec opined that in the camps, women were better at affiliating and forming close relationships of mutual aid than men.[2]

Those prisoners who were not killed immediately and who didn't survive the camps were often the victims of chance. In other cases, those who knew or believed that they were the only survivors of their families and had no current social relationships often lost their will to survive. Survivors recognized these inmates as the walking dead and used the word *Muselmann* to describe them. The origin of this slang word is not known precisely.[3] Muselmann was a person who was at the last stage of dehumanization, physical destruction, and emptiness, who had lost the will to live. He or she might suicide by grabbing onto a strand of the electrified barbed wire fences surrounding most camps or would simply cease to eat or function and drop dead or else get noticed by a guard who would beat him or her to death. A Muselmann was a skeletal, walking dead; he or she just didn't know it yet.

Having some control over a situation, even just *believing* you have control when in reality you don't or having control over your *reaction* to aversive or traumatic situations lessens the stress and your reaction to it. Our background and early experiences teach us whether or not we generally have or think we have control over life events, and this feeling of control or lack of it, *gives* us the confidence or *limits* our feeling of confidence in our ability to cope with the stressors we face.

Obviously, inmates of the Nazi camps had very little, if any, control over their environment, even over whether they lived or died. Many survivors reported that they made efforts to find ways to feel like they had control. Reportedly, some Jewish prisoners fasted on *Yom Kippur*. Given the starvation rations that barely kept them alive, it's noteworthy that they refrained from eating on that Jewish fast day, if only to prove to themselves that they had some control over their own behavior and lives, despite the overwhelming control the Nazis had over them.

Sonia believed she had a purpose in living. But, more than that, she planned and executed acts of survival in the ghetto and in the camps, looking for opportunities to do something that might keep her alive.

Gloria and I discussed and compared the types and intensities of the respective sufferings of her parents. Abe knew that terrible things were happening to his family and Europe, and there was nothing he could do about it. Abe was a man of action. He came up with ideas and operationalized them. During the war, he was faced with his biggest challenge: to accept that he had no control over his family's fate in Europe. He couldn't protect them. He had no way to rescue them and spirit them out of Europe. Added to that, albeit of secondary concern, he experienced the trauma of losing everything he had built up in Warsaw. In America, he faced a future with no money, no means of making a living, not even knowing the language.

In the ghettos, camps and forced labor facilities, Sonia was physically debilitated. She had to suffer the trauma of losing her children and the guilt of not having been able to protect them. Worst of all, unlike Abe, she lived in an upside-down world. There was no morality. No humanity. Only the logic of terror, suffering and death. Sonia faced the danger of sudden death for six and a half years.

255

What is most remarkable about Sonia and Abe is their private and, in some ways public, heroism. They survived disaster and trauma of the worst sort without losing their honor or humanity. They both loved people and they loved life. For both of them, family came first above all else.

Dr. Leo Eitinger, Professor of Psychiatry at the University of Oslo, and himself a survivor of Auschwitz, presented a similar perspective to the U.S. Holocaust Council in 1987. He suggested that camp inmates who somehow managed to retain their self-respect and maintained their ability to care for others as well as for themselves, who kept alive their hope to live, suffered less psychological damage and survived their camp experience with fewer psychological disturbances "and with one's personality intact – as far as this was possible at all."[4]

Abe and Sonia didn't consider themselves victims. They saw themselves as survivors. They flourished. Their story is a little bit like the biblical story of Joseph advising Pharaoh. They had nearly seven years of plenty in Warsaw. This was followed by seven years of suffering for Sonia in Europe while Abe struggled to survive as a stranger in an alien land in New York. Unlike the *Children of Israel*, they didn't wander in the desert for 40 years after liberation. For more than 40 years they lived productive and happy lives in the United States. They raised two happy and productive children and they lived long enough to enjoy two loving grandchildren. They always maintained a positive outlook towards life. While they lived well, they actually had very few possessions. Material things meant little to them. They enjoyed fine things but did not treasure them. Their home in Lido was burglarized twice and beautiful silver and *objets d'art* were stolen. After the first burglary, Abe installed an alarm system in the home. Police believed the same burglars hit them again; after the first burglary, the burglars waited until the things from the first burglary were replaced. When the burglars hit the second time, they found a way to bypass the alarm system. After the second burglary, the defects in the alarm system were corrected, but the things were not replaced. Abe and Sonia believed that material comforts were to be enjoyed, but they were not the goal of life. It was much more important to live like a *Mentsch* than a millionaire.

I never heard Abe or Sonia complain about or regret the loss of this or that *thing*. Even more telling, they showed no fear of a home invasion. They had no weapons for self-protection. They were not ignorant of crime; after all they were victims of burglaries. But they both felt that they wouldn't live in fear. And nothing that could happen to them could be worse than what they had already experienced.

It is claimed that optimists often survive difficult circumstances better than pessimists – that is, with less distress. Why should this be so? Optimists are believed to face problems with active coping skills; they take control to the best of their ability of the problem situations. They accept reality and try to change it rather than hoping it will go away. Pessimists, on the other hand, are more likely to avoid changing their situation and are more likely to give up (thinking, for example "what's the use?").[5] Similarly, those who can generate coping thoughts that combat hopeless thoughts can fight depressive emotions, activate coping behaviors and reduce the effects of traumatic experiences.[6] Having said this, it is important to emphasize that no premorbid personality nor personality disorder was necessary in the face of catastrophic trauma to leave for many survivors a permanent if not indelible impact, mostly but not entirely negative on the survivor.[7]

Abe, himself, couldn't explain how he and Sonia escaped death. He formed for himself the answer often expressed to his family, which he noted in a brief, hopeful yet anguished reminiscence in 1979:

I say that we are miracle people. Every one of us survived by miracles. We are survivors from the ashes of the Holocaust. We are living witnesses against the Nazi murderers, who killed so many millions of innocent people because our names were Jewish.

For those who knew them personally or have got to know them from this book, it's impossible to not admire Sonia and Abe for surviving devastating traumas without becoming cynical and angry at the world. They were happy people in the years prior to 1939 and happy and grateful in the years after 1945. They did not allow their traumas of the Holocaust to change them for the worse. They didn't just survive traumas, but thrived after surviving them. They both felt tremendous gratitude for what they had, and little regret over the things they had lost.

One of the most important characteristics they shared was acceptance. They had the ability to accept "what is" with equanimity. Abe often illustrated his thoughts in conversation with sayings he had heard and remembered or had generated himself. One of his favorites reflected how he lived his life without regrets and with purpose:

There are three days: yesterday, today and tomorrow. Yesterday is a lost day. There is nothing you can do about it. It is like a cancelled cheque. It is gone. It is worthless. Tomorrow doesn't belong to you. There is no assurance you will be here. You can plan, but who knows? It is like a promissory note. Maybe it will be paid. Or maybe it will not. But today is important. Today is like you are holding cash in your hand. Don't waste it. Use it well. You can do wonderful things with it. Be good to others. Help others who can use your help. Take advantage of today. Take good care of it. Because today belongs to you.

In a significant sense, both Sonia and Abe were quite flexible in adapting to their lifetime changes. Neither one was paralyzed into fantasy and inaction. Both of them rose to the occasions in which they found themselves and adapted to their new environments. In a totally different context, Bret Stephens of the *Wall Street Journal* wrote a meaningful turn of phrase that seems relevant to Sonia and Abe. Stephens writes about how Israelis have adapted to an environment of war, terrorism and murder, carrying on their daily lives, while a "… sense of normality was achieved through an effort of will and a touch of fatalism."[8]

Fatalism implies acceptance of "what is," which, in turn, can be verbalized as *gam zu l'tovah* (a Rabbinical saying, meaning "this too is for the best"). Abe mailed us a letter after Gloria's third pregnancy ended in a miscarriage. It is a loving letter that illustrates Abe's intuitive, psychological insight into comforting someone after a loss.

Dear, Dear Gloria

Ken just told us the news. You should be happy it happened now, not in the last months. Gam zu l'tovah.

Sarah and David made my 83rd birthday worthwhile living. The credit is due to you and Ken. For teaching them respect and kindness to me and others. Very few children have so much love for others as your children. I am very proud and privileged to be your father and father-in-law, and Papa of a great and lovely family. I love you all very, very much. God bless you all. The tears which now drop from my eyes are sharing the pleasure from my great love for you.

Your father and your Papa.

Abe and Sonia were separated physically for seven years. They survived the war *because* they were separated from each other. Had Abe not traveled by chance to America but had remained in Warsaw, he more likely than not would have been killed in the Ghetto uprising or murdered by the Nazis along with the other men of the family. Knowing that Abe was alive in America kept Sonia alive. Expecting that Sonia would survive the war and join him in America never left Abe's thoughts. That forced him to start working again from the bottom of the business world, which kept him from despair and inaction. Each of them experienced his and her own personal physical and emotional trauma. They survived because of their commitment and love for each other and their courage in the face of catastrophe. They both actively refused to give up hope.

Abe refused to fail in America. And Sonia refused to die.

After the war, Abe and Sonia revived their pre-war, life-affirming, optimistic and happy outlook on life. They refused to live in a past of sadness and grief. They lived in a future of hope and joy.

I think of some words Abe and Sonia wrote that may explain it all, far above my own poor power to add or detract or to understand, let alone explain.

On January 29, 1976, while vacationing in Palm Beach, Florida, Abe sat down at his dining room table and committed his thoughts to paper:

My Thanks to God

I am thankful to God for keeping me alive for 71 years

I am thankful to God for helping me in making the right decision in selecting my partner in my life

I am thankful to God for saving my wife from Hitler's gas chambers

I am very thankful to God for blessing me with a wonderful son

I am thankful to God for blessing me with a wonderful daughter

I am thankful to God for leading my Gloria in making her decision to marry her wonderful husband

I am thankful to God for blessing me with so many wonderful friends

I am begging you, dear God, please protect my family, watch over them

Lead them in the right direction

Guide them in making the right decisions

I am begging you, dear God, my children should live in a world of peace.

In an essay Sonia wrote in 1948 for a night school assignment to write about her life, she concluded with the following stunning words:

I was happy I had the children until 1943.

1. Maddi; Price; Seligman; Siebert.
2. Friedrich, p. 29; Tec. pp. 175f.
3. U.S. Holocaust Memorial Museum Library, Lexicon of Camp Slang. Cited in Wittman, p. 304, n. 28.
4. Chamberlin, pp. 197f.
5. Scheier, et al.
6. Burns.
7. Krell, p. 13.
8. Stephens.

BIBLIOGRAPHY

Arad, Yitzhak, *The Operation Reinhard Death Camps: Belzec, Sobibor, Treblinka*. Revised and expanded Edition. Bloomington IN: Indiana University Press. 1987. Updated English version © 2018 Indiana University Press.

Bailey, Ronald H., "Made in America" in: *World War II*. Vol. 28, No. 6. March/April 2014. pp. 48-55.

Bartov, Omer, *Anatomy of a Genocide: The Life and Death of a Town Called Buczacz*. NY: Simon and Schuster, 2018.

Bartov, Omer, *Hitler's Army: Soldiers, Nazis, and War in the Third Reich*. NY: Oxford University. Press, 1992 (paperback).

Bendersky, Joseph W., *The Jewish Threat. Anti-Semitic Politics of the U.S. Army*. NY: Basic Books, 2000.

Blatman, Daniel, *The Death Marches: The Final Phase of Nazi Genocide*. Cambridge, MA: Belknap Press of Harvard University Press: 2011.

Bower, Tom, *Nazi Gold*. NY: Harper Collins, 1997.

Breitman, Richard, *Official Secrets*: *What the Nazis Planned What the British and Americans Knew*, N.Y.: Hill and Wang, 1998.

Breitman, Richard, *The Architect of Genocide: Himmler and the Final Solution*. NY: Alfred A. Knopf, 1991.

Browning, Christopher, *The Origins of the Final Solution*. Lincoln Neb., Univ. of Nebraska Press and Jerusalem: Yad Vashem, 2004.

Bukey, Evan Burr, *Hitler's Austria: Popular Sentiment in the Nazi Era, 1938-1945*, University of North Carolina Press, 2000.

Burns, David D., M.D., *Feeling Good. The New Mood Therapy*. NY: Harper Collins, 1999.

Chamberlin, Brewster and Feldman, Marcia (Eds.), *The Liberation of the Nazi Concentration Camps 1945: Eyewitness Accounts of the Liberators*. U.S. Holocaust Memorial Council, Washington, D.C., 1987.

Chesnoff, Richard Z., *Pack of Thieves*. NY: Anchor Books, A Division of Random House, 1999.

Churchill, Winston, *The Gathering Storm*, Vol. I of *The Second World War*. Boston: Houghton Mifflin Co., 1948.

Chylinski, T. H., *Poland Under Nazi Rule*. Confidential report by U.S. Vice Consul in Warsaw, completed November 13, 1941. Declassified by CIA in 2001 under the Nazi War Crimes Disclosure Act.

Citino, Robert M., *The Wehrmacht's Last Stand: The German Campaigns of 1944-1945*. University Press of Kansas, 2017.

Cohen, Roger, *Soldiers and Slaves*. NY: Alfred A. Knopf, 2005.

Cwiklinski, Jan, *The Captain Leaves His Ship*. NY: Doubleday & Company, 1955.

Czech, Danuta, *Auschwitz Chronicle 1939-1945*. NY: Henry Holt, 1990 (English Translation.)

Dawidowicz, Lucy, *The War Against the Jews*. NY: Holt, Rinehart and Winston, 1975.

Department of State, Intelligence Research Report. Distributed by the Office of Intelligence Coordination and Liaison (OCL)-2312, *The Jews in Poland Since the Liberation*, May 15, 1946. Declassified 06/12, 1979, NARS date 08/22/1983.

Desbois, Father Patrick, *In Broad Daylight: The Secret Procedures Behind the Holocaust by Bullets*. NY: Arcade Publishing, 2015.

Desbois, Father Patrick, *The Holocaust by Bullets: A Priest's Journey to Uncover the Truth behind the Murder of 1.5 Million Jews*. Palgrave Macmillan, 2008.

Edelman, Marek, *The Ghetto Fights*. Published in a pamphlet *The Warsaw Ghetto: The 45th Anniversary of the Uprising*. Interpress Publishers. pp. 17-39.

Encyclopedia of Camps and Ghettos, 1933-1945. Vol. I, Indiana Univ. Press in association with the United States Holocaust Memorial Museum, 2009.

Evans, Richard J., *The Coming of the Third Reich*. NY: Penguin Books, 2003.

feldgrau.com/WW2-German-Military-Soviet-Union accessed July 10, 2017

Ferencz, Benjamin B., *Less Than Slaves*. Cambridge MA: Harvard Univ. Press, 1979.

Fleming, Gerald, *Hitler and the Final Solution*. University of California Press (translated English edition), 1984.

Frankl, Viktor E., *Man's Search for Meaning*. Boston: Beacon Press, 2006 (orig. © Viktor E. Frankl, 1959).

Franklin, Benjamin, *Plain Truth*. November 17, 1747.

Friedrich, Otto, *The Kingdom of Auschwitz*. Harper Perennial, 1982, 1994.

Frieser, Karl-Heinz, *The Blitzkrieg Legend* (translator John T. Greenwood). Naval Institute Press, Annapolis Maryland 2012.

Gellately, Robert, *Backing Hitler: Consent and Coercion in Nazi Germany*. NY: Oxford Univ. Press, 2001.

Gensicke, Klaus, *The Mufti of Jerusalem and the Nazis: The Berlin Years*. Translated from the German by Alexander Fraser Gunn. London & Portland OR: Valentine Mitchell first paperback edition 2015.

Gilbert, G.M., *Nuremberg Diary*. Da Capo Press, 1995 (Republication of 1947 edition published by Farrar, Strauss).

Gilbert, Martin, *Winston S. Churchill*. Companion Volume V. Part 3, *The coming of war 1936-1939*, William Heinemann, 1982.

Goldensohn, Leon, *The Nuremberg Interviews*. Edited and with Introduction by Robert Gellately, NY: Vintage Books a Division of Random House, 2005.

Grabowski, Jan, *The Polish Police: Collaboration in the Holocaust* (Ina Levine Annual Lecture November 17, 1976). Washington, DC: United States Holocaust Memorial Museum, Jack, Joseph and Morton Mandel Center for Advanced Holocaust Studies, 2017.

Gross, Jan T., *FEAR. Anti-Semitism in Poland After Auschwitz*. NY: Random House, 2006.

Gutman, Yisrael, *The Jews of Warsaw*. Indiana University Press, 1982, Midland Book Edition (PB), 1989.

Hale, Christopher, *Hitler's Foreign Executioners: Europe's Dirty Secret*. UK: The History Press, 2011.

Hanson, Victor Davis, *The Second World Wars: How the First Global Conflict was Fought and Won*. NY: Basic Books, 2017.

Hart, Bradley W., *Hitler's American Friends: The Third Reich's Supporters in the United States*. NY: St. Martin's Press, 2018.

Hastings, Max, *Inferno: The World at War, 1939-1945*. NY: Vintage Books, A division of Random House, 2011.

Hausner, Gideon, *Justice in Jerusalem*. NY: Harper & Row, 1966.

Heilman, Anna, *Never Far Away: The Auschwitz Chronicles of Anna Heilman*. University of Calgary Press, 2001.

Helm, Sarah, *Ravensbrück: Life and Death in Hitler's Concentration Camp for Women*. Anchor Books: 2016.

Hett, B.C., *Burning the Reichstag*. NY: Oxford University Press, 2014.

Hirsh, Michael, *The Liberators: America's Witnesses to the Holocaust*. NY: Bantam Books, 2010.

Hobbes, Thomas, *Leviathan*. 1651. "The Second Part: Of Commonwealth," Chapter XVII, paragraph 2.

Huberman, Abraham, *Letters*. "Meeting one of the 'Three Josephs'" in: *Long Beach Independent Voice*. July 5, 1979, p. 4.

Jaglom, Henry, The Third Stone on the Second Row: A Family Memoir and a Brief History of the Jewish People. Unpublished manuscript. Revised, 2018.

Jansen, Christian and Weckbecker, Arno, *Der "Volksdeutsche Selbstschutz" in Polen 1939/40*. München: R. Oldenbourg Verlag, 1992.

Jasinski, Dr. Grzegorz, *Polish Cultural Losses in the years 1939-1945*. Polishresistance-ak.org/28, Accessed 01/21/2018.

Jenkins, Holman W. Jr., column in: *The Wall Street Journal*. 2018, March 24-25, p. A17.

Jewish Encyclopedia 1906.

Kaplinski, Baruch, *et al.* (Eds.), *Memorial Book of Kozienice (Kozienice, Poland). Translation of Sefer Zikaron le-Kehilat Kosznitz*. Published by JewishGen, Inc. An Affiliate of the Museum of Jewish Heritage A living Memorial to the Holocaust 36 Battery Place, New York, NY 10280, 2016.

Kassow, Samuel D., *Who Will Write Our History?* Penguin Books and Indiana Univ. Press, 2007.

Klee, Ernst; Dressen, Willi; Riess, Volker (Eds.) *The Good Old Days.* NY: The Free Press, 1991 (translated from German Schöne Zeiten © 1988)

Kochanski, Halik, *The Eagle Unbowed: Poland and the Poles in the Second World War.* Cambridge, MA: Harvard University Press, 2012, PB edition: 2014.

Koskodan, Kenneth K., *No Greater Ally.* NY: Osprey Publishing, paperback edition, 2011.

Krakowski, Shmuel, "The Fate of Jewish Prisoners of War in the September 1939 campaign" in: *Yad Vashem Studies*, Vol. XII, Yad Vashem, Jerusalem, 1977, pp. 297-333.

Krell, Robert, "Psychiatry and the Holocaust" in: Robert Krell and Marc I. Sherman (Eds.) *Medical and Psychological Effects of Concentration Camps on Holocaust Survivors.* Vol. 4 Genocide: A Critical Bibliographic Review. New Brunswick: Transaction Publishers, 1997.

Laquer, Walter (Ed.), *The Holocaust Encyclopedia.* New Haven: Yale University Press, 2001.

Laquer, Walter and Breitman, Richard, *Breaking the Silence.* Brandeis University Press, paperback, 1994.

Lindbergh, Charles, *The Wartime Journals of Charles A. Lindbergh.* N.Y.: Harcourt Brace Jovanovich, Inc., 1970.

McDonald, James G., *My Mission in Israel.* N.Y.: Simon and Schuster, 1951.

Maddi, Salvatore R. and Kobasa, Suzanne C., *The Hardy Executive.* Homewood, I: Dow Jones-Irwin, 1984.

Marszalek, Jozef, *Majdanek; The Concentration Camp in Lublin.* Warsaw: Interpress, 1986.

Matthaus, Jürgen; Bohler, Jochen and Mallmann, Klaus-Michael, *War, Pacification and Mass Murder, 1939: The Einsatzgruppen in Poland.* MD: Rowman & Littlefield, 2014.

Medoff, Rafael, *Blowing the Whistle on Genocide.* West Lafayette, Purdue University Press, 2009.

Mendelsohn, Ezra, "Interwar Poland: good for the Jews or bad for the Jews?" Chapter 11 in: C. Abramsky, M. Jachimczyk and A. Polonsky, *The Jews in Poland.* NY, NY. Basil Blackwell Ltd., 1986.

Miller, Peter N., "What we know about murdered peoples", book review in: *The New Republic,* April 9, 2008, pp. 34-39.

Miller, Richard Lawrence, *Nazi Justiz: Law of the Holocaust.* Westport, CN: Praeger, 1995.

Mlynarczyk, Jacek Andrzej, "Between the German Authorities and Polish Society: The Polish "Blue Police", Chapter 6, "Eastern Europe" in: Jochen Bohler and Robert Gerwarth (Eds.), *The Waffen-SS: A European History.* NY: Oxford University Press, 2017 (Kindle Edition).

Motadel, David, *Islam and Nazi Germany's War.* Cambridge, MA: The Belknap Press of Harvard University Press, 2014.

Müller, Ingo, *Hitler's Justice: The Courts of the Third Reich.* Cambridge, MA: Harvard University Press, 1991.

Müller, Rolf-Dieter, *The Unknown Eastern Front: The Wehrmacht and Hitler's Foreign Soldiers.* Translated by David Burnett. London: I.B. Taurus, 2012.

Namier, L. B., *Diplomatic Prelude.* London: Macmillan & Co., Ltd. 1948.

Neitzel, Sonke and Welzer, Harald, *Soldaten. On Fighting, Killing and Dying: The Secret World War II Transcripts of German POWs* (translated from German by Jefferson Chase). Alfred A. Knopf, 2012.

Noakes, J. and Pridham, G. (Eds.), *Nazism 1919-1945: A History in Documents and Eyewitness Accounts*. Vol. I, The Nazi Party, State and Society 1919-1939. Schocken Books (original © University Exeter, 1983, 1984). Vol. II Foreign Policy, War and Racial Extermination, 1988.

Ozsvath, Zsuzsanna, *When the Danube Ran Red*. Syracuse University Press: 2010.

Overy, Richard, *1939 Countdown to War*. NY: Penguin Books, 2009.

Overy, Richard, *Interrogations: The Nazi Elite in Allied Hands 1945*. Viking, 2001.

Paillole, Paul, *The Spy in Hitler's Inner Circle*. Oxford and Philadelphia: Casemate, 2016 (translated from the French, *Notre espion chez Hitler*, Nouveau Monde editions, 2011).

Parssinen, Terry, *The Oster Conspiracy of 1938: The Unknown Story of the Military Plot to Kill Hitler and Avoid World War II*. NY: Harper Collins Publishers, 2003.

Paskuly, Steven (Ed.), *Death Dealer: The Memoirs of the SS Kommandant at Auschwitz*. (translated by Andrew Pollinger). Da Capo Press (A member of the Perseus Book Group: 1996; first published NY: Prometheus Books, 1992 © Steven Paskuly, 1992).

Patterson, David, *A Genealogy of Evil: Anti-Semitism from Nazism to Islamic Jihad*. NY: Cambridge University Press, 2011.

Patterson, David, *Along the Edge of Annihilation: The Collapse and Recovery of Life in the Holocaust Diary*. Seattle: University of Washington Press, 1999.

Paulsson, Gunnar S., *Secret City: The Hidden Jews of Warsaw 1940-1945*. New Haven: Yale University Press, 2002.

Pool, James, *Who Financed Hitler: The Secret Funding of Hitler's Rise to Power, 1919-1933*. NY: Pocket Books, a division of Simon & Schuster, 1997.

270

Price, Kenneth P., and Tryon, W., and Raps, C.S., "Learned Helplessness and Depression in a clinical population: A test of two behavioral hypotheses" in: *Journal of Abnormal Psychology*, 1978, 87, pp. 113-121.

Pringle, Heather, *The Master Plan: Hitler's Scholars and the Holocaust*. NY: Hyperion Books, 2006.

Reitlinger, Gerald, *The Final Solution*. 2nd revised and augmented Edition. NY: Thomas Yoseloff, 1968.

Richardson, William and Freidlin, Seymour (Eds.), *The Fatal Decisions: First Hand Accounts by Hitler's Generals*. Barnsley South Yorkshire, England: Pen & Sword Military, 2012 (originally published by Michael Joseph Ltd., 1956).

Rigg, Bryan Mark, *Hitler's Jewish Soldiers*. University Press of Kansas, 2002.

Ringelblum, Emmanuel, *Polish-Jewish Relations During the Second World War*. Edited and with footnotes by Joseph Kermish and Shmuel Krakowski. Evanston: Northwestern University Press, 1992 (published posthumously).

Roberts, Andrew, *The Storm of War*. NY: Harper Perennial (paperback edition) 2012.

Rossino, Alexander B., *Hitler Strikes Poland: Blitzkrieg, Ideology, and Atrocity*. University Press of Kansas ,2003.

Rubin, Barry and Schwanitz, Wolfgang, *Nazis, Islamists, and the Making of the Modern Middle East*. New Haven: Yale University Press, 2014.

Scheier, M., et al., "Optimism, pessimism, and psychological well-being" in: Edward C. Chang (Ed.) *Optimism & Pessimism: Implications for Theory, Research, and Practice*. Washington, D.C.: American Psychological Association, 2000.

Seligman, Martin E.P., *Learned Optimism*. NY: Pocket Books, a Division of Simon & Schuster, Inc., 1990.

Shepherd, Ben H., *Hitler's Soldiers: The German Army in the Third Reich*. New Haven: Yale University Press, 2016.

Siebert, Al., *The Survivor Personality*. NY: Berkley Publishing Group, A division of Penguin Putnam, 1996.

Singer, Isaac Bashevis, *Shosha*. NY: Farrar, Straus and Giroux, 1978.

Smelser, Ronald and Davies, Edward J. II, *The Myth of the Eastern Front*. UK: Cambridge University Press, 2008.

Snyder, Timothy, *Bloodlands: Europe Between Hitler and Stalin*. NY: Basic Books, 2010 (paperback edition 2012).

Sofsky, Wolfgang, *The Order of Terror: The Concentration Camp*. Translated by William Templer. English translation, NJ: Princeton University Press, 1997.

Sprecher, Drexel A., *Inside the Nuremberg Trial: A Prosecutor's Comprehensive Account*. NY: University Press of America, Inc., 1999.

Stahel, David, *Joining Hiter's Crusade: European Nations and the Invasion of the Soviet Union, 1941*. UK: Cambridge University Press, 2018.

Stargardt, Nicholas, *The German War: A Nation Under Arms 1939-1945*. NY: Basic Books, 2015.

Stephens, Bret, "Life During Wartime," column in: *Wall Street Journal*, September 20, 2016, p. A13.

Stone, Lewi, "Quantifying the Holocaust: Hyperintense kill rates during the Nazi genocide" in Stone, *Sci. Adv.* 2019;5: eaau7292 2 January 2019.

Taber, George M. *Chasing Gold*. NY: Pegasus Books, 2014.

Taleb, Nissim Nicholas, *The Black Swan*. NY: Random House, 2010.

Taylor, Telford, *Munich The Price of Peace*. NY: Doubleday & Company, 1979.

Tec, Nechama, *Resilience and Courage.* New Haven: Yale University Press, 2003.

Tedeschi, Richard G., *Posttraumatic Growth.* Mahwah N.J.: Lawrence Erlbaum Associates, 1998.

The Holocaust Chronicle. Lincolnwood IL: Publications International, Ltd. 2003.

The Nation Associates, *The Record of Collaboration of King Farouk of Egypt with the Nazis and Their Ally, The Mufti: The Official Nazi Records of the King's Alliance and of the Mufti's Plans for Bombing Jerusalem and Tel Aviv.* Memorandum Submitted to the United Nations, June 1948. Babel.hathitrust.org/cgi/pt?id=mdp.39015028745217 Accessed July 3, 2018.

The Stroop Report: A facsimile edition and translation of the official Nazi report on the destruction of the Warsaw Ghetto. Translated from the German and annotated by Sybil Milton. NY: Pantheon Books, 1979.

Thucydides, 5th Century B.C.E. Book III: *Revolution at Corcyra.*

Time Magazine, Vol. 38, Issue 12, September 22, 1941. pp. 13-14.

Ullrich, Volker, *Hitler: Ascent 1889-1939.* NY: Alfred A. Knopf, 2016.

Van Ells, Mark D., "Americans for Hitler – The Bund" in: *America in WWII*, August 2007.

Van Pelt, Jan, The *Case for Auschwitz: Evidence from the Irving Trial.* Indiana University Press: © 2002 (first paperback edition 2016).

Von Lang, Jochen (Ed. in collaboration with Claus Sibyll; translated from the German by Ralph Manheim), *Eichmann Interrogated: Transcripts from the Archives of the Israeli Police.* NY: Farrar, Straus & Giroux, 1983.

Wachsmann, Nikolaus, *KL A History of the Nazi Concentration Camps.* NY: Farrar, Straus and Giroux, 2015.

Watt, Richard M., *Bitter Glory: Poland and its Fate 1918-1939.* NY: Hippocrene Books, 1998.

Weber, Thomas, *Hitler's First War*. Oxford University Press, 2010, 2011 (paperback edition).

Weinberg, Gerhard L., *A World at Arms: A Global History of World War II*. NY: Cambridge University Press, 1994 (paperback edition 2005).

Weinberg, Gerhard L. (Ed.) *Hitler's Second Book: The Unpublished Sequel to Mein Kampf by Adolf Hitler* (translated by Krista Smith). Enigma Books, 2003.

Weiss, Ann, *The Last Album: Eyes from the Ashes of Auschwitz-Birkenau*. NY: W.W. Norton & Company, 2001.

Westerman, Edward B., *Hitler's Police Battalions: Enforcing Racial War in the East*. University Press of Kansas, 2005.

Whitlock, Flint, *Given Up for Dead: American GI's in the Nazi Concentration Camp at Berga*. Westview Press, 2005.

Wills, Matthew B., *The Lindbergh Report*. UK Ltd.: Author House, 2008.

Wistrich, Robert S., *Hitler and the Holocaust*. NY: Random House, Modern Library Edition, 2001.

Winik, Jay, *1944 FDR and the Year that Changed History*. NY: Simon & Schuster, 2015.

Wittmann, Rebecca, *Beyond Justice: The Auschwitz Trial*. Cambridge, MA, Harvard University Press, 2005 (paperback edition 2012).

Yahil, Leni, *The Holocaust: The Fate of European Jewry*. NY: Oxford University Press, 1990.

Zimmerman, Joshua D., *Contested Memories: Poles and Jews During the Holocaust and its Aftermath*. New Brunswick, N.J.: Rutgers University Press, 2003.

ACKNOWLEDGMENTS

I was able to write this book because Abe and Sonia wrote letters, essays, diary-like entries and reminiscences from which I quoted liberally. They also sat for video interviews. In the few instances in which there were discrepancies among these sources, I did my best to resolve them based on my memories and those of Gloria's of the stories Abe and Sonia had related and on relevant, outside historical records and documents.

By chance, I came across Danuta Czech's *Auschwitz Chronicle 1939-1945* while browsing in a Dallas "Half Price Books" store many years ago. While flipping through the pages I found a reference to Sonia's Auschwitz camp tattoo number and the date she arrived at Auschwitz. This find would encourage me to embark on further research in primary sources and documents to flesh out Sonia's and Abe's personal histories.

I am grateful to Ann Weiss for her labor of love in producing *The Last Album: Eyes from the Ashes of Auschwitz-Birkenau.* In this book, Dr. Weiss reproduced photographs that she found in a locked room on the grounds of Auschwitz, of Jews who had been deported to the camp. My good friend Reid Heller owned the book and brought it out to show me while we were celebrating a Shabbat meal at his home. My eyes came to rest on a photo on page 41. I turned to my wife, Gloria, unable to hide my excitement, "Honey, there's a picture of your mother here. She, Lunia the nanny, and the two children are out for a walk on a Warsaw street sometime in 1939." The photo, which we had never seen before, must have been brought to Auschwitz by Lunia during her deportation to

Auschwitz from Warsaw or from another camp. The next day, Gloria brought out the book and showed the picture to Sonia. Sonia put on her reading glasses and peered at the picture. Without any hesitation, she immediately confirmed my find. "Yes, that's me and the children and Lunia." That night, Sonia passed away. Gloria remarked to me that her mother's confirmation of the previously unknown – to us – photo was Sonia's last gift to her.

My thanks to Ms. Michlean Lowy Amir, archivist at the United States Holocaust Memorial Museum in Washington, D.C., who found documentary material in the museum's archives that were helpful to me, in particular learning that Sonia had spent a brief time in Ravensbrück. Thanks are due to Mr. David A. Langbart, archivist at the National Archives, Washington, D.C., Textual Records Division, whose sleuthing helped me identify the name of the American Vice Consul in Warsaw who provided the U.S. visa to Abe that allowed Abe to enter the United States in August 1939. Mrs. Barbara Ferraro of New Jersey and Mr. John Korpal of Dallas were kind enough to translate various Polish documents and inscriptions on photographs from Polish into English, which have provided me important personal information on Abe and Sonia. My cousin, Isaac Cable diligently deciphered and translated from Yiddish to English nearly indecipherable copies of letters that Abe sent to his cousin in Bogota in 1940 and 1944. George Kremer is a Dutch art collector, founder of the Kremer Virtual Museum and publisher of some five books. He offered many helpful suggestions regarding the historical sections of this text and although English is not his native language, he corrected a number of grammatical and spelling errors. I am grateful to historians Reid Heller, J.D., and Zsuszanna Ozsvath, Ph.D., Leah and Paul Lewis Chair in Holocaust Studies at the University of Texas at Dallas, for their suggestions. Many thanks to Nils Roemer, Ph.D., Stan and Barbara Rabin Professor of Holocaust Studies at the University of Texas at Dallas, who read several drafts of my manuscript, pointed out some errors and made valuable suggestions and critical comments that have vastly improved this work. Bryan Mark Rigg, Ph.D., noted military historian and author, corrected a number of errors in the manuscript and made useful suggestions for improving the text. Sonia's two grandchildren, Sarah Lucia Price-Brown, journalist and mother of four children whom Abe and Sonia did not have the pleasure of knowing, and David A. Price, himself a talented writer, both made valuable suggestions to me. I also appreciate their giving me permission to print excerpts from eulogies they wrote for Mark and Sonia.

Helen Schary-Motro, J.D., Gloria's cousin and daughter of Zalman Schary, the relative who convinced Abe to come to the U.S. in July 1939, is a journalist and published author. She carefully read at least four drafts of my manuscript and made insightful, critical comments, questions and suggestions on nearly every page of the manuscripts. Her advice has made this book far better than it would have been without her contributions as a reviewer, and I remain in her debt.

I am grateful to my very dear friend, Gerri Alpern-Patterson, a scholar in her own right of Jewish history and the Holocaust, who knew Abe and Sonia and independently conducted videotaped oral histories of their testimonies, which I reviewed again while preparing this book. David Patterson, Ph.D., holds the Hillel A. Feinberg Chair in Holocaust Studies in the Ackerman Center for Holocaust Studies at the University of Texas at Dallas. More importantly, he holds a very special place in my life as one of my closest friends. He also read at least four drafts of my manuscript. I asked him to read my manuscript as an anonymous critic and not as a friend. His many trenchant comments were invaluable in improving this book. I also thank him for his help in translating various passages in source works from German to English. Words cannot express my gratitude to David for his unselfish contributions to improving this book.

I have not always followed suggestions made by my generous readers. Any remaining errors of commission or omission in this book remain my responsibility and I apologize in advance for them.

Finally, and most of all, I remain in debt to the love of my life, Gloria, for marrying me, allowing me to spend my life with her and granting me the honor of writing her parents' story. She read and reread many drafts. She has always been my best and most honest critic. I greatly appreciate her understanding and emotional support during the six years that I have been writing this book. Gloria was a devoted daughter to Abe and Sonia. She remains a loving wife and partner, wise counselor to our children and a patient and devoted grandmother.

ABOUT THE AUTHOR

Dr. Kenneth P. Price grew up in Brookline, Massachusetts. His parents were teachers and inculcated in Dr. Price a lifelong love of learning, reading and writing. After high school, he spent a year studying at the Hebrew University and the Hayyim Greenberg Institute in Jerusalem, Israel.

He graduated *magna cum laude* with honors in psychology from Brandeis University. He earned his Ph.D. in psychology from SUNY at Stony Brook, where he was a Herbert Lehman Fellow. He worked as a psychologist at the Northport VA Hospital and was on the faculty of the University of Texas Southwestern Medical School. He has evaluated more than 300 military veterans for psychological injuries incurred during their service and has served as a consulting or expert witness in dozens of legal cases.

An avid student of human nature, politics and history, Dr. Price has authored some two dozen scientific articles in psychology and medical journals.

Dr. Price lives in Dallas with his wife, where they both enjoy their four grandchildren.

Dear Reader,

If you have enjoyed reading my personal-historical memoir, I would very much appreciate your posting a short review on Amazon or other book review site such as Goodreads. If you have been reading this as an ebook and have limited time, you are kindly asked to leave a rating.

Thank you very much.

Dr. Ken Price

AMSTERDAM PUBLISHERS HOLOCAUST LIBRARY

The series **Holocaust Survivor Memoirs World War II** consists of the following autobiographies of survivors:

Outcry. Holocaust Memoirs, by Manny Steinberg

Hank Brodt Holocaust Memoirs. A Candle and a Promise, by Deborah Donnelly

The Dead Years. Holocaust Memoirs, by Joseph Schupack

Rescued from the Ashes. The Diary of Leokadia Schmidt, Survivor of the Warsaw Ghetto, by Leokadia Schmidt

My Lvov. Holocaust Memoir of a twelve-year-old Girl, by Janina Hescheles

Remembering Ravensbrück. From Holocaust to Healing, by Natalie Hess

Wolf. A Story of Hate, by Zeev Scheinwald with Ella Scheinwald

Save my Children. An Astonishing Tale of Survival and its Unlikely Hero, by Leon Kleiner with Edwin Stepp

Holocaust Memoirs of a Bergen-Belsen Survivor & Classmate of Anne Frank, by Nanette Blitz Konig

Defiant German - Defiant Jew. A Holocaust Memoir from inside the Third Reich, by Walter Leopold with Les Leopold

In a Land of Forest and Darkness. The Holocaust Story of two Jewish Partisans, by Sara Lustigman Omelinski

Holocaust Memories. Annihilation and Survival in Slovakia, by Paul Davidovits

From Auschwitz with Love. The Inspiring Memoir of Two Sisters' Survival, Devotion and Triumph Told by Manci Grunberger Beran & Ruth Grunberger Mermelstein, by Daniel Seymour

Remetz. Resistance Fighter and Survivor of the Warsaw Ghetto, by Jan Yohay Remetz

My March Through Hell. A Young Girl's Terrifying Journey to Survival, by Halina Kleiner with Edwin Stepp

---

The series **Holocaust Survivor True Stories WWII** consists of the following biographies:

Among the Reeds. The true story of how a family survived the Holocaust, by Tammy Bottner

A Holocaust Memoir of Love & Resilience. Mama's Survival from Lithuania to America, by Ettie Zilber

Living among the Dead. My Grandmother's Holocaust Survival Story of Love and Strength, by Adena Bernstein Astrowsky

Heart Songs. A Holocaust Memoir, by Barbara Gilford

Shoes of the Shoah. The Tomorrow of Yesterday, by Dorothy Pierce

Hidden in Berlin. A Holocaust Memoir, by Evelyn Joseph Grossman

Separated Together. The Incredible True WWII Story of Soulmates Stranded an Ocean Apart, by Kenneth P. Price, Ph.D.

The Man Across the River. The incredible story of one man's will to survive the Holocaust, by Zvi Wiesenfeld

If Anyone Calls, Tell Them I Died. A Memoir, by Emanuel (Manu) Rosen

The House on Thrömerstrasse. A Story of Rebirth and Renewal in the Wake of the Holocaust, by Ron Vincent

Dancing with my Father. His hidden past. Her quest for truth. How Nazi Vienna shaped a family's identity, by Jo Sorochinsky

The Story Keeper. Weaving the Threads of Time and Memory - A Memoir, by Fred Feldman

Krisia's Silence. The Girl who was not on Schindler's List, by Ronny Hein

Defying Death on the Danube. A Holocaust Survival Story, by Debbie J. Callahan with Henry Stern

A Doorway to Heroism. A decorated German-Jewish Soldier who became an American Hero, by Rabbi W. Jack Romberg

The Shoemaker's Son. The Life of a Holocaust Resister, by Laura Beth Bakst

The Redhead of Auschwitz. A True Story, by Nechama Birnbaum

Land of Many Bridges. My Father's Story, by Bela Ruth Samuel Tenenholtz

Creating Beauty from the Abyss. The Amazing Story of Sam Herciger, Auschwitz Survivor and Artist, by Lesley Ann Richardson

On Sunny Days We Sang. A Holocaust Story of Survival and Resilience, by Jeannette Grunhaus de Gelman

Painful Joy. A Holocaust Family Memoir, by Max J. Friedman

I Give You My Heart. A True Story of Courage and Survival, by Wendy Holden

Monsters and Miracles. Horror, Heroes and the Holocaust, by Ira Wesley Kitmacher

Flower of Vlora. Growing up Jewish in Communist Albania, by Anna Kohen

Zaidy's War, by Martin Bodek

In the Time of Madmen, by Mark A. Prelas

―――

The series **Jewish Children in the Holocaust** consists of the following autobiographies of Jewish children hidden during WWII in the Netherlands:

Searching for Home. The Impact of WWII on a Hidden Child, by Joseph Gosler

See You Tonight and Promise to be a Good Boy! War memories, by Salo Muller

Sounds from Silence. Reflections of a Child Holocaust Survivor, Psychiatrist and Teacher, by Robert Krell

Sabine's Odyssey. A Hidden Child and her Dutch Rescuers, by Agnes Schipper

The Journey of a Hidden Child, by Harry Pila with Robin Black

―――

The series **New Jewish Fiction** consists of the following novels, written by Jewish authors. All novels are set in the time during or after the

Holocaust.

The Corset Maker. A Novel, by Annette Libeskind Berkovits

Escaping the Whale. The Holocaust is over. But is it ever over for the next generation? by Ruth Rotkowitz

When the Music Stopped. Willy Rosen's Holocaust, by Casey Hayes

Hands of Gold. One Man's Quest to Find the Silver Lining in Misfortune, by Roni Robbins

There was a garden in Nuremberg. A Novel, by Navina Michal Clemerson

Aftermath: Coming-of-Age on Three Continents, by Annette Libeskind Berkovits

The Girl Who Counted Numbers. A Novel, by Roslyn Bernstein

The Butterfly and the Axe, by Omer Bartov

The series **Holocaust Books for Young Adults** consists of the following novels, based on true stories:

On the Run. A True Story, by Suzette Sheft

The Boy behind the Door. How Salomon Kool Escaped the Nazis, by David Tabatsky

The Precious Few. An Inspirational Saga of Courage based on True Stories, by David Twain with Art Twain

Want to be an AP book reviewer?

Reviews are very important in a world dominated by the social media and social proof. Please drop us a line if you want to join the *AP review team*. We will then add you to our list of advance reviewers. No strings attached, and we promise that we will not be spamming you.
info@amsterdampublishers.com

Made in the USA
Columbia, SC
25 February 2023

12972226R00167